M

DATE DUE

NOV 2 5 2007	

DEMCO, INC. 38-2931

OCT 0 1 2007

DEATH AND THE MAIDENS

worth, and talents, a perhaps also because I found the
thought you I loved you the more. What ever friend
may know I am not loud or vulgar. I love g[...]
your selves alone — I endeavour to be as frank to
as possible that you may understand my real cha[...]
I understand from mamma that I am your long
stock — and the content beyond your ~~friends~~ satis[...]

ANGLETERRE

B. Shelly Esq
Poste Restante
Genève
Switzerland

May 29th 1816

at the time of Fanny Woodstock[...]. I have not room
to tell you more particulars I will write and tell
when I see him every thing — I believe however
I shall go to Ireland instead of to France at least
short time. Mary gave a great deal of [...]
I write from [...] I believe my few friends [...]
my attachment to you known out of your [...]

DEATH AND THE MAIDENS

FANNY WOLLSTONECRAFT
AND THE SHELLEY CIRCLE

JANET TODD

COUNTERPOINT
Berkeley

A CIP catalog record for this book is available from the Library of Congress.
ISBN-13: 978-1-58243-339-4
ISBN-10: 1-58243-339-9

Printed in the United States of America

Counterpoint
2117 Fourth Street
Suite D
Berkeley, CA 94710
www.counterpointpress.com

9 8 7 6 5 4 3 2 1

CONTENTS

In memory of Lois Tilbrook

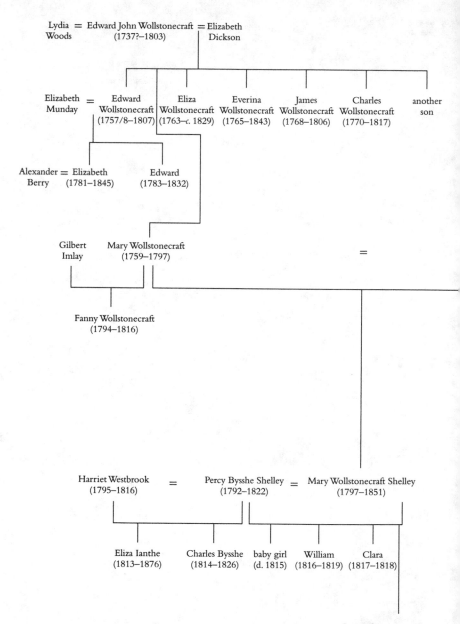

Lydia = Edward John Wollstonecraft = Elizabeth
Woods   (1737?–1803)   Dickson

Elizabeth = Edward   Eliza   Everina   James   Charles   another
Munday   Wollstonecraft Wollstonecraft Wollstonecraft Wollstonecraft Wollstonecraft son
          (1757/8–1807) (1763–c. 1829) (1765–1843)   (1768–1806)   (1770–1817)

Alexander = Elizabeth   Edward
Berry   (1781–1845)   (1783–1832)

Gilbert   Mary Wollstonecraft   =
Imlay   (1759–1797)

Fanny Wollstonecraft
(1794–1816)

Harriet Westbrook   =   Percy Bysshe Shelley = Mary Wollstonecraft Shelley
(1795–1816)   (1792–1822)   (1797–1851)

Eliza Ianthe   Charles Bysshe   baby girl   William   Clara
(1813–1876)   (1814–1826)   (d. 1815)   (1816–1819)   (1817–1818)

Percy Florence = Jane St. John
(1819–1889)

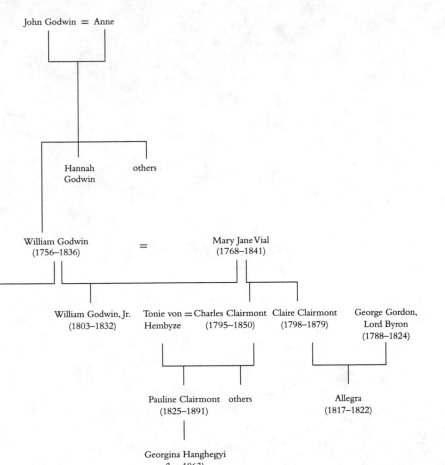

John Godwin = Anne

Hannah Godwin   others

William Godwin   =   Mary Jane Vial
(1756–1836)   (1768–1841)

William Godwin, Jr.   Tonie von = Charles Clairmont   Claire Clairmont   George Gordon,
(1803–1832)   Hembyze   (1795–1850)   (1798–1879)   Lord Byron
                                                                              (1788–1824)

Pauline Clairmont   others   Allegra
(1825–1891)   (1817–1822)

Georgina Hanghegyi
(b c. 1863)

She indeed rewards me, for she is a sweet little creature; for, setting aside a mother's fondness (which, by the bye, is growing on me, her little intelligent smiles sinking into my heart), she has an astonishing degree of sensibility and observation ... She is all life and motion ... Her eyes follow me every where, and by affection I have the most despotic power over her.

Mary Wollstonecraft on Fanny

Duty kept her with us: but I am afraid her affections were with them.

William Godwin on Fanny

Her voice did quiver as we parted,
Yet knew I not that heart was broken
From which it came — and I departed —
Heeding not the words then spoken.
Misery — oh misery
This world is all too wide to thee!

Percy Bysshe Shelley on Fanny

His whole existence was visionary, and there breathed in his actions in his looks and in his manners that high and superhuman tone which we can only conceive to belong to a superior being ...

Claire Clairmont on Shelley

Shelley was certainly a man of Genius and great feeling — but the effects of both were perverted by some unhappy flightings of mind that led him to cause much unhappiness to his connections.

Everina Wollstonecraft on Shelley

PREFACE

For many years I have been haunted by the figure of Mary Wollstonecraft's eldest daughter, Fanny – the child who travelled with her mother through Norway, Sweden and Denmark and who featured so vibrantly in Mary Wollstonecraft's final works. Biographers of Percy Bysshe Shelley, Mary Shelley and William Godwin have sometimes allowed Fanny to intrude into their narratives. They say she was always melancholy, morbidly anxious and lacking her mother's compensating energy. In their readings she becomes a small, tragic figure, destined to live only in the margins of the Wollstonecraft–Godwin–Shelley story; she is pronounced docile, quiet and depressive even as a child. I come to Fanny, however, through Mary Wollstonecraft's pictures of the bouncing girl, all spirits and energy. I want to avoid any assumption that she was always depressed and that her early death was almost inevitable.

There was never a more documented group of people than those who made up the households of the Godwins and the Shelleys in 1814–16; Fanny was involved in both. The records concerning her are contradictory, competing and often, despite their apparent transparency, secretive or lying. When she was definitely in Wales, Fanny was declared in Ireland; long after her death was known, she was said to be staying with relatives. Many authentic letters have been destroyed and what are left have been manipulated, made manipulative or overwritten. I have marshalled all the facts I can, but some links must be speculative.

Beyond letters and journals there are creative works, the novels and philo-sophical writings of William Godwin, the fiction of Mary Shelley, Godwin's daughter and Fanny's half-sister, and the poetry of Mary's husband, Percy Bysshe Shelley. To scour these for hints of life is considered bad form in biographies but what is distinctive in the lives of these extraordinary young people is their literariness, exactly their refusal to separate life and literature. They created themselves through the fictions of each other and wrenched life into serving fiction, their own and other people's. When living, Fanny felt the power of her mother's writings and in death was overshadowed by them.

There is no extant picture of Fanny; the portraits reproduced in this book are of those who surrounded her: Mary Wollstonecraft, Godwin and the Shelleys. Their lives impacted on Fanny, illuminating and circumscribing her at every turn. So her story must be a group story, a narrative of one of the first families of Romanticism.

ACKNOWLEDGEMENTS

MANY SCHOLARS HAVE been immensely helpful in answering my queries. While not wishing to associate any of them with my conclusions, I would like to thank the following: B. C. Barker-Benfield, Pamela Clemit, Nora Crook, Maurice Hindle, Abigail Mason, Nicholas Roe, Wil Verhoeven and Ann Wroe. I owe gratitude also to David Brownridge, Daphne Johnson and Noel King for much genealogical and geographical help, and to Elizabeth Spearing, Diana Birchall and Derek Hughes for patient readings of the manuscript. My thanks are also due to Antje Blank for her usual careful and enthusiastic involvement, and to the University of Aberdeen for allowing me time to pursue this project.

I appreciate help from the librarians and archivists at the British Library and the Cambridge University Library; from William Hodges of the Bodleian Library, University of Oxford; from Helen Harrison of the State Library of New South Wales; Richard Morgan of the Glamorgan Record Office; Kim Collis of the West Glamorgan Archive Service; Niclas L. Walker of St Fagans: National History Museum, Cardiff; Caroline Mason from the Cambrian Indexing Project; and Alex Effgen for help with the Silsbee Family Papers.

I am grateful to the Bodleian Library, University of Oxford, for granting me permission to quote from the Abinger manuscripts; to the Peabody Essex Museum, Salem, Massachusetts, for the Silsbee Family Papers; and to the Mitchell Library, State Library of New South Wales, for the Berry, Wollstonecraft and Hay papers.

For their generous help with the illustrations I would also like to thank Lady Bally-Clairmont, Bernice Cardy, Charles C. Carter, Lady Clairmont von Gonzenbach, Helen Drinkwater and Haidee Jackson.

LIST OF ILLUSTRATIONS

16. George Gordon, 6th Baron Byron by Henry Hoppner Meyer, after George Henry Harlow (*c.* 1816); National Portrait Gallery, London.
17. Fanny Wollstonecraft's handwriting; Bodleian Library, Oxford.
18. Advertisement for the Cambrian Coach.
19. Coroner's bill for inquests, quarter sessions roll for 1816; Glamorgan Record Office, Cardiff.
20. The Mackworth Arms in Wind Street, Swansea, by William Butler (*c.* 1840); City & County of Swansea: Swansea Museum.
21. Shelley's verses on Fanny's suicide; Bodleian Library, Oxford.
22. Shelley's drawings; Bodleian Library, Oxford.
23. Marble memorial to Mary and Percy Bysshe Shelley in Christchurch Priory Church, Dorset, England; Helen Drinkwater.
24. William Godwin by William Brockedon (1832); National Portrait Gallery, London.

Frontispiece
Fanny's letter from London to Mary and Shelley in Geneva, written in the summer before her death; Bodleian Library, Oxford.

PART I

CHAPTER 1

DEATH

ON 12 OCTOBER 1816 the *Cambrian* newspaper in Wales reported the suicide of an unknown young woman in the upstairs room of a coaching inn called the Mackworth Arms in Wind Street, Swansea. She had arrived three days earlier from Bristol on the evening coach; the following morning she had been found dead by the maid. Next to the body was a note; the signature had been torn off, so nobody knew the woman's identity. It was, however, clear that she was not the most common female suicide, a poor girl in the family way, but a 'most respectable' lady.

The newspaper printed the note as part of a good story – suicide accounts were popular. It read:

> I have long determined that the best thing I could do was to put an
> end to the existence of a being whose birth was unfortunate, and
> whose life has only been a series of pain to those persons who have
> hurt their health in endeavouring to promote her welfare. Perhaps
> to hear of my death will give you pain, but you will soon have the
> blessing of forgetting that such a creature ever existed as

The words stopped abruptly at the tear.

Nobody came forward to claim the body and it was buried, probably at the parish's expense in a pauper's grave.

So ended the existence of Fanny Wollstonecraft, half-sister of Mary Shelley, stepchild of William Godwin and eldest daughter of the celebrated feminist Mary Wollstonecraft. Who tore off the signature, so preventing identification of the body, and why?

One suggestion of Shelley and Godwin biographers is that the maid did it, instructed by the innkeeper to avoid the taint of suicide on the premises. But there seems no obvious point to this. The note and laudanum bottle made clear what had happened.

Possibly Fanny herself tore it off, suddenly feeling her own lack of identity – like Mary's Creature in *Frankenstein* she had no secure name. Illegitimate child of Mary Wollstonecraft, she was, strictly speaking, Fanny Wollstonecraft. Yet she had been registered at her birthplace in France as Françoise Imlay, using her father's name. For most of her short life she had been called Fanny Godwin courtesy of her stepfather. When he married again the second Mrs Godwin rather resented the fact, and Fanny knew it.

Or perhaps she wished on reflection to spare the Godwins embarrassment, knowing as she did how their lives had been dogged by scandal. But the mimicry of what she must have heard at home – 'hurt their health in endeavouring to promote my welfare' – sounds bitter, and she died with items that could tell the suspicious who she was: stays marked 'MW' and a Swiss gold watch, as well as the aggrieved note. It seems unlikely that she tore off the name she had written.

There remains another option: Percy Bysshe Shelley, her sister Mary's lover.

What follows is an attempt to understand why Fanny Wollstonecraft/ Imlay/ Godwin should have killed herself and written her note and why Shelley, acting on behalf of Godwin and Mary, probably defaced it.

CHAPTER 2

GENIUS

FANNY'S DEATH WAS not inevitable but it was resolutely planned.
It required a long journey to find a concealed and private place – a journey
which gave ample opportunity for second thoughts. The day before she set
out to kill herself, I believe she spoke to Shelley in Bath. He would then
be the last of her friends and relatives to see her alive. His response in their
unrecorded conversation almost certainly finalised her decision to die. It
gave new and fatal weight to the many private slights and rejections which
over the past two years since 1814 had fed her insecurity and shadowed her
intense hopes.

Hers was not an idiosyncratic pain: it came from an involvement – more
marginal than she would have wished – in a major and decisive shift in
the nature of European culture. This was the emergence of a cult of genius
– the veneration of genius as something that exempted its possessor from the
moral and social principles that governed everyday humanity. Genius was a
new form of aristocracy. Beethoven reproved Goethe for his social deference
to a nobleman: Goethe was, he declared, the far greater of the two.

Paradoxically, the first two meteoric geniuses to emerge in Britain –
Byron and Shelley – were both upper class, their glamour as Romantic artists
inseparable from the old glamour of the aristocrat. Shelley was an egalitarian,
and his social and emotional entanglements with bourgeois characters would
have been impossible had he not taken this character. Yet his egalitarianism

was also one of the privileges of his high social standing. The combination inspired him to moral experiments unthinkable to bourgeois radicals like William Godwin from whom he imbibed many of his principles.

The four geniuses who dominated Fanny's short life of twenty-two years are, from the earlier generation, her dead mother Mary Wollstonecraft and her stepfather William Godwin, both Enlightenment eighteenth-century thinkers, and from the second generation the Romantic nineteenth-century figures of her half-sister Mary with her lover, then husband, Percy Bysshe Shelley.

৩

Fanny was the daughter of Mary Wollstonecraft, famous for her daring feminist manifesto of 1792, *A Vindication of the Rights of Woman*. This pleaded for an austere, rational womanhood to replace the emotional femininity then in fashion: with proper education women could prove they were intellectually equal to men. It was not an entirely novel idea but it was expressed dramatically in the revolutionary rhetoric of the time. Women, Mary Wollstonecraft declared, should aim at controlling not men but themselves; they should become independent beings, not artful mistresses.

For a while the work received excited and enthusiastic response. Christian liberal women such as Anna Seward called it a 'wonderful book' which applied 'the spear of Ithuriel' to patriarchal systems; the respectable playwright Hannah Cowley, though thinking any politics 'unfeminine', encountered in it a 'body of mind as I hardly ever met with'. Subscribers to circulating libraries complained that the book was so much in demand that 'there is no keeping it long enough to read it leisurely'.[1] But the tide soon turned, most violently when people learnt about the miserable private life of the book's author. Mary Wollstonecraft became a 'philosophical wanton' and an unsexed female whom no decorum had checked. It was, it seemed, difficult to exist entirely by reason. Sex and jealousy had a way of scrambling lives.

Fanny's father was more obscure. In Paris, a year after the publication of *The Rights of Woman*, Mary Wollstonecraft had fallen passionately in love with a tall handsome American entrepreneur from New Jersey called Gilbert Imlay. He promised an entrancing family life in the wilds of unspoilt America once he had made his fortune. In fact, after minimal engagement with the American War of Independence – which allowed him to term himself 'Captain Imlay' – and after being involved in the murky land speculations of the notorious James Wilkinson in Kentucky, Imlay had fled the United States leaving a trail of debts and unanswered court writs. Despite a past which included slave-dealing in the 1780s, he surfaced in Europe as a republican primitive from Kentucky with impeccable libertarian views: anti-slavery, anti-marriage, anti-religion. Sometimes he traded in French royalist silver; sometimes he dealt in frontier property he did not entirely own. Having written a book describing how idyllic (and affluent) life might be on the far side of the Alleghenies, he seduced disillusioned Europeans (and perhaps himself at times) with dreams of places elsewhere – much as he seduced Mary Wollstonecraft. For all his distinction from the geniuses who dominated his daughter's life, Imlay shares with them their talent for peddling non-existent destinations and fictitious utopias.

By contrast with Gilbert Imlay, Mary Wollstonecraft's second partner – Fanny's stepfather – was one of the most celebrated thinkers of his age. William Godwin had come from a poor Dissenting family in rural Norfolk into the centre of metropolitan political debate with his book *An Enquiry Concerning Political Justice*, a *cause célèbre* in 1793. For a few years in this revolutionary decade he became one of London's most renowned intellectuals, blazing 'as a sun in the firmament of reputation'. His writings contained 'the oracles of thought': 'Throw aside your books of chemistry,' the young poet Wordsworth exclaimed, 'and read Godwin on Necessity.'[2] Copies were bought by subscribers and read aloud in political meetings. Samuel Taylor Coleridge 'hymned' Godwin with 'an ardent lay':

> For that thy voice, in Passion's stormy day,
> When wild I roam'd the bleak heath of Distress,
> Bade the bright form of Justice meet my way –
> And told me that her name was HAPPINESS.[3]

Political Justice believed in the future improvement of humanity, not through the violent communal actions of revolutionary France but through individual effort. Raised to become a Dissenting minister, Godwin had

replaced his faith in Christianity with a belief in reason and human poten-
tiality: he brought to his opinions all the fervour of a former Puritan divine
– and all the fundamentalism of a convert. In place of hope for heaven and
a Christian millennium he provided a millennial vision of the ordinary
world transformed through reason into a state without war, crime, disease
or selfishness.

The book taught philosophical anarchism; it doubted the value of arti-
ficial human institutions – monarchy, party government, law and religion
– all of which ossified thought. They would fade away, Godwin believed, as
people became wiser and more rational and sought the good of all. Private
familial affections were at base selfish: marriage was a monopoly, 'an affair
of property, and the worst of all properties'; its abolition 'will be attended
with no evils'. 'The supposition that I must have a companion for life, is the
result of a complication of vices. It is the dictate of cowardice, and not of
fortitude. It flows from the desire of being loved and esteemed for something
that is not desert.'[4]

In more conservative times, after the bloody trajectory of the French
Revolution had made radicalism suspect in England, Godwin became more
cautious. 'I have fallen (if I have fallen) in one common grave with the cause
and love of liberty,' he wrote as he toned down later editions of his great
book.[5] The versions of 1796 and 1799 now declared that different stages of
history required different institutions: marriage was a contract that must be
honoured; it could not be disdained in society as it now existed.

He acted out his more pragmatic view when, as a bachelor of forty in
1797, he gave in to Mary Wollstonecraft's pleas once she found herself pregnant by him. The pair were married a few months before their daughter
was born. Ten days after the birth Mary Wollstonecraft died. The new baby
was baptised Mary Wollstonecraft Godwin: she would grow up to become
Mary Shelley – after Jane Austen, the most talented woman novelist of the
early nineteenth century. Her most famous work, *Frankenstein,* was a muted
celebration of her father's great book.

❧

Had a matchmaker been called in to find a wife and soulmate for the young
radical thinker and poet Percy Bysshe Shelley, passionate republican heir of

a baronetcy, she would surely have lighted on Mary Wollstonecraft Godwin, an attractive, clever girl of lower but respectable social class and the daughter of two famous republican parents.

As a schoolboy Shelley had imbibed and come to revere Godwin's principles. However, the two men's class difference ensured that they lived out those principles quite differently. On the one hand Godwin was a bourgeois radical. If in their earliest and fieriest form in *Political Justice* his social theories committed him to reject marriage and espouse sexual freedom, in practice he had heeded public opinion. In one area alone he held by his radical principles: in the sphere of finance. He believed that the world owed intellectuals a living and must relieve him in particular from the consequences of his own imprudence. Hence the mutually parasitic tie with Percy Bysshe Shelley, disciple, patron and, to his horror, seducer of his sixteen-year-old daughter.

On the other hand, Shelley's egalitarianism was sustained by his secure sense of gentry privilege. If the corrosive need of money became the dominant factor in Godwin's middle-class married life, Shelley, grandson of a rich baronet, could always feel that his own money problems should not by right be happening to him at all: they should not interfere with the *droit de seigneur* of a genius.

The newly radicalised gentleman could bear a striking resemblance to the old-style eighteenth-century aristocratic libertine. Yet the artistic glamour of the genius gave Shelley the cult-leader's ability to draw young women of middle-class background not simply into his bed but into the insecurity and infamy of an itinerant sexual commune.

He knew inside out the incendiary first version of *Political Justice* which he thought gave him licence to find love and sex where he could – especially with Godwin's daughter. For this act he had had to separate the great author William Godwin from the outraged father and disregard the caveats in later editions, that an individual flouted conventions at his (or usually her) peril. In Godwin's view Shelley ignored the fact that *Political Justice* in all its versions preached reason, not the self-interested passion with which the young man left England with two sixteen-year-old girls. Shelley's living out of Godwin's abstract principles in ways that horrified their creator is a tale with many casualties.

In 1816 Shelley's 21-year-old wife Harriet, whom he had deserted for

Godwin's daughter Mary, committed suicide. Her death came only a few weeks after 22-year-old Fanny's. In the world of pragmatic compromise envisaged by Jane Austen at about the same time, enthusiastic Harriet as Marianne Dashwood from *Sense & Sensibility* should have lived to find a kinder man, while compassionate Fanny could and should have gained the rewards earned by her namesake Fanny Price in *Mansfield Park*. Instead both encountered Shelley's utopian absolutism.

⚜

To a perhaps unprecedented degree the lives of Shelley and his circle were interchangeable with texts. Its members saw the world not only through *Political Justice* but also through books such as *Paradise Lost* and the eighteenth-century European bestsellers, Goethe's *Sorrows of Young Werther* and Rousseau's *La Nouvelle Héloïse,* with their stories of extreme and indulged emotions. Real lives implemented literary theories and in time Shelley and Mary even, recursively, wrote about characters who tried to understand existence from the precepts of the books they read and reread rather than from their own experience: Frankenstein's Creature, for example, in part pieces together his past from *Paradise Lost*.

People had always lived by books: by various bibles, by romances and tales, but also, less often, by treatises. A century and a half earlier, men such as the Earl of Rochester were thought to have been corrupted into atheism and licentiousness by Thomas Hobbes's *Leviathan*. But Hobbes was in the end a theorist of the established order, offering an alternative theory for what existed. Godwin's work, if translated from theory into practice, would affect all action, public and private, and take the actor out of ordinary society and its conventions. Yet his book provided no personal gratification as the Bible or romance – or indeed Hobbes – did. Shelley would seek to remedy this fact.

The younger generation had their lives turned into texts almost as they were living them: Fanny, for instance, read about her own conception, birth and infancy in her mother's published writings. Both she and her half-sister Mary may have seen themselves in characters William Godwin drew in his novels as they grew up within his house. Much of what Mary wrote to Fanny of her European journeys was published later as a travelogue. Yet, amidst all this frenzy of literary production, Fanny in Swansea left behind for publication only a suicide note – to which an anonymous hand denied her an author's rights.

∾

Fanny's short life is defined by two symmetrical journeys, both to goals as imaginary as any marketed by her two fathers Gilbert Imlay and William Godwin. In the first Fanny was present but unknowing; in the second absent but very much aware. Both were transmuted into enduring literature, the first into Mary Wollstonecraft's published love letters to Imlay, believed by Godwin to equal the fictional love letters Goethe imagined for his hero Werther, as well as the engaging travel book *Letters from Sweden*. The second, the elopement of her daughter Mary and Shelley in 1814, had its most durable literary consequence in Mary's novel *Frankenstein,* a work much about utopian journeying – as well as about suicide and motherless children.

Mary Wollstonecraft's journey was to Scandinavia, an area little known to English travellers, rarely visited by a woman and her baby. It followed her abandonment by her lover Imlay; its ostensible purpose was to recover his stolen cargo of royalist silver, its ulterior one to regain his lost affection. She had only partial success with the first goal, none with the second.

In 1814 the journey of her daughter Mary with Shelley once more displayed idealism dissolving into disappointment. It had been inspired by Godwin's imaginary picture of free Switzerland in his novel *Fleetwood*, but it foundered on insolvency and jealousy. As one of Shelley's acquaintances would remark, 'His journeys after what he has never found have racked his Purse & his Tranquillity.'[6]

Both journeys would haunt and determine Fanny's short life. In her own, final, one, to a Welsh coaching inn, as so often she provided a reverse image of the exotic travelling of the two Marys, mother and sister. Old family connections perhaps gave South Wales comforting familiarity, but the place had nothing in common with the mirages on offer in Godwin's Switzerland or Imlay's Kentucky. Indeed, the status of Swansea in the nineteenth-century imagination seems roughly equivalent to that with which Dylan Thomas invested nearby Laugharne when he renamed it Llareggub. 'Have you been looking after me?' asks a character in Douglas Jerrold's play *Beau Nash, The King of Bath*.

'In every corner of the world,' is the reply.

'Have you been at Swansea?'

'No.'

After a life shadowed by literature Fanny could scarcely have contrived a less literary death.

CHAPTER 3

MARY

THE LOVE STORY of Mary and Shelley accelerated in 1814, two years before Fanny travelled to Swansea to die.

Between four and five in the morning of 28 July 1814 in London the sixteen-year-old Mary Godwin, slight, light-haired younger daughter of the dead Mary Wollstonecraft, wrote a note of farewell to her father William Godwin and left it in his room propped up where he would see it. She paid no mind to her half-sister Fanny, who was away in Wales. The absence suited the runaway, since Fanny, had she been at home, would have been up by then – she was a known early riser. She would have tried to prevent Mary leaving and causing such pain to her father. Or, just possibly, she might have gone with her – and her life story would have been quite different.

Mary woke her stepsister Claire Clairmont, daughter of the second Mrs Godwin, Mary Wollstonecraft's much criticised successor. Claire was a pretty girl, with dark hair and eyes, a little younger than Mary. Then the pair crept out of 41 Skinner Street. They were dressed in sombre silk gowns and carried bundles of their clothes, letters and writings. They walked along the road to the edge of Hatton Garden where Percy Bysshe Shelley, a tall, lanky figure with thick, wild hair, 'flexible' face, and large very blue eyes, had been watching 'until the lightning & the stars became pale'.[1] He had a hired coach and horses in readiness. Mary was eloping from her father's house.

She may already have been pregnant, her poor health over the next days a possible sign, although she had a tendency to travel sickness, and impregnation may have occurred on the journey. Shelley, Mary and Claire were planning to go to Switzerland, which Claire regarded as her native land since her mother, who was given to colourful stories, said rather implausibly that her father had been Swiss. Shelley was inspired by *Fleetwood*, in which the hero describes Switzerland as an idyllic place of liberty and primitive manners – Godwin himself had never been beyond the British archipelago but an imaginative vision was as good as a guidebook for these literary young people. Godwin's Switzerland seemed to Shelley a proper location to establish a community of free love and kindred spirits, of physical and intellectual fulfilment.

Claire had been chaperone at the clandestine meetings of Shelley and her stepsister by the side of Mary Wollstonecraft's tomb and was eager not to be outdone in act and attitude. She knew French, so could be useful when they reached the Continent. Although he could read and quote extensively from books, Shelley, like Mary and Fanny, spoke the language haltingly, as Claire gleefully noted. But Shelley had also invited Claire for her own sake. He liked the company of many girls – he had grown up in a court of admiring sisters. This was not the first pair of women he had rescued. Three years earlier, in 1811, he had eloped with Harriet Westbrook, just turned sixteen; soon he brought her sister to join them. He was now abandoning Harriet for another sixteen-year-old girl and bringing along her sister at once.

Mrs Godwin, who disliked her stepdaughter, said Claire was tricked into the elopement by Mary, who invited her to take a walk 'to breathe a little morning air in Marylebone fields'; Shelley then pushed Claire into the carriage – it was virtually a kidnapping.[2] But everything points to a voluntary exit. Still a week short of his twenty-second birthday, Shelley fascinated all the girls in Skinner Street – Fanny, Claire and Mary; he was charismatic, transfiguring with his personality and smile. According to Claire, it was 'as if he had just landed from Heaven'.[3] Shelley would often inspire this kind of comment.

At Dartford Shelley hired four new horses to speed them to Dover. Nonetheless the journey took all day and the heat was so oppressive it made Mary faint. They had missed the boat to France but, in the evening after dinner, instead of waiting for the next packet Shelley hired two sailors who carried them out to sea in an open fishing craft. It tossed on the waves like the paper boats he loved to sail on rivers and lakes.

They travelled through the night. The evening was calm but just before morning a heavy storm ended the oppressive heat and almost overturned them. Mary was sea-sick and lay across Shelley, who could hardly stay awake to support her. Exhausted, he mused on death, wondering 'what will befall this inestimable spirit when we appear to die'. As the storm subsided the wind blew them towards Calais, where they arrived in the morning. Mary felt wretched after a 'comfortless sleep' but Shelley's spirits soared with the light: 'the broad sun rose over France'.[4]

Back in Skinner Street, Godwin read the note propped up on his dressing table and saw the empty beds. He was appalled. As Mrs Godwin would later write to her Irish acquaintance, Lady Mount Cashell, it would have been better if the girls had never read books and imbibed free principles. If she and Godwin had brought them up 'on an inferior footing as befitted our poverty they would never have attracted Mr S's attention and they might now be safe at home'.[5]

Mrs Godwin did not expect to prevail on a girl like Mary, whom she regarded as spoilt and self-willed. But her own daughter Claire, only just sixteen, might be rescued. She had not been Shelley's prime target and possibly could be persuaded to return intact. So Mrs Godwin set off for France in hot pursuit of the trio. She travelled all night, then made the Channel crossing by day, alighting in Calais in the evening after their arrival. She was tired but resolute. It was usually the habit of Shelley, grandson of a baronet and heir to a fortune, to stay at the best lodgings in town. She easily found him and the girls in rooms in Dessein's hotel, made famous by Laurence Sterne's *Sentimental Journey* nearly half a century earlier. Literary associations always appealed to them.

Soon they heard that a fat lady was calling for her daughter with whom Shelley had run away.

Claire spent the night alone with her mother, who worked to persuade her that she had been abducted by Shelley. By morning Claire was won over by Mrs Godwin's 'pathos' (Shelley's word, perhaps Claire's as well) and was ready to return to Skinner Street. But after some talk with Shelley she felt anew the glamour of wandering through Europe unparented. Claire and Mary were competitive, and Claire baulked at the idea of her stepsister having such an adventure without her.

When she heard her daughter's decision Mrs Godwin said nothing;

she simply went home alone. With some satisfaction Shelley watched her waddling down to the Dover boat. He had never liked her. Back in Skinner Street she felt embarrassed that she had not been more persistent, that her husband had not come with her and that her daughter had withstood her pleas. So, when she wrote to Lady Mount Cashell, she made a more acceptable version, substituting James Marshall, one of Godwin's oldest friends, for herself. He was said to have tried but failed to see Claire, then to have proceeded to Paris after the runaways. Mrs Godwin was desperate to present her own daughter in the best possible light.

❦

Shelley was steeped in the works of Mary Wollstonecraft. He had arrived at the Godwin household so full of admiration for the dead feminist that he was already half in love with her children. Through their childhoods Fanny and Mary had been encouraged almost into idolatry of their mother, and as they grew up they made frequent visits to her grave. All had probably by now read her account of the French Revolution and were familiar with the early promises of regeneration.

She had described a dramatic Paris, for she had arrived there in early 1793 just in time to see the Bourbon monarch Louis XVI travelling to his trial for treason; he would be executed a few weeks later. She was frightened and alone, wishing she had even kept a cat for company. As the Terror took hold of Paris over the next months she walked near the new guillotine and found the streets running with blood. The abrupt change outside from hope to horror mirrored her own intense moods with Imlay, of happiness and misery as she discovered love and sex for the first time, then lost both.

To Mary, Claire and Shelley her accounts breathed of epic emotion and more heroic times than those they inhabited. Her Paris had been terrible and dramatic. Theirs in 1814 was less exciting.

The French Revolution had given way to dictatorship and empire. After years of conquest, Napoleon had surrendered unconditionally to Britain and her allies on 11 April and been exiled to Elba. To the disgust of many British liberals, the Bourbon monarchy under Louis XVIII, fatter even than their own Prince Regent, was re-established in Paris. In London months after the victory there were still commemorations in St James's Park, but in France the newly dispossessed were disgruntled. Returning émigrés were eager to put back the clock, pretending that the tumult of nearly thirty years had never happened.

Peace would soon be interrupted by Napoleon's astounding return and final defeat at Waterloo in 1815, but for the moment the city swarmed with English tourists, shut out from trips to Paris since the brief peace of Amiens a decade before. One person who had been there all along was Helen Maria Williams, chronicler of the entire history of France from the Revolution to the Bourbon Restoration. She had welcomed Mary Wollstonecraft to her republican salon in the early 1790s. From her Mary and Shelley had hoped to hear personal stories of a mother Mary had never known. But Helen Maria Williams was away in the country, or at least 'not at home'. Perhaps she meant to be unavailable. Despite her own unconventional lifestyle, Helen Maria Williams was always keen to keep up proprieties.

Underlying their disappointment with the dingily grand city was their lack of money. Shelley had expected funds from his bookseller acquaintance, Thomas Hookham. Instead he found a letter of reproach. Yet he managed to prise £60 out of a moneylender. With this they could get to Switzerland if they walked. So on 8 August Shelley, with Claire, bought a donkey from the market. It would carry their baggage, including the load of books they felt necessary for any journey: Mary Wollstonecraft's first novel for example, *Mary, A Fiction,* about a woman who, unsuitably married off, is unable to follow her heart with another and in the end welcomes death as the only exit. They would read it together on the rocks among the French hills.

They were poor judges of donkeys and a few miles from Paris their animal sank down and refused to budge. They swapped it for a mule, paying over the odds. The £60 was not going to take them far. Nonetheless Shelley took this moment to dispatch a letter to his wife Harriet suggesting she might find her own solitary way to Switzerland to join them. Their friend, Thomas Love Peacock, would advise her on how to travel alone and use her money wisely, and she should bring the deed of separation between herself and Shelley being prepared by his lawyers, as well as a copy of her marriage settlement.

She would come not as his wife – though she was five months pregnant with their second child – but as a member of a commune presided over by her replacement, Mary Godwin. Harriet did not reply but the letter, though hurtful, gave her hope that, after the adventure, Shelley would return to her. It was well she did not set out, since they themselves would long since have left Switzerland by the time she arrived.

No invitation went to Mary's half-sister Fanny, for Shelley knew her deep respect for her stepfather Godwin. The previous year, before being tainted with the scandalous elopement and before he had actually met the admired author of *Political Justice*, Shelley had written to Godwin suggesting Fanny come to join his family, then consisting of his wife Harriet and her sister. To his amazement Godwin had not lived up to the principles of his great work but, instead, following convention had refused the offer on her behalf.

The journey to Switzerland was hot, especially for Mary and Claire, still in their black silk dresses. The land, devastated by what Shelley called the 'liberticide' war, was stripped of trees and the impoverished peasants provided bad food and uncomfortable shelter. The mule was traded for a carriage and more of their money disappeared. But Shelley continued to feel expansive. They encountered a pretty child; he at once offered to take her with them. The father refused. Such acts were not uncommon – Mary Wollstonecraft had adopted a girl, Ann, abandoned only after she found that the child had been habitually filching sugar. But Shelley's sudden enthusiasms were more idiosyncratic; when still in school he had wanted to adopt a travelling acrobat and in the year of his elopement with Harriet he wished to shut himself away with two poor girls aged four or five: he would educate them, he claimed, so that he could see the effect of impressions on unprejudiced minds.

Feeling increasingly attracted to Shelley and jealous of Mary, Claire made niggling remarks. On one occasion she complained so bitterly of rats and a lecherous host that the lovers had to take her into their bed. Mary and Shelley were composing a journal together; Shelley soon abandoned it since he was not a natural diarist. For Mary, however, everything had to be recorded: she had the itch of scribbling habitual at home, and rarely did anything without thinking how it would read on the page. Competitive as usual, Claire too began a diary in one of Shelley's old notebooks. In it he had jotted down in various languages some erotic thoughts of lovemaking. It was heady stuff for a teenaged girl who had lost her reputation without the pleasure of doing so.

Claire would use the diary to record her own sensations. By now she was employing her famed hysteria – or 'horrors', as Mary named the episodes – to some effect. They had been reading Shakespeare's *King Lear* together and Mary suspected her stepsister of trying to attract Shelley with a display of sensitivity. In her diary Claire described how Cordelia's question 'What shall poor Cordelia do – Love & be silent' struck a chord in her: 'Real Love … courts the secret glades,' she wrote.[6]

The experiment in communal living had turned out less rapturous than Shelley had hoped. Sexual and emotional tensions surfaced as Mary tried to assert her exclusive hold, while Claire, entranced by her stepsister's lover, vied for his attention. On one occasion they came close to a stream beside some trees; Shelley bathed 'as if he were Adam in Paradise before the fall' and suggested that Mary bathe naked also – he would dry her with leaves. Mary thought it 'most indecent', Claire recorded, suggesting that she herself would have done this willingly. She felt altogether closer to Shelley's ideal of liberated woman than her favoured stepsister. She rather than Mary would be a new Mary Wollstonecraft.

To onlookers, Mary and Shelley gave a rather bedraggled impression and a Swiss man took them for runaways from their parents. When Claire confirmed this he asked her if she too was a fugitive for love. 'Oh! Dear No,' she replied. 'I came to speak french.'[7] There had always been runaways but this trio was unusual. Perhaps only children like Mary and Claire brought up in Godwin's household could be quite so contemptuous of convention, and an heir to a grand fortune like Shelley quite so cavalier about money.

In Switzerland they had again expected something from Hookham but nothing awaited them. They had less that £30 between them, just enough to return to England if they went cheaply down the Rhine. This they decided to do and their extreme reaction to the people they met en route shows their discomfort with themselves by now: Mary called their smoking German fellow-travellers 'uncleansable animals' and 'loathsome creepers'. Later she would look back on the remembered beauties of the Rhine as paradise, something akin to her mother's pictures of Scandinavia purged of the 'dark shades'.[8]

Unconcerned as they often seemed about paying debts, they all noticed they could not pay for the Channel crossing. The captain made a boatman row them up the Thames and follow them through the London streets until they found the fare. They tried various sources, including Hookham, without success, then went round to Chapel Street where Shelley obtained £20 from the wife he had abandoned three months before. Mr and Mrs Godwin were out of the question and they did not approach Fanny, knowing she had no money.

Yet this jaunt of her sister, stepsister and Shelley, this journey for which she had had no invitation and no warning, would affect Fanny's life quite as much as it would theirs. Godwin said that it unsettled her mind, while Claire later remarked, '[A]fter [Shelley] carried off Mary and me – there came a change ... [Fanny] suffered deeply.'[9] Indeed the elopement, seemingly so hare-brained with its squabbling girls and inadequate donkeys, altered the lives of everyone in 41 Skinner Street.

CHAPTER 4

MARY WOLLSTONECRAFT

THROUGHOUT THEIR JOURNEY Mary and Shelley had been accompanied by Mary Wollstonecraft's most appealing work, *Letters from Sweden, Norway and Denmark*, which described her daring voyage to Scandinavia with her baby. The book, her last completed one before her death following childbirth in 1797, was based in part on letters sent to Imlay and, since so much concerned their child Fanny, it served to give the infant a literary, textual life long before she could talk or write herself. Fanny would always live for others, and indeed for herself, in this seductive work, which, together with the published love letters to Imlay, would reveal both the magnificence of Mary Wollstonecraft and the abjection that made her twice intend to abandon the child she so much loved. For before and after the voyage to Scandinavia, Mary Wollstonecraft had tried to kill herself.

In 1796, when it had first been published, Godwin read *Letters from Sweden* and commented: 'If ever there was a book calculated to make a man in love with its author, this appears to me to be the book.'[1] Mary, Shelley and Claire shared his admiration and in 1814 they carried the work through France and into Switzerland. When others were left behind, this precious book was always packed, finding a place on their donkey, on their mule, in the carriage and on the river. On the cargo boat going down the Rhine Shelley read it aloud to Mary and Claire. They had just celebrated Mary's seventeenth birthday and she was pregnant. Thinking on her own birth and future she may have wanted to hear again this northern voyage of the heart and visualise Mary Wollstonecraft as mother.

In the early letters to Imlay written in France before the Scandinavian voyage Mary had tenderly displayed her pride in baby Fanny, her 'quantity of brains', her health and spiritedness: 'the little damsel ... has been almost springing out of my arm,' she told him. Fanny was 'a little sprite' and a 'little Hercules'. She negotiated smallpox with ease although badly marked by the disease. She would not be a beauty, but her mother was pleased to note her sunny vibrant disposition – the Wollstonecrafts were a moody, over-sensitive family. Perhaps Fanny would have her father's breezy temperament

She would not, however, have his care, for Imlay soon tired of fatherhood. Bitterly Mary Wollstonecraft remarked, 'Amongst the feathered race, whilst the hen keeps the young warm, her mate stays by to cheer her; but it is sufficient for man to condescend to get a child, in order to claim it.' Alone in France she experienced motherhood as draining, sometimes feeling 'almost a slave to the child'. But when she found a robust Parisian nursemaid called Marguerite, Fanny, 'as gay as a lark', became her only comfort as Imlay retreated from them both. The child responded to her love: 'Her eyes follow me every where, and by affection I have the most despotic power over her,' the mother wrote.

At intervals she threatened to go off with Fanny but the threats were idle – Imlay, ebullient as ever, simply did not mind. The baby cut her teeth and made 'good use of them to gnaw a crust ... she is just like a little squirrel ... nothing can equal her life and spirits.' Certainly her mother could not: 'I am sick at heart; and, but for this little darling, I would cease to care about a life, which is now stripped of every charm.'[2] She envied mothers who had been killed with their children by the guillotine.

In spring 1795, with Fanny and her nurse Marguerite, Mary Wollstonecraft arrived back in London from France. Imlay tried to live with them, then abandoned the attempt. Now not even one-year-old Fanny could bind her mother to life. In May she tried suicide, probably with an overdose of laudanum, but was discovered in time by Imlay.

His curious answer to their predicament was for Mary Wollstonecraft to travel to Scandinavia as his 'wife' and business representative to see what had happened to a stolen ship carrying French silver in which he had a large commercial interest. He promised to meet her and Fanny in Switzerland at the end of their journey; then they would all live together as a family. Again he fed her dream of rescue, of a safe domestic haven.

In June Mary with baby Fanny and the nurse Marguerite set off for Scandinavia. She conducted her business, sometimes with Fanny in tow and sometimes alone while the baby stayed behind with Marguerite; feeling solitary, she would see traces of Fanny wherever she went, hearing her soft cooing in the air and seeing her little footprints on the empty sands. Melancholy and weary herself, she pitied her child grown to adulthood in a world she herself had found so harsh:

> I feel more than a mother's fondness and anxiety, when I reflect on the dependent and oppressed state of her sex. I dread lest she should be forced to sacrifice her heart to her principles, or principles to her heart. With trembling hand I shall cultivate sensibility, and cherish delicacy of sentiment, lest, whilst I lend fresh blushes to the rose, I sharpen the thorns that will wound the breast I would fain guard – I dread to unfold her mind, lest it should render her unfit for the world she is to inhabit – Hapless woman! what a fate is thine!

Mother and child became interchangeable as Mary quoted from Sterne's cruelly optimistic *Sentimental Journey*: 'Poor lamb! It may run very well in a tale, that "God will temper the winds to the shorn lamb!"'; then capped it with a tragic echo of *King Lear*: 'but how can I expect that she will be shielded, when my naked bosom has had to brave continually the pitiless storm?'[3]

In September Mary Wollstonecraft, Fanny and the nurse arrived in Dover; Imlay was not there to meet them but he had provided lodgings in London. Mary begged him to live with her for the sake of their 'interesting child' but he refused. When she learnt he was cohabiting with an actress, she could bear life no longer. She determined to kill herself in earnest. A suicide letter gave directions for Fanny to be delivered to a friend in Paris: 'I write you now on my knees; imploring you to send my child and the maid with ——, to Paris, to be consigned to the care of Madame ——, 2 rue ——, section de ——. Should they be removed, —— can give their direction. Let the maid have all my clothes, without distinction.'[4]

The main message in the note was Mary's bitterness at her abandonment and hope of psychological revenge: 'Should your sensibility ever awake, remorse will find its way to your heart; and, in the midst of business and sensual pleasure, I shall appear before you, the victim of your deviation from rectitude.'

Then she went to Putney Bridge and threw herself in the Thames. She was rescued by fishermen as she drifted unconscious down the river.

She felt no guilt. When she recovered she declared her attempted suicide a rational act. For her final unfinished novel *Maria, or The Wrongs of Woman*, she left multiple endings, most of which allow the heroine to succeed in killing herself as the most appropriate thing to do. The child, if still alive, would be abandoned. In life, however, she felt her responsibility: 'I daily labour to remember that I still have the duty of a mother to fulfil.'[5]

She was not ashamed of love outside marriage but thought it politic now to pass as Mrs Imlay, especially as she had to earn her living as an author. Her image as unhappy mother (but not fallen woman) was one of the charms of *Letters from Sweden*. It presented herself and baby Fanny as wayfarers in a romantic wilderness.

PART II

CHAPTER 5

FANNY

LETTERS FROM SWEDEN attracted several men to its melancholy writer. These included the famously austere bachelor, William Godwin, then forty, who had, some years before, found the author of *The Rights of Woman* quite overbearing when at a dinner party he had come to hear the radical activist Tom Paine speak, rather than the 'assertrix' of female rights. For all his philosophical radicalism Godwin believed in separate spheres and liked some gentleness and deference in women.

He was no Gilbert Imlay. In appearance he was rather unprepossessing: of middle height and stocky, he had a large head and nose and he parted his hair in unflattering revolutionary style. He seemed cold, the embodiment of his own anti-passionate rational theories, and he displayed a mixture of awkwardness and vanity, shyness and pomposity.

On closer inspection some women found him appealing. Recently he had become more susceptible and his most romantic feelings had been aroused by a married lady called Maria Reveley, whose husband for a time found him importunate and forbade him their house. He was also attracted to Elizabeth Inchbald, a playwright and novelist in her forties, still beautiful and still enjoying the admiration of many men. Shortly after re-meeting Mary Wollstonecraft, Godwin entered a quite new phase of life: he became her lover.

By now Fanny was walking and talking. Sometimes she played with

Maria Reveley's seven-year-old son Henry, who would remember her as 'a most amiable loving little girl, though plain and ... pitted with small-pox'. Amelia Opie, another young friend of Godwin's, admired her 'strong, well-formed limbs and florid complexion', while Godwin's sister Hannah thought she resembled her mother in appearance.[1]

Godwin's relationship with Mary Wollstonecraft was never placid. He was new to sex and habitual affection, and she remained emotionally vulnerable. She upset him with her moodiness and he annoyed her with his ponderous self-centredness. But with Fanny he was patient and Mary Wollstonecraft worked hard to include him within the family – 'give Fanny a biscuit – I want you to love each other,' she told him.

Godwin fell easily into the role of surrogate father, and he and Mary sometimes jocularly called each other 'Mama' and 'Papa'. Fanny grew fond of him and he gave her cakes and pudding when she called on him with her nurse; sometimes she stayed with him in his messy lodgings. When she and her mother neared them on their walk, she would pipe up, '[G]o this way Mama, me wants to see Man.' But she had to control herself as well: Fanny 'wishes to ask Man's pardon – She won't cry any more,' Mary wrote. Godwin responded by occasionally signing himself 'Man'.[2]

Fanny could probably recall little of her biological father but she had the security of her mother. Only once in Mary Wollstonecraft's extant letters was there any conflict between her new love and her duty to her child. She and Godwin went away for a night while Fanny was recovering from chicken pox. Missing her mother, the little girl fretted herself into renewed fever and scratched the spots. Already pitted with smallpox, her face was now further damaged.

The short absence had scarred Fanny's emotions as well as her face. When her mother stayed in bed one morning Fanny showed how deep was her fear of abandonment and she clung obsessively. The power was, as Mary Wollstonecraft once described, 'despotic'.

In December 1796 Mary realised she was pregnant for the second time. Although she was passing as Mrs Imlay, her child could not be Imlay's and she would be ostracised by almost everyone. Also, a new baby could only make her financial situation worse. A bond reluctantly accepted for Fanny from Imlay had not been paid – despite all his talk of large sums of money and speculations in American land and royalist silver, Imlay had nothing in London but debts. Meanwhile the publisher Joseph Johnson, who had helped Mary Wollstonecraft's writing career and lent her money over the years, noted her relationship with Godwin and offered no more help. She needed marriage and money.

Ignoring his own severe theories, Godwin rose to the occasion. '[T]he comfort and peace of a woman for whose comfort and peace I interest myself would be much injured if I could have prevailed on her to defy those prejudices,' he wrote to his friend Tom Wedgwood of Wedgwood china, his generous patron for many years.

The wedding took place on 29 March 1797 in St Pancras' church. When it became public some friends dropped Mary Wollstonecraft, realising now her earlier unmarried status; others mocked Godwin for so blatantly severing theory and practice. Others were impressed – they were the 'most extraordinary married pair in existence', declared his old radical friend Thomas Holcroft. To his pious mother in Norfolk he had no need to justify himself; yet, when he announced his marriage, he failed to mention Fanny's existence. 'You might have been so good as told me a few more particulars about your conjugal state,' wrote Mrs Godwin when fully informed, 'as when you were married, as being a father as well as a husband; I hope you will fill up your place with propriety in both relations.'[3]

With Tom Wedgwood's financial help, Mary, Godwin and Fanny moved together into the newly built Polygon in Somers Town, one of a group of tall, narrow, rather jerry-built but elegant terraced houses near fields and nursery gardens, but a little too close to the brickyards for fashionable people. Godwin also took lodgings nearby to use as a study, so avoiding complete immersion in family life; often he would be away all day, returning only for dinner in the late afternoon.

Fanny loved the Polygon, planning to make hay in the nearby fields with her new toy rake. Sometimes she and her mother walked together into the flat open country nearby. Often, however. they were forced to stay indoors for it was a stormy summer of squalls and comets, more turbulent than any time in living memory. Mary Wollstonecraft felt her bulk and longed for the birth to be over.

In June 1797, accompanied by his disciple Basil Montagu, Godwin visited Tom Wedgwood in Staffordshire. He wrote back to Mary, 'Take care of yourself, my love, & take care of William' (they had decided the 'creature' was a boy). 'Tell Fanny something about me. Ask her where she thinks I am. Say I am a great way off, & going further & further, but that I shall turn round & come back again some day. Tell her I have not forgotten her little mug & that I shall chuse a very pretty one. Montagu said this morning about eight o'clock upon the road, Just now little Fanny is going to plungity plunge. Was he right?'

In her response Mary reported: 'Fanny wanted to know "what you are gone for,"'; she was talking of 'Poor papa' and was 'turning your letter on all sides'. Godwin replied at once, 'Kiss Fanny for me; remember William; but (most of all) take care of yourself. Tell Fanny, I am safely in the land of mugs.' He had chosen a Wedgwood mug with an F on it. Back in London Fanny played with Henry Reveley; her head was running on 'Papa', and, when she lost her toy monkey, she announced that it had 'gone into the country'.[4]

The baby was due at the end of August. Godwin favoured having a male physician present but his wife, remembering the ease of Fanny's birth and believing women should minister to women, chose a midwife. On Wednesday 30 August labour began and late that night a puny baby was born – not William but a new Mary Wollstonecraft. At two in the morning of 1 September Godwin saw his new daughter; no one recorded whether three-year-old Fanny was introduced.

Then things went wrong. Mary Wollstonecraft's placenta failed to follow and began to rot inside her. Godwin sent Fanny away with Maria Reveley and, when his wife's milk became unsuitable for the new baby, it was drawn off by puppies; baby Mary followed Fanny to the Reveleys where a wet nurse was hurriedly engaged. Death approached with agonising slowness. Maria Reveley went to the Polygon for a final visit, taking her son Henry with her; probably Fanny was thought too young to see her mother in such straits.

Towards the end, Godwin thought he ought to talk to his wife about the future education of her two daughters but she was too weak to attend to him. She had, however, written 'Lessons' about the upbringing of very young children, based on life with Fanny; it could serve as some guide.

Mary Wollstonecraft died on 10 September. Fanny was to all intents and purposes an orphan. Yet her mother's 'despotic power' over her daughter would linger on.

⚬⧸

At her death Mary Wollstonecraft left an unfinished novel, *Maria*. Little Fanny was as central to it as she had been to *Letters from Sweden*. It describes a mother whose baby has been snatched from her, leaving her with a longing for her lost child whose tiny fingers she imagines pressing her full breasts. Much of the story is an account written for this child, and it sounds very like Mary Wollstonecraft writing to little Fanny:

> The tenderness of a father who knew the world, might be great;
> but could it equal that of a mother – of a mother, labouring under a
> portion of the misery, which the constitution of society seems to have
> entailed on all her kind? It is, my child, my dearest daughter, only such
> a mother, who will dare to break through all restraint to provide for
> your happiness – who will voluntarily brave censure herself, to ward off
> sorrow from your bosom.

And she added, 'Death may snatch me from you, before you can weigh my advice, or enter into my reasoning.' Maria in the novel well knew the effect of a mother's premature death: 'I, alone, by my active tenderness, could have saved … from an early blight, this sweet blossom,' she wrote, while her orphaned friend remarks, 'Now I look back, I cannot help attributing the greater part of my misery, to the misfortune of having been thrown into the world without the grand support of life – a mother's affection.'[5]

In one of her last letters to Imlay Mary Wollstonecraft had written, 'When I am dead, respect for yourself will make you take care of the child.' She was mistaken. Imlay had shown no fatherly feelings for Fanny and had no intention of taking or providing for her. Godwin may have feared his claim since he and Johnson enquired after the character of any current mistress but Imlay seems easily to have accepted another man's guardianship – so long as he himself was not asked for money. In 1796 he had offered a bond, the interest of which was supposed to be used for Fanny's support. Neither Johnson nor Godwin saw the money, even though they tried to shame him into providing it.

While making no effort to pay up, Imlay was acutely aware of the figure he was cutting in London and he begged Johnson not to humiliate him further: 'I believe the opinion of the world is always sufficiently secured by an upright & unequivocal conduct, though one should refuse to conform to some of its narrow & censorious maxims,' he wrote. 'I believe this observation will apply in my case – if so, I beseech you to reflect how brotherly & considerate a conduct it is, to begin the senseless cry of scandal, & incite the world to consider that conduct as faulty, which, I believe, it is inclined to consider as innocent – observe also, that what is done is irremediable.' There was much concerning his image here, nothing about his daughter. Johnson, who had never rated Imlay highly either for character or handwriting, remarked when he forwarded the scrawled letter to Godwin that it was 'the most intelligible one that I have seen from that quarter'.[6] Imlay's brisk ability to see situations as 'irremediable' was one source of his repeated self-fashioning and survival.

It is a pity that he did not keep in touch with Fanny, however. Father and daughter would have had little temperamentally in common but perhaps he might have lightened her serious, sensitive Wollstonecraft legacy. Through Imlay she could have had a feeling of paternal ancestry to put beside her sister's secure one, and some knowledge of respectable relatives in New Jersey who might even have wanted to meet her. But no further contact is recorded.

Imlay was in London after the final parting with Mary Wollstonecraft and saw Godwin on several occasions, and he managed to notch up more debts. Apparently he came down in the commercial world – no longer a republican dealing in royalist silver but a tradesman in fruit and groceries, real or imaginary. Around 1800 the trail of lawsuits in America and Europe against him peters out. Perhaps he solved his debt problems by assuming a new name. By then Fanny had also taken a new name: she was Fanny Godwin.

෴

There were, however, other near relatives who maintained a close interest in the child: her mother's two younger sisters, her aunts Eliza Bishop and Everina Wollstonecraft.

After Fanny had been born in France in May 1794 at the height of the Terror, Mary Wollstonecraft could not be sure that the news of her birth had reached her sisters, then unhappy governesses in Wales and Ireland. She wrote several letters repeatedly giving the news, hoping one would get through. None mentioned her unmarried status, but Eliza and Everina guessed it, being aware of their sister's advanced views. Mary Wollstonecraft did not oppose marriage as such but she did believe in easy divorce when it failed to contribute to the happiness of both partners. When Eliza had had a post-partum breakdown back in 1783 after the birth of her first child, her sister had had no scruples in taking her away from both her husband, Meredith Bishop, and her new baby (the baby died soon after). Although Eliza had wavered, Mary had opposed reconciliation with a man she thought unworthy. Marriage was not a sacred state. Then she set Eliza up as an independent teacher. Soon they had been joined by the youngest Wollstonecraft sister, Everina, who had found life with a feckless father and unwelcoming brother worse alternatives even than teaching. So Mary Wollstonecraft had rescued and organised the lives of both her sisters without help from a husband, father or brothers.

Over the next years Eliza and Everina came to depend heavily on the energetic Mary. They admired her intellectual life in London and envied her trip to revolutionary France. Sometimes desperately jealous of her brilliant sister, Eliza Bishop in particular could also be proud of her success – even her notoriety. On one occasion when she was a governess in Wales and Mary was in Paris after writing *The Rights of Woman*, Eliza was thrilled to find herself dancing with a man who imagined her the famous Mary Wollstonecraft. Both younger sisters dreamed that Mary would rescue them from work they hated and whisk them off to more glamorous lives abroad. Eliza declared she would even prefer the Terror to the boredom and petty humiliation suffered in provincial Wales. She yearned for an invitation to France and scrutinised Mary's letters for any hint of welcome, elated whenever her sister held out a promise of Paris. She even left her job to learn French in preparation. Occasionally, to her bemusement, she and Everina were treated to Imlay-inspired visions of life in utopian America, where apparently Eliza would find ease and Everina a husband.

Then, to their huge disappointment, Mary returned to London. Not knowing her desolation, they failed to understand her needs and thought only of their own. In fact by now the burden of hope and dependence they had placed on her was simply too great. Terrified that Eliza would rush to London to join the sister she believed happy and rich, Mary wrote a tactless letter repelling her – a third adult destroyed marital pleasure, she said. Would Eliza accept money instead? The money was presumably dangled before all their eyes by Imlay in lieu of fidelity. Needless to say there was no money to disperse.

Eliza was stung to the quick. The relationship never recovered and the sisters never again met. Everina, however, did visit Mary Wollstonecraft in February 1797, after the liaison with Godwin had begun but before the pair openly lived together. There was little sisterly confiding and no mention of Everina playing with her small niece Fanny. On this visit Everina realised that some of Mary's 'essential sentiment' had 'changed sorrowfully during her Paris residence' but it was too late to establish intimacy.

The marriage to Godwin, which Everina regarded as 'woeful and most afflictive to her many many Friend[s]', helped wean the Wollstonecraft sisters from dependence on Mary.[7] Despite her sense of their incompetence to run their own lives, the pair in time managed to establish small schools in Hume Street, Dublin: Everina a boarding establishment for girls and Eliza a day one for boys. They remained obscure women but there are glimpses of them in the recollections of fellow Dubliners, Mary Hutton, William le Fanu and an old friend of their sister's, Hugh Skeys.

Those who knew both declared Eliza Bishop the more congenial and open of the two. Mary Hutton found her attractive with 'beautiful brown eyes and most winning gentle manners: her whole bearing gave the idea of a perfectly lady-like and refined person'. She found the younger, tall, and now formidable Everina 'a great contrast to her sister': she was 'an overbearing, disagreeable, ill-tempered woman, very sarcastic and very clever'.

William Le Fanu recalled knowing the sisters as a child: Eliza liked treating him to sugar plums while Everina would affront his parents, as she did in the following incident:

One day Everina came to his father's house to dinner.

'Of course we are very glad to see you,' said the host, 'but there is no one to meet you; it was for to-morrow we invited you.' *Everina.* 'You write such an abominably bad hand that it is impossible to know what day one is invited for.' *Mr Le Fanu.* 'But it was my wife who wrote the letter.' *Everina.* 'Well, if you *had* written it, it would have been in such an abominably bad hand that I could not have made it out.'[8]

Hugh Skeys thought highly of neither Eliza nor Everina, noting their 'infirmities of temper' – but, then, Mary Wollstonecraft had not thought highly of *him,* believing him selfish and parsimonious; so the feelings were probably mutual.

When Mary Wollstonecraft died in September 1797 Eliza and Everina, with their hard-won independence and reasonably settled existence, considered that they would be the best carers for their little niece, Fanny. Much later, commenting on Mary Shelley's character as an adult, Everina praised her good principles, which, 'considering who brought her up', spoke 'in favour of her disposition'.[9] Presumably she thought Godwin's intimidating personality and unconventional views unsuitable in a guardian of girls, especially of one unrelated to him by blood. So Everina wrote on behalf of herself and her sister, offering to take Fanny and raise her in Ireland.

Godwin did not hesitate. He had not met Eliza Bishop and did not like Everina. He had seen her when she visited her sister in London and again at the Wedgwoods in Staffordshire; on both occasions relations had been frosty. Fanny thought of him as her 'papa'; in his house she would be living with his half-sister, his own daughter. He replied at once to her aunts that he would adopt Fanny and give her his name.

Blood was unimportant: 'It is of no consequence that I am the parent of a child,' he had written in *Political Justice,* 'when it has once been ascertained that the child will receive greater benefit by living under the superintendence of a stranger.'[10] There was 'no friend upon whose heart she had so many claims as upon mine', he declared of himself and Fanny. Henceforth the girl, who in England was legally a Wollstonecraft while registered as Françoise Imlay in France, would be Fanny Godwin (her stepfather believed that, when society was perfected, all surnames would be abolished). The resolution distressed Fanny's aunts. Years later Everina would comment bitterly on a widower who, on the basis of his principles, refused to give up his little children to their kindly aunt to raise.

Godwin's decision was a generous and troubling one. A bachelor only a few months before, he now faced life as a lone parent of two small children. In education he was a theorist, not a practitioner, and he worried that he was unfitted by experience and temperament for the upbringing of girls. His wife had left hints in her 'Lessons' on how to develop intelligence and self-esteem in small children, and his mother suggested he use these when she wrote from Norfolk, 'You will follow your wives direction, give them a good deal of air, and have a good opportunity [sic], as yo. live out of the Smoke of the city.'[11]

But his 'wives direction' required much parental input. Godwin was used to a life of frugal expense, rigid habit, study, writing, constant visiting and theatre-going, and he could not and would not change. '[W]hen the wild cries of baby Mary fill the house, threatening to shatter the glass in the windows, I succumb to unreasoning panic,' he wrote. Whatever he felt about his duties to the children, he believed his work came first, both because he owed much to his talents and because he desperately needed to make money. Mary Wollstonecraft's long dying had been costly and he now had her debts to pay as well as his own.

Yet Godwin also prided himself on assuming the role of parent. In the new year following his wife's death he wrote to one of her importunate creditors that he had taken upon himself 'the care & support of her two children', so it was not to be expected that he could pay much of his debt: 'More than this, under my circumstances, cannot, I think, be expected from me.'[12] With a flourish he announced, 'My own domestic scene is planned and conducted solely with a view to the improvement and gratification of children ... Are not my children my favourite companions and most chosen friends?' An American visitor in 1803 wrote that Godwin was 'in his family, affectionate, cordial, accommodating'. [13]

◈

Despite the unpromising beginning, baby Mary continued to strengthen. It would not have been surprising if three-year-old Fanny, suffering both the loss of her mother and the arrival of a competitor for her stepfather's affections, should have felt occasional hostility — especially to a sister who, she would soon know, bore her mother's name. On one occasion when sending Fanny's love, Hannah Godwin remarked of the little girl, 'She behaved like an angel to Mary yesterday.' Perhaps such behaviour was unusual in the early months.

Fanny had some continuity of care: her nurse Marguerite stayed on for a while, and her mother's friends Maria Reveley and Eliza Fenwick dropped into the Polygon to see her and the baby, as did Hannah Godwin. But there was no substitute for a beloved mother. Mary Wollstonecraft remained an overwhelming presence in the household not only for Fanny but for almost everyone who came there.

The first person to offer to take the dead woman's place was the new housekeeper. Louisa Jones was a friend of Hannah, and Godwin employed her for the first year or so after his wife's death. She cared for the two children and ran the household. Friends regarded her as very much part of the Polygon family; Fanny was always dubious.

Soon Louisa wanted to be more than a housekeeper: a foster mother to the girls – and probably a new wife to Godwin. She played energetically with the children and relayed their little messages to their father when he was away. She tried to pacify Fanny, who was fretful whenever Godwin left. Maybe it was for this reason and because Louisa Jones presumed sometimes to stand in for her mother that Fanny came to dislike her and counted the months she was at the Polygon. Yet together the pair went on outings and Miss Jones encouraged Fanny to speak up for herself. When she did so, it was almost invariably to bid for Godwin's attention.

Louisa Jones could be touchy and jealous. When Godwin was staying with Louisa's sisters in Bath for a few days he wrote that he hoped she was looking after the children. Of course she was, she snapped and blamed him for not asking instead to hear directly from these children – and about herself. 'Well Fanny have you any thing to say to Pappa? Yes. I have waited for the answer, it is only a kiss and a shake hands. They are her own words I assure you – May Jones shake hands too! Pray dont refuse her, for she is very silly and wants to be reassured by such acts of kindness that she is not totally undeserving of some tho ever so little regard from Fannys and Marys Pappa.' Later she finished a letter: 'Farewell return soon and make us happy.'

Godwin was unresponsive – Louisa Jones was not to be the successor of the marvellous Mary Wollstonecraft. A year later she had given up hope. She stopped having 'glorious' fun with the children and wanted to leave the Polygon as soon as possible.

Uninterested in her emotions, Godwin was desperate to retain her services. Her going would be 'desertion', he thundered, a blow directed at himself. Louisa remained adamant, but the tension affected her ability to cope, especially with Fanny. '[I]nstead of being of advantage to the children I am become quite the contrary,' she told Godwin. 'Fanny does not love me nor do I think she ever would, Mary, my heart aches at the idea, would I am sure love me very dearly' but 'I have not even the spirit to amuse her and much more to endear or attach her to me – in fact I am fit for no one thing I am become useless in body & mind.' She continued sadly, 'I am so convinced that I am not calculated to make the children particularly Fanny happy that if I followed the present impulse say that I ought to have left the Polygon at the time I first felt this.'

Whether Fanny loved her or not, Miss Jones knew her going would affect a little girl who had lost her father, then her mother; Godwin should let her prepare for the moment by speaking openly. In refusing this, Godwin was being 'deliberately cruel', in Miss Jones's view.

He ignored her opinion, continuing instead to threaten and badger. Louisa pleaded to be allowed to stay in close contact with the Polygon after she left – the idea of sometimes hearing Fanny read lightened her heart: 'If circumstances do not forbid I think I may yet be of some service to Fanny – I anticipate a great deal of happiness in the experiment & I am sanguine enough to think it will not fail – and that as a visitor a frequent one if it meets approbation I can produce double the effect I could ever hope to do by living with her – for I am sure at present I should be the ruin of her temper and her habits in general.' Back came the reply, 'all connection must cease' between Miss Jones and the children once she had left.

She remained determined – even though her letters stating the fact became illegible and incoherent with grief: 'my god how shall I bear the moment of parting with you but will it be for ever, oh no it cannot be –'.[14] She left as planned and went off to live in Bath with George Dyson, a clever, sometimes violently drunken young friend of Godwin who had become infatuated with her. Whether or not Fanny loved Miss Jones, she would have felt this further parting.

CHAPTER 6

GODWIN

SOON AFTER HER death, Godwin had moved into his wife's old study and, when Joseph Johnson sent him the portrait of Mary Wollstonecraft painted by John Opie during her last pregnancy, her auburn hair set off by a soft white gown and her hands free of book or pen, he placed it over the mantelpiece. It was the most attractive, gentle and serene of the images. Anyone who entered his private domain would have to compete with this portrait.

'I must endeavour to provide in the most eligible manner for the dear pledges this incomparable woman has left behind her,' Godwin wrote. One method was to honour and exploit his dead wife. So a few weeks after her death he began sorting out the passionate and complaining love letters she had written to Gilbert Imlay and which Imlay had returned at her request; he intended to publish them, together with her unfinished novel *Maria*. He also began a biography, to be entitled *Memoirs of the Author of a Vindication of the Rights of Woman*; for this he would follow the principle proposed in *Political Justice*, of speaking truth without fear of consequences.

Primarily using his personal knowledge of Mary Wollstonecraft and what she had told him of her early life, he sought more details from those who knew her as a young adult. Hugh Skeys, the widower of her beloved friend Fanny Blood, shared some memories. But most important for his project would be information from her closest relatives, Everina Wollstonecraft and Eliza Bishop. He wrote to them at once for assistance.

Aware of their brother-in-law's penchant for frankness, the sisters received the request with misgiving. It would be wise to be uncooperative. But, when they learnt that Godwin was in touch with the unsympathetic Skeys, they wrote to insist on what they felt might be underplayed – the affection of Mary Wollstonecraft for her sisters. But they gave little else away about their young lives together and he had to press on without their memories and without the copious letters his wife had written to them through most of her adult life.

The sisters' uneasiness at the project was justified. Godwin composed a biography of unprecedented openness, letting the world know of Mary Wollstonecraft's intimate and until then largely secret past: her infatuation with the married artist Henry Fuseli, her sexual affair with Imlay (who, perhaps for Fanny's benefit, he treated leniently – and romantically: with Imlay she was 'like a serpent upon a rock, that casts its slough, and appears again with the brilliancy, the sleekness, and the elastic activity of its happiest age'), her two suicide attempts, her illegitimate child and her extramarital relationship with himself. For this he admitted that both of them had been equally eager: neither was the 'agent or the patient, the toil-spreader or the prey'.[1] As a result of this frankness, whatever name she was given – Imlay, Wollstonecraft, or Godwin – everyone would now know that Fanny was a bastard – and that her half-sister Mary had been conceived outside marriage. When he delivered the manuscript, Godwin was advised by Joseph Johnson to be more evasive, but he refused. He saw nothing unfeminine in his wife's frank admission of her needs and emotions.

꿍

He had thoroughly misjudged the public mood. Instead of admiring his subject and the unsparing treatment, readers were aghast at the revelations about Mary Wollstonecraft and at her husband's lack of shame – the *Anti-Jacobin Review* for July 1798 summarized the work: this 'account of his wife's adventures as a kept mistress … informs the public that she was concubine to himself before she was his wife'. Only a few readers combined sympathy and sadness. An anonymous admirer from Lancashire, who much regretted Wollstonecraft's 'frailties' and poor support of 'Modesty', wrote that she hoped Godwin would never make her children aware of their mother's misfortunes or let them read the *Memoirs*, which she called a record of Mary Wollstonecraft's failings. He should merely set before them all 'her amiable qualities'. She was 'particularly interested for the Infant she had when surrounded by distress in a strange land – the affection you have [for] this dear lamented Woman will tend to produce a tenderness to the Orphan Daughter'.[2]

Facing a chorus of abuse Godwin made some changes for the second edition, omitting names of people who did not want to be associated with him, Mary Wollstonecraft or the notorious work. But the damage had been done.

When they read the book in Ireland, Eliza Bishop and Everina Wollstonecraft were appalled. Their sister, whose robust but moral *Rights of Woman* they had rather admired, had been exposed as abject, suicidal and immoral. Their name had become even more notorious now than at the height of her fame in 1792. It was harder than ever to make their modest living; they would never forgive Godwin. Matters were made worse by the scandal of Mary King, who, along with her sister Lady Mount Cashell, had been Mary Wollstonecraft's former pupil in Ireland. Mary King's lover had just been killed by her father, Lord Kingsborough, whose trial for murder occurred in this same year: her moral failings were ascribed to her time with Mary Wollstonecraft.[3]

Despite the furore over the *Memoirs,* Godwin had to write on – it was the only way he knew to make money. So he began a new novel, *St Leon.* To many readers, the portrait of Marguerite appeared a more seemly tribute to Mary Wollstonecraft as wife and mother rather than mistress.

The description of Marguerite's early married life resembled Godwin's expurgated memories of his short time with his wife. But, as miseries fall fast on her through her obsessed spouse, Marguerite parts company with Mary Wollstonecraft, not known for her exemplary resignation. Indeed, the character comes close to the fictional ideal of patient and suffering womanhood which Wollstonecraft had found so dangerous as a model for women. Godwin had been chastened by the reception of the *Memoirs* but already in that book he had leaned towards a sentimental, emotional and very gendered vision of woman. In *St Leon* he went further, perhaps preparing a suitable picture of their mother for his two little girls to emulate in the new, more conservative era of the nineteenth century. The picture fitted well with the beautiful mellow portrait in his study and with the changing times – but rather less with *A Vindication of the Rights of Woman.*

Within the novel there is a curious portrait of St Leon's daughter. Although the girl is older than Fanny when he wrote, Godwin may have drawn a little on what he apprehended of his stepdaughter. The fictional character was

> uncommonly mild and affectionate, alive to the slightest variations
> of treatment, profoundly depressed by every mark of unkindness, but
> exquisitely sensible to demonstrations of sympathy and attachment ...
> Her chief attachment was to her mother, though she was by no means
> capable of her mother's ... heroic fortitude.[4]

If this recalls the real Fanny, it may refer to her being overwhelmed by the trauma of Mary Wollstonecraft's early death. With his rational views on the control of the emotions, Godwin may have felt that the child grieved more than was proper. He would also find his daughter Mary inadequate in this respect when, as an adult, she grieved intensely for the death of her little son.

⚬❧

The widower did not make the same mistake. Soon he was on the lookout for a wife – he had grown used to love and sex: 'A judicious and limited voluptuousness is necessary to the cultivation of the mind,' he now declared. Although he assured Tom Wedgwood, 'I have not the least expectation that I can ever know happiness again', he knew he could not manage alone. As he wrote in *St Leon*, 'I never gave credit to that axiom of a sickly sensibility, that it is a sacrilege, in him who has been engaged in one cordial and happy union, ever to turn his thoughts to another ... He that dedicates his days to an endless sorrow is the worst and most degraded of suicides ... I should hold that in many cases he who entered into a second marriage, by that action yielded a pure and honourable homage to the manes of the first.'[5] Since this sentiment is largely irrelevant to the novel, Godwin was presumably arguing his own case with the various women he almost immediately approached.

When she grew up, his daughter Mary insisted on her father's long-term grief – 'he mourned [Mary Wollstonecraft] to the verge of insanity; but his grief was silent, devouring, and gloomy' – even as she glossed his frantic search for a new woman:

> The happiness he had enjoyed with his wife instilled the opinion that he might at least in a degree regain a portion of the treasure he had lost if he entered into a new engagement with a woman of sense & of an amiable disposition. Instead of as heretofore guarding himself from the feelings of love, he appears rather to have laid himself open to them. The two orphan girls left in his charge of course weighed much in the balance – he felt his deficiency as the sole parent of two children of the other sex.[6]

Within hours of Mary Wollstonecraft's death Godwin was writing to Elizabeth Inchbald, a woman who had disliked his wife and whom she had thoroughly disliked – she mocked Inchbald as 'M[rs] Perfection'.[7] He was not naturally tactful and his approach foundered. A couple of years later he tried again. The response was frosty: 'it will always give me great pleasure to meet you in company with others', Elizabeth Inchbald wrote, 'but to receive satisfaction in your society as a familiar visitor at my own house I never can.'[8]

The most serious early candidate as replacement was the author and teacher Harriet Lee, whom Godwin met in Bath less than six months after his wife's death when he was staying with Louisa Jones's sisters – a fact of which the susceptible Louisa might have been apprised: 'The feeling of love was awakened in their first acquaintance, & his immediate desire was to study her mind.'[9]

Through the summer of 1798 he bombarded Harriet Lee with letters, arguing that 'Celibacy contracts and palsies the mind' and trying to persuade her of the insignificance of their religious differences – he was an atheist, she piously Christian. He did not stress his children's needs but expatiated much on his own. In the end Harriet rejected him, '[I]t gives me great pain to have disturbed the quiet of your mind,' she wrote, 'but I cannot remedy the evil without losing the rectitude of my own.'[10] No doubt she blessed her firmness when she heard the outcry that greeted the *Memoirs*.

The most obvious candidate as both wife and stepmother was the 29-

year-old Maria Reveley, whose husband died suddenly in July 1799 leaving Maria with her ten-year-old son Henry, Fanny's playmate. Godwin moved speedily – too speedily for Maria, who retreated pleading grief and the proprieties of mourning. Godwin countered by blaming her convention-ality, and badgered her to convert her admitted intellectual attraction into physical. He sounded rather like Mr Darcy importuning Elizabeth Bennet in *Pride & Prejudice*: 'You are invited to form the sole happiness of one of the most known men of the age ... This connection, I should think, would restore you to self-respect, would give security to your future peace, and insure for you no mean degree of respectability.'

Maria found the badgering unseemly and begged him to stop. Only now did he bring forward one of her attractions: 'You always professed the highest regard for Mrs Godwin; naturally it would be expected you should feel some interest in her children & mine'; on his own behalf he added, 'There is nothing upon earth that I desire, so ardently, so fervently, so much with every sentiment & every pulse of my heart, as to call you mine.' [11]

Maria closed the episode by taking up with an old friend, John Gisborne, a merchant with literary leanings whom she married in May 1800, less than the conventional twelve months after her husband's death. The following year the Gisbornes settled in Italy. Fanny saw neither Maria Reveley nor her little friend Henry again, although both would become important in her sister Mary's peripatetic life.

CHAPTER 7

FANNY

CHILDREN WERE MORE expensive and demanding than Godwin could have known. Mary needed a wet nurse for eight months after her birth, and childhood ailments of both girls required doctors who had to be paid. When Godwin's mother in Norfolk sent 'a new piece of print for my grand-daughter Mary for a gown, with 2/6 to pay for the making, a pr. little Stockens and Hat for yr. Ch.' she reminded her son of still other needs: 'It's a mercy your children have got over the measles so well but there is a great duty belongs to you to instruct them in the word of God in their youth for they are naterally [sic] prone to vanity & idleness there is no need to teach them that.'[1] It would be difficult to square the advice with her earlier suggestion that he follow his dead wife's directions for cultivating self-respect and reliance in children.

In the last resort, they were *girls*; they must learn to read and write well, but exacting formal education was not essential. Never a great admirer of his wife's *Rights of Woman,* Godwin did not believe in the identity of the sexes. 'Till the softer sex has produced a Bacon, a Newton, a Hume or a Shakspeare, I never will believe it,' he wrote.[2] Among the four people who had influenced him intellectually – the list included Coleridge and Dyson – he failed to note Mary Wollstonecraft.

Godwin did what he could for Fanny. He read to her Sarah Trimmer's popular 'Story of the Robins', Anna Laetitia Barbauld's graded lessons for small children, and perhaps some of her mother's frightening tales, which taught young people that there was grief, loneliness and guilt in the world as well as love and compassion. He walked her along the path to St Pancras' churchyard to see her mother's grave and took her to play by the Fleet river; he carried her to the theatre to watch *The Children in the Wood,* to the burlesque tumbling and clowning show in semi-rural Sadler's Wells, which so delighted the young Wordsworth with its giants, dwarfs, conjurors and harlequins; at Astley's Amphitheatre on Westminster Bridge Road they saw trick horse-riding, spectacles and panoramas of disasters and battles. On one occasion he took both children to the glittering shell grotto at Twickenham created by the poet Alexander Pope. When he went to dine with an old radical friend, Horne Tooke, five-year-old Fanny went with him, as she did on many other occasions.

But in general he was too pressed to be much concerned with educational theories and he later admitted he took little notice of Mary Wollstonecraft's 'Lessons'. If the children kept well and Fanny learnt her letters, it was as much as he could truly answer for. 'The poor children!' he exclaimed shortly after his wife's death. 'I am the most unfit to direct the infant mind.'

He hated being disturbed by Fanny's noise and needs, and he demanded complete quiet in the house when he worked. When he visited Coleridge's home, the poet's little son Hartley, who called Godwin 'Mister Gobwin', knocked Godwin so hard on the shin with his toy, a wooden ninepin, that Godwin complained to Coleridge's wife about the child's 'boisterousness'. Coleridge agreed his children might be a touch 'rough & noisy' but he found 'the cadaverous Silence of Godwin's Children … quite catacomb-ish: & thinking of Mary Wolstonecroft I was oppressed by it the day [Humphry] Davy & I dined there.'[3] When Shelley's friend Miss Hitchener called on Godwin on her journey to join the Shelleys, she too was critical of the way he isolated himself from his children, 'only seeing them at stated hours'.[4] Godwin admitted to Coleridge, 'When Fanny interrupts my reading with a request to hold her on my knee and tell her a fanciful tale, I confess I must curb my temper.'

Fanny could be demanding. A month after her mother's death, the *Monthly Visitor* learnt that the child was far from passive and obedient in the way she should be: 'This girl is a sufficient antidote to the mistaken speculations of her mother.' And, in the months after the death, Louisa Jones also noted that four-year-old Fanny's 'spirits and animation exceed any description'. The little girl's spirits were helped by good health. Apart from her beauty-ruining attacks of smallpox, chicken pox, and perhaps measles, there is no record of serious illnesses; Amelia Opie commented on her 'habitual hardihood'.

In the summer of 1800 Thomas Holcroft's daughter wrote to Godwin, 'How are your Fanny and Mary? No doubt they afford you many many happy hours. Yes: social affections are the solace of life: the world may be unjust, and fortune may frown but they can not rob us of the infinite and exquisite delights that arise from sympathy of soul and purity of heart.'[5] Hannah Godwin anticipated the delight he would have in Fanny and Mary as they grew up. Godwin probably agreed in the main, and he included the girls in his new friendships, for example the one he made with Charles Lamb, essayist and clerk in the East India Office. Like Godwin, Lamb knew about domestic troubles – he kept house with an intermittently insane sister who had killed their mother. And always the girls were part of the friendship with the roly-poly, garrulous Coleridge, who when he came to the Polygon talked incessantly to anyone; visiting for dinner he sometimes stayed for days. 'Kisses for Mary and Fanny – God love them!' he wrote later from the Lake District while awaiting the birth of another child. Despite criticising Godwin's home life, Coleridge had noticed the recent softening in his friend's opinions. He ascribed this less to philosophy, poetry and intercourse with himself than to the influence of 'dear little Fanny and Mary'. He relayed his small son's love to the girls: 'Hartley sends his love to Mary: "What? & not to Fanny?" "Yes – and to Fanny – but I'll *have* Mary." – He often talks about them.'[6]

Yet Godwin also acknowledged the burden of his family, and an invitation to Ireland from a new friend, the Irish lawyer John Philpot Curran, arrived just when needed. He was feeling financially easy, for *St Leon* had brought him in 400 guineas, although most of this had been swallowed by debts. To the indignation of his remaining creditors, Godwin set out for Dublin at the end of June 1800 intending to have a short holiday. Among other things he wanted to mend bridges with his late wife's sisters after his refusal to send Fanny to them and after the furore over the *Memoirs*.

He left both children in the care of his housekeeper and James Marshall, his oldest and closest male friend, almost his factotum, whom his daughter would later remember affectionately as a benevolent man with a 'kind intelligent countenance'.[7] The choice of Marshall annoyed his sister Hannah. As a result she refused to visit the girls.

Although Everina had written most of the letters to Godwin about the adoption of Fanny and tended to take the lead in conversation, it was Eliza Bishop whom Godwin most saw during his stay. He found her warm and lovable, quite different from her sister. Everina was aware of her propensity to antagonise everyone, of her 'unskilfulness in conveying any feeling of disappointment without its seeming to imply censure', as she described it in a letter of semi-apology to Godwin.[8] Despite her admission, however, he had made up his mind: he told Marshall he thoroughly hated Everina.

Nevertheless he visited about town with her. Together they went to see Mrs Le Fanu, probably a relative of his good London friend, the playwright Richard Brinsley Sheridan, and on several occasions he met Hugh Skeys, Fanny Blood's widower, who had helped him with the *Memoirs*. Skeys's low opinion of the sisters, coupled with his own dislike of Everina, may well have hardened Godwin's determination to hold on to both of Mary Wollstonecraft's children.

But he cannot much have wavered before he left, else he would have taken Fanny with him. And his letters home suggest it would have been a wrench to part with the little girl. In his own eyes as well as hers he was her 'papa'. So he simply paid his dues to the aunts by taking the presents they sent back to the girls. As the eldest, Fanny should have the right of choosing Eliza's gift, which he assumed the preferable of the two.

The letters Godwin wrote to his friend Marshall while he was holding the fort back in London were in part for the children to hear. They were the most affectionate and tender he ever wrote to or about Fanny – and they contrast with the tetchy ones he was writing to almost everyone else at the time. In them the little girls Fanny and Mary are together, learning, running, playing and waiting anxiously for his return.

He had felt a little guilty at leaving them: 'they lost their mother, & I feel as if it was very naughty in me to have come away so far, & to have put so much land, & a river sixty miles broad between us, tho, as you know, I had very strong reasons for coming,' he told Marshall. More than his own guilt, he felt *their* absence. He imagined them thinking of him thinking of them. He wanted to know if his friends continued to be interested in them: 'You do not tell me whether they have received or paid any visits ... I should be glad to hear of that.'

He had expected to feel relief at getting free of the noise and constant demands, but in fact he missed the girls. Little Fanny was affectionate and very eager to please him; he thought of her fondly. He wrote back to London asking for detailed news and he visualised the homecoming; some of his words Marshall was to read aloud or Fanny to read for herself:

> papa is gone away, but papa will soon come back again, & look out at
> the coach-window & see the Polygon across two fields, from the trunks
> of the trees at Camden Town. Will Mary & Fanny come to meet me?
> I will write them word, if I can, in my next letter or the letter after
> that, when & how it shall be. Next Sunday, it will be a fortnight since
> I left them, & I should like if possible to see them on the Sunday after
> Sunday the 20th July.

He deputed to Fanny the care of the garden and if he returned to find it spruce and if she kept some strawberries and beans for him she should get six kisses.

He was concerned with her reading and writing. 'I hope you have got Fanny a proper spelling book,' he wrote to Marshall. 'Have you examined her at all, & discovered what improvement she has made in her reading?' The repeated reference to her reading suggests that at six she had perhaps not progressed as he expected since Louisa Jones praised her facility two years earlier: 'Fannys progress in reading astonishes as much as it pleases me, all the little words come as freely from her as from a much older child & she spells pig, bog, cat, box, Boy, without seeing them when asked.' Still, Godwin hoped, 'next summer, if I should ever again be obliged to leave them for a week or two, that I shall write long letters to Fanny in a fine print-hand, & that Fanny will be able to read them by herself from one end to the other. That will be the summer 1801.'[9]

Three weeks later Godwin was still in Ireland, hoping the girls had not forgotten him. He told Marshall, 'I think of them every day, & should be glad, if the wind was more favourable, to blow them a kiss apiece from Dublin to the Polygon.' He had seen many children, among them those of Lady Mount Cashell, and they were 'very nice children'. But he had 'seen none that I love half so well, or think half so good as my own. I thank you a thousand times for your care of them.'

The following day he wrote again:

Ah, poor Fanny, here is another letter from papa, & what do you think he says about the little girls in it? Let me see! Would pretty little Mary have apprehension enough to be offended if I did not put in her name? Look at the map! This is Sunday, that I am now writing. Before next Sunday I shall have crossed that place there, that you see marked as sea, between Ireland & England, & shall hope indeed to be half way home. That is not a very long while now, is it? My visit to Ireland is almost done. Perhaps I shall be upon the sea in a ship, the very moment Marshall is reading this letter to you. There is about going in a ship in Mrs Barbauld's book. But I shall write another letter that will come two or three days after this, and then I shall be in England. And in a day or two after that, I shall hope to see Fanny & Marshall & Mary, sitting on the trunks of the trees …[10]

Although he wanted to return to his girls, Godwin had stayed far longer than he at first intended, for there was seduction in Dublin. In *Political Justice* he had declared the love of fame a delusion; yet he was finding it difficult to adapt to his changed public position, no longer London's pre-eminent intellectual but simply a cultural anachronism, his great work, which had seared the minds of so many in the radical 1790s, now largely unread and his frank *Memoirs* a byword for indelicacy. With some reason he had begun to feel persecuted: 'I see that there is a settled and systematical plan in certain persons, to render me an object of aversion and horror to my fellow-men,' he complained. But here in Ireland he felt a celebrity again.

He enjoyed being fêted. He was delighted with the attention of witty, ugly John Philpot Curran, whom he accompanied to the county assizes when he should have set out for home. He relished visiting Lady Mount Cashell's grand house – despite his republicanism a title always charmed Godwin and he boasted to Marshall, 'I have kept pretty good company here. Last Wednesday I dined with three countesses.'[11]

Lady Mount Cashell's poised eccentricity bemused him – she was very tall and forceful; her severe, unadorned dress reminded him of his dead wife's poor friend Eliza Fenwick, though the aristocrat exposed her 'gigantic arms' with less modesty, 'almost up to the shoulders'. He discussed with her how to bring up his girls – later the pair continued the conversation by post.

While Godwin fell back on general theory, trying to hold for a little while longer to the radical notion of equal *potentialities* – at least within one sex – Lady Mount Cashell suggested that different children needed different treatment from the start. 'It is easy for people to lay down rules but often impossible to follow them & in education above all things it is disadvantageous to adhere strictly to any particular system,' she wrote. She wanted nothing but 'the health and happiness' of his 'little girls'.

Godwin boarded the packet for Wales on 12 August; en route he wrote again affectionately of Fanny and Mary, once more imagining the delicious moment of first encounter. Calling on his favourite book by his dead wife, *Letters from Sweden,* with its picture of Mary Wollstonecraft's rapturous meeting with baby Fanny after a short absence, he found the child so present to him that he began addressing her again within Marshall's letter:

> I think I will contrive to be in town so as to be able to give you an accurate previous notice of the time, for the sake of the dear little girls & the trunks of the trees … Will not Fanny be glad to see papa next Tuesday? It will then be more than seven weeks since papa was at the Polygon: I hope it will be a long, long while, before papa goes away again for so much as seven weeks. What do you think F.? But he had to come over the sea, & the sea would not let him come when he liked: look at it in the map …'[12]

He arrived back a few days later and the letters ceased.

⟡

A year after the Irish trip and his visits to the Wollstonecraft sisters, Godwin was quarrelling with Everina and Eliza by post, this time concerning some dilapidated rental houses in Primrose Street, Spitalfields, near the original Wollstonecraft home. The rents had descended to the brothers and sisters and to their father's widow, Lydia, living in her native town of Laugharne in South Wales. Since the sisters all distrusted the eldest brother, Edward, a grasping, now retired, lawyer, Mary Wollstonecraft had, through Joseph Johnson and then Godwin, taken over administration of the houses, remitting the income from the rents to her various siblings and her father; Johnson and Godwin continued to carry out the thankless task when she died, and Everina and Eliza always suspected that Godwin in particular mismanaged matters.

Now the youngest Wollstonecraft brother, Charles, working in America, had asserted his right to some of the income. The sisters disputed his claim: he owed them all large sums, to be paid back through his share of the rents. Godwin and Johnson felt he had a claim and were planning to act without consulting them further. Everina protested sharply but, when Godwin accused her of being unjust and 'unhandsome', she backed down, desperate not to lose connection with Fanny and Mary by being too severe. Still, the sisters had to assert their rights and they planned to come to London, even though Eliza was, as so often in these days, feeling unwell.

The trip was a chance to meet seven-year-old Fanny, whom Eliza had never seen. They had been sending presents over, most recently some fossils. Everina was trying to get Fanny interested in one of her own lifelong fascinations – nearly forty years later an old acquaintance in Wales knew she would still be delighted with the gift of 'a great Curiosity which is a pettry-fied Mushroom'[13] – but she complained that the little girl had not thanked her for the present. Indeed, Fanny's failure to write was more than once a theme of Everina's letters. Godwin often stood over the children when notes were required – and insisted they be written well – but clearly had not done so here. Fanny, with not much sense of either aunt, could not motivate herself very easily.

In the event Eliza remained poorly and Everina came to London alone. No one kept a record of the visit and the formidable Everina's interaction with her sensitive little niece.

Yet Fanny must have made a good impression for in 1804, four years after Godwin's trip to Dublin, both sisters arrived in London to make a serious bid for her. Probably they even envisaged taking her home with them to Ireland. She was growing up and Godwin might now be more receptive to their proposal, finding her a burden on his straitened finances. They would place her in a boarding school, and in due course let her teach in their schools. Fanny was present at many of the dinners and meetings and may well have been there when the aunts discussed what they proposed. Now that she had met the gentler, more winning Eliza, did she have any desire to live with her aunts? It seems unlikely for, once again, Godwin rejected the offer.

The sisters returned disconsolate to Dublin. An old friend of Mary Woll-stonecraft's wrote to comfort them: 'I was sorry for your Disappointment about poor little Fanny – yet perhaps the additional anxiety you would have felt from having withdrawn her from the protection of Mr G — might have given you more pain than you are aware of – & I suppose he must mean well to the Child, or he wd have been ready enough to give her up.'[14]

In July 1806 the sisters asked for money from Godwin (as manager of the Primrose Street properties) and came over again, to see Fanny no doubt but also to consider the problems of their houses. They now had a greater share through the recent death of yet another brother. In their dealings they made contact with their eldest brother Edward Wollstonecraft. He was not invited to dine with Godwin, but Everina and Eliza took Fanny to meet him and his two children, Edward and Elizabeth, on several occasions. Eliza-beth, thirteen years older than Fanny, found her cousin 'very amiable', an adjective frequently used for Fanny. Unfortunately when Everina was not in town encounters between the cousins ceased.[15] The Godwin and Edward Wollstonecraft households can have had little in common, the one valuing intellect and ideas, the other concerned – if Mary Wollstonecraft is to be credited – with status and respectability.

The Primrose Street properties continued troublesome and Godwin hired workmen for repairs. But he could do nothing right and in the following summer of 1807 Everina was complaining about his plans to spend 'so much of the income of the rents on repairs when their circumstances currently do not allow it'. The problem prompted another visit in 1808 by Aunt Everina alone.

All in all, during these years of her growing up Fanny was exposed a good deal to her aunts. Primarily the interaction was with Everina, the more severe of the pair, and she seems rarely to have had a chance of being alone with the warmer Eliza. If she had, perhaps like William Le Fanu she would have been offered sugar plums by this comfortable lady instead of being lectured on her inadequacies as a correspondent. A prospect of life with so stern a critic as Aunt Everina may well not have seemed attractive.

Godwin knew his stepdaughter's fondness for him and this no doubt had lain at the base of his decision to retain her in 1804 against her aunts' pleas, and despite his relative poverty. Yet, before she saw them again, he needed to talk seriously with her about her position and what she might expect in the future. The decisions he took for her should be in part her own and based on rational as well as emotional grounds. So on 8 February 1806 he recorded in his diary an 'explanation' with eleven-year-old Fanny. Many biographers assume this to have been the moment when he told her she was illegitimate and not his daughter.

The assumption is reasonable but unlikely. Charles Lamb had called her Fanny Imlay, the name used initially by her mother, while the 'Lessons' for children which Mary Wollstonecraft had left unfinished at her death and which Godwin was urged to use for her upbringing were addressed to 'my unfortunate girl'. In such a bookish house, it is hard to imagine the frank *Memoirs* did not reach Fanny's hand before this moment, when she was close to twelve, or that she did not read her mother's Swedish travels or *Posthumous Works*, including the passionate letters written to Gilbert Imlay. Had she done so she would have known more of her conception and birth than most girls could ever have done, and she would have been very definitely aware that she was not Godwin's child. She would have read exactly where she was conceived – the Paris barrier during the Terror – and known her mother's emotions throughout pregnancy and in the weeks following her birth. She would have seen letters portraying the long decline of the relationship between her parents and perhaps responded to her mother's imaginings: 'My child may have to blush for her mother's want to [sic] prudence – and may lament that the rectitude of my heart made me above vulgar precautions.'[16] (The 'precautions' she should have taken were financial rather than physical, and they would have been pointless since no promises of support from Imlay would have been honoured.) Surely, too, Fanny would have remembered a little of the time before Godwin lived with her and her mother: he and Mary Wollstonecraft married when she was three. In their many visits which declared their particular interest in her, had her aunts never alluded to the fact that she was not Godwin's daughter? If it had been otherwise, they could have had little expectation of detaching her from him.

But, although she must have known something of how she had, in the *European Magazine*'s phrase, been so 'disgracefully brought into the world', the serious conversation probably drove home the problem of her birth. Illegitimacy was no great matter in the Godwin household, and the fact that she had been kept and raised by him when she had close maternal relations made her presence his choice not a necessity. Yet the need to discuss her future at so early an age cannot have made her feel more secure, added as it was to her lack of 'the grand support of life – a mother's affection'. There is no similar recorded 'explanation' with her sister Mary.

❧

Fanny's consolation was her 'papa', Godwin. It was not an entirely comfortable one. He had had no trouble showing his fondness when the girls were little, as his letters from Ireland reveal, but as they grew older he became more remote, more insistent on his own needs. In *St Leon* the self-centred hero observes that the joy of children has to come from the affection of two parents. Without it, feeling towards them is 'comparatively cold, selfish, solitary, and inane', rather an extreme characterisation of the single parent. 'In their early years we are attached to our offspring, merely because they are ours ... But as they grow up, the case is different. Our partiality is then confirmed or diminished by qualities visible to an impartial bystander as real as to ourselves,' he wrote.[17]

Godwin set high standards for the children and demanded constant consideration for himself. During their short months of marriage Mary Wollstonecraft had objected to her husband's assumption that his intellectual work should take precedence over hers. He had not changed his attitudes with her death and for most of each day when he was not visiting he shut himself in his study demanding quiet, as Coleridge had noted. He knew his needs and their effect: 'There never can be a perfect equality between father & child,' he wrote, '& if he has other objects & avocations to fill up the greater part of his time, the ordinary resource is for him to proclaim his wishes & commands in a way somewhat sententious & authoritative, & occasionally to utter his censures with seriousness & emphasis. It can therefore seldom happen that he is the confidant of his child, or that the child does not feel some degree of awe & restraint in intercourse with him.'[18]

CHAPTER 8

MARY JANE

IN IRELAND IN the summer of 1800 Godwin had seen himself primarily as a father and imagined that, if he went away again the following year, he would write long letters to Fanny. But by the time the summer of 1801 came round, the life of all of them had irrevocably changed, for, between the two seasons, Godwin had found another wife.

He could later declare that one of the motives that led him to choose a second marriage 'was the feeling I had in myself of an incompetence for the education of daughters'. Neither Fanny nor Mary would endorse this feeling or its solution.

In the evening of 5 May 1801 as he sat on his balcony in the Polygon Godwin was interrupted by a new tenant in the neighbouring house, a Mrs Clairmont. Had she the honour of beholding the immortal author of *Political Justice,* she asked. A later detail sounds a little fanciful: from then on whenever Godwin came into his garden she hurried out to 'walk up and down clasping her hands and saying to herself, "You great Being, how I adore you!"'[1]

Three weeks after the meeting, seven-year-old Fanny and Mary, close to four, were being introduced to the two Clairmont children, fair, clear-eyed Charles, nearly six, and dark, exotic three-year-old Claire. Actually at this time Claire was called Jane, but she was a flamboyant child who later experimented with styles of names and behaviour. Working with the euphonious name of Clairmont she would try out 'Clara' before settling on 'Claire': it gave her a French aura and had a literary ring.

Frequent tea parties with all the children followed and outings were arranged to let the families get to know each other. Yet Godwin still sometimes took Fanny and Mary out alone – they were not yet overwhelmed by the Clairmonts. Their old housekeeper Louisa Jones, perhaps by then disillusioned with Dyson and still hoping to stir Godwin's romantic interest, had been forgiven her earlier desertion and had reappeared around Christmas. Unaware of Mrs Clairmont's progress, she too visited the Polygon regularly.

On 6 July both Godwin and Clairmont families packed into a hackney carriage to attend a spectacular performance of *Puss in Boots* at Astley's Amphitheatre. It had a full orchestra to accompany the acts with clowns and horse-riders. The outing would help unite the families. A week after, in Godwin's diary began to appear tell-tale marks that revealed that sexual intercourse had occurred between himself and Mrs Clairmont without the benefit of marriage. Louisa Jones's visits petered out.

There was no problem for either partner. Godwin's views were well known and, despite her self-presentation, Mrs Clairmont had never been married: she was in fact Miss Mary Jane Vial and her two children were illegitimate, with different fathers. More circumspect than her predecessor, she had not allowed the circumstance to be generally known – and possibly Godwin was unaware of the unconventional parentage of the children – but it did mean that, when she too became pregnant and wanted marriage, she had to marry twice, once for public consumption as the widow Clairmont and an hour later for legal purposes as what she was: the spinster Mary Jane Vial.

Godwin had agreed easily to the weddings; he had taken to heart his mother's response to the *Memoirs*: that without marriage there would be 'children and wives crying ab[ou]t the streets without a protector'.[2]

Mary Jane Clairmont, now Mrs Godwin, had had a chequered life. Born in Exeter, probably to a French father, she had, she said, run away from home to live with his relatives in France. Two extramarital relationships ended in desertion and she even spent time in debtors' prison.[3] But she was a resourceful woman and her French background may have allowed her to make money teaching the language and translating. However she did it, she managed in 1801 to present herself as a respectable widow lodging in a respectable house. But she needed a husband as much as Godwin needed a wife. Both must have hoped the other had rather more money than was the case.

When Godwin's friends saw the replacement for Mary Wollstonecraft they were mostly appalled. Charles Lamb despised her portly appearance, big bottom, and coarse mind: he called her a 'bad baby' and 'a damn'd infernal bitch'. Mary Lamb saw her as the spiteful sister in a fairy tale. Many people noticed her inability to tell the truth and her childish tantrums, which made visiting painful. The diarist Henry Crabb Robinson, once – though no longer – a great admirer of *Political Justice* and now a close friend of the author, judged her 'querulous of attentions'.[4] What they all found difficult to stomach was that Godwin himself seemed fond of her; he had, they concurred, been shorn of any remaining dignity in marrying 'an Infernal devil'.

Some of this feeling honoured Mary Wollstonecraft, but the frequent dislike does suggest a woman with considerable power to displease. Young Mary loathed her and her noisy brood; they overwhelmed her and Fanny. At the same time it would have challenged a person of easier temper than Mrs Godwin's to keep her new composite household peaceful and loving. Blamed for favouring her own children, she felt especially irritated at Fanny's tenuous claim on the household and envious of the attention clever Mary drew away from her own daughter.

The child who had provoked the marriage died at once but on 28 March 1803 another was born, a William at last. Six years earlier Godwin had been a bachelor – now he had seven people to support. No two children shared a father and mother. In the circumstances his decision in 1804, against her aunts' pleas, to keep Fanny in his house is a remarkable one and suggests that she herself must have had a hand in it.

In many ways the Godwins were an oddly matched couple, he careful of speech, she voluble; he tending to reserve, then obstinacy, she to constant volatility; she growing hysterical when angry, he becoming cold and remote. She worked hard for all the family and felt underappreciated, although Godwin was grateful for her 'courage under calamities'. There is affection in the odd surviving communication between them. Godwin called his wife 'Dear mamma – my dearest love!' and 'the sympathising ... partner of my fire-side'. And she would later write, 'Your dear balmy letter, brought stump-a-stump upstairs at half past 9 by Willy, has set my mind at ease … Charles smiled in the most heavenly manner at your kiss and a half. Fanny stood quite still. – Jane capered.'[5]

She was not used to curbing her tongue or her temper, especially with Godwin's children. There were frequent rows with them and with her husband, sometimes followed by separations – one occurred just before the 'balmy letter' and lasted most of the summer. In an earlier threatened separation Godwin wrote, 'You part from the best of husbands … the best qualified to bear & be patient toward one of the worst of tempers.' On her side she lamented. 'How cruel, how more than cruel you are to make me seem unkind! If you could be a woman and a *managing* woman but for a single day you would understand better what the most affectionate of wives could or could not do.'[6] An anecdote suggests how the pair could carry on in public. A few months after they got back together they were out visiting, and their host 'asked Madame how the weather was; very cold, indeed, said she. No, indeed, said Mr., it is quite sultry; so she drew her chair close to the fire, and he removed to the farthest part of the room.'

Shortly after Godwin's serious talk with Fanny, Mary Jane felt in need of a break from family tasks and tensions. She took Fanny with her to visit an old friend of Godwin's, the now crippled novelist Charlotte Smith in Tilford, Surrey. Whilst apart, the Godwins wrote almost daily letters; so a window opens briefly on this extraordinary household.

Despite the liberal educational theories Godwin and Wollstonecraft had espoused, punishments – whippings and learning by rote – were evidently used to keep the children in line. Charles, the closest in age to Fanny, had upset his mother before she left and wished to avoid a whipping from his stepfather; also he wanted Godwin to celebrate his birthday properly. After the event had gone off fairly well he wrote an account of his special day to Fanny. Godwin insisted that he also write to his mother, but after much prodding the sulky boy produced 'the most soulless thing you ever saw'. As punishment his stepfather made him learn 'My Mother' a poem out of *Dalton's Original Poetry*, a sentimental piece by Ann Taylor:

Who ran to help me when I fell,
And would some pretty story tell,

Or kiss the place to make it well?
My Mother.

The image was laughably far from Mrs Godwin's. Nonetheless, as corrective the poem worked well and Charles managed a second, more suitable letter to his mother.[7]

On her side, Mary Jane missed none of the children except baby William, 'my beauty boy, my angel'. But she wondered whether the others 'go on as I wish'. She sent 'loves & kisses to every good child'.

Charles may have missed Fanny, for she was by now often the peace-maker in the family, smoothing things not only between her sister and their stepmother but also between Charles and his stepfather. Mary and Claire were not unhappy to have Fanny away since they managed to avoid music lessons in her absence.

✒

There was never enough money in the household, and both Godwin and Mary Jane trawled their brains for methods of gaining it. Although his great books had been his treatise *Political Justice* and his haunting obsessive novel *Caleb Williams,* Godwin found such works made little money. So he tried writing drama, a more profitable genre. His tragedy *Antonio,* when performed, was a disaster, and two attempts later he accepted he was no playwright. Neither he nor Mary Wollstonecraft had much skill in creating characters very different from themselves. There would have to be another way.

Soon after his first wife's death, he had contributed some pieces to a magazine for children called the *Juvenile Library,* which provided useful knowledge for middle-class boys and girls – science, geography, some botany and pictures of heroic characters to emulate. Possibly, thought the new Mrs Godwin, they might sustain the family by starting their own press publishing imaginative and liberal children's books and textbooks based on the lessons and learning of the various young people in their care. As an abstract philosopher with a disdain for the 'shopkeeping and traffic-trained character', Godwin was as little fitted for business as abstract principles for

60

ordinary quotidian life – but she herself was a 'managing woman', energetic and determined; with her green-tinted spectacles in place she would be the centre of the operation.[8] As the man of the house Godwin would have to raise and deal with money, however.

Initially the business did well. Intending to expand, in 1807 – when Fanny was thirteen, Mary ten and Claire nine – they all moved from the Polygon to Skinner Street in the City of London. The narrow corner house they took had been recently but not well built; it had four storeys with space for a shop on the ground floor and good bow windows to display books. Upstairs there was a corner study for Godwin and on the top floor a school-room for the girls facing east to take the morning sun – when it managed to shine through the smoke and gloom. For the moment the house appeared rent free since there was a dispute about ownership. So at first the Godwins felt better off.

For the children it was a difficult move. The Polygon was on the edge of London and close to open country; Skinner Street, on the corner of Snow Hill, Holborn, was in the polluted centre, a bookselling district near Smith-field cattle market close to three prisons, including the Fleet for debtors. The New Drop of the Old Bailey held public hangings every few weeks, some attracting great crowds. Smells wafted into the house, from the covered sewer of the Fleet Ditch, from the millinery shops, from meat, fish, fur and oil prepared and sold close by; sounds of slaughtered animals pierced the air.

For Fanny, who had spent most of her short life wandering the wilds of Scandinavia, then playing near fields on the edge of London, it was a huge shock. It told at once on Claire's health and the following summer she was sent off to the seaside resort of Margate for three months to benefit from the sea air and bathing – she was back in time for the winter jaunt to Astley's. Mary deeply resented the move. She blamed it squarely on her stepmother.

The bulk of the work in the bookshop fell on Mrs Godwin. 'The inglo-rious transaction below-stairs', Godwin commented airily, 'furnishes me with food, clothing and habitation and enables me to proceed.' Later an acquaintance who knew his affairs well remarked of Godwin, 'he is not a man of the world in the sense he ought to be to obtain a living by business'.[9] He had been in debt much of his life, seriously so since he moved in with Mary Wollstonecraft, and he had depended on others such as Joseph Johnson and Tom Wedgwood to get him out of scrapes. Indeed, noticing Godwin's lack of business acumen together with Fanny's undefended position in his household, Johnson in his will directed a bond of £200 to be paid to her on his death.

In the shop mismanagement occurred from the outset: a roguish first manager was soon dismissed and Eliza Fenwick, Mary Wollstonecraft's impoverished friend, installed in his place. She enjoyed the work but complained of the conditions: the shop lacked a proper fire and the Godwins never asked her to join them for dinner upstairs – perhaps they were just stingy with their employees or perhaps they disapproved of her poor dress, for she could not afford to have linen visible beneath her grey gown. (Their friend Lady Mount Cashell was similarly austere but Godwin took this as aristocratic singularity.) In January 1808, when they grew more concerned about the shop's profitability, the Godwins decided to 'discard' her 'without much ceremony', as she complained to their common friend Mary Hays. Eliza Fenwick never forgave them – years later she declared she abhorred Godwin: while 'of all human beings' Mrs Godwin was the object of her 'sincerest detestation'.[10]

Yet the Godwins could be generous as well. Aaron Burr discovered this when he first visited England in 1808. An exile from the new United States, Burr had long admired Godwin and Wollstonecraft and, when vice-president of the nation, he had sent to England to obtain copies of their portraits. His was more than passing admiration and he raised his daughter Theodosia according to the principles of *The Rights of Woman*; perhaps because her mother had died so early, he even wrote her frank, rather alarming, letters about sex and relationships. In 1804 his career faltered when he killed his political enemy Alexander Hamilton in a duel, then was discovered plotting an invasion of Mexico. He was tried for treason in 1807 and, although found not guilty, felt it politic to leave the country.

During his four years of exile, partly spent in England, he was intrigued by the composite Godwin family and grateful for hospitality and for the newspapers and books he borrowed. In time he understood that the Godwins were in financial trouble too, but he found them welcoming nonetheless. 'We starve at four,' Godwin had written to one dinner guest.

Burr felt more admiration for the second Mrs Godwin than was usual among Godwin's friends; he found her sensible and amiable, and he took

many strolls alone with her. He was grateful to both Godwins for understanding and being tactful about his financial position – having held such
high office in America, he was embarrassed to let most people know how
poorly he lived in his sordid furnished lodgings in Clerkenwell Close for
only eight shillings a week. When the time came to leave, he needed help to
raise enough money for his passage back to America. Mary Jane tried to sell
his watch for him and Godwin his books.

⋘

Unhampered by his first wife's feminist notions – and indeed his own earlier
antagonism to institutional education for either sex – Godwin with Mary
Jane arranged formal instruction as day boys at nearby Charterhouse for
Charles Clairmont and young William, but little was provided for the girls.
Claire had just over three months in a Kentish boarding school and about
fifteen months in the nearby village of Walham Green – where she studied
music and French in particular. Mary had six months in Ramsgate, primarily for her health. Fanny seems to have stopped going to school almost as
soon as the new Mrs Godwin came on the scene and there were no further
periods of formal education provided for her.

Godwin's first biographer and family acquaintance reported that his
second wife tried to have her own children educated at the expense of Fanny
and Mary, and the record seems to bear this out. Only Claire among the girls
grew up fluent in French, which suggests that Mrs Godwin, although bilin-
gual, took few pains with the children she had inherited, who, since they
would probably have to earn their livings, would have been advantaged by
having a good command of the language. Years before, Mary Wollstonecraft
had paid money out of her small earnings to give her sisters Eliza and
Everina a grounding in French, so that they could become governesses in
more genteel households.

Yet the girls were not neglected. Fanny was more than once praised for
her drawing and probably had training in art. All of them were learning
music. Mrs Godwin boasted that the girls had been 'taught by Mr Godwin
Roman Greek and English history, French and Italian from masters'. After
the disaster in the summer of 1814, she regretted her boast.

When Godwin was asked whether he was bringing up Mary

Wollstonecraft's daughters according to her educational system, he responded: 'The present Mrs Godwin has great strength and activity of mind, but is not exclusively a follower of the notions of their mother; and indeed having formed a family establishment without having a previous provision for the support of a family, neither Mrs Godwin nor myself have leisure enough for reducing novel theories of education into practice.'[11]

For many readers the most shocking aspect of the *Memoirs* had been Godwin's insistence that, even in death, the once pious Mary Wollstonecraft expressed no religious sentiments. When the *Monthly Visitor* criticised Fanny, it implied that little could be expected from a daughter who had spent her first years with such a mother. The second Mrs Godwin was a Roman Catholic and, before she married Godwin, her two illegitimate children attended the Chapel of St Aloysius in Somers Town. Little concerned with doctrine, she easily slipped over to the state church when married and, after years of mocking ritual, the notorious atheist Godwin found himself presiding over a household of regular prayers, while the children were sent for a time to Sunday morning service at St Paul's Cathedral. Drawing on his own miserable childhood, he insisted on testing them on the sermon when they returned, although he never commented on the material.[12]

The training was half-hearted and the children showed little orthodox Christian belief – though in later years Mary conformed in religion as in other matters and Claire at the very end of a long life slipped back into her mother's Catholicism. Godwin himself did not waver; in his final years he remained dismayed at the 'oppressive weight of religious prejudice'.[13] From his publications for children, the girls would know the Bible as a series of adventure stories, not divine truth. Faith would be no crutch for them in aching adolescence. Art, literature, and genius came to take its place – while lacking religion's clear, conventional guidance. In Skinner Street the phrase 'superior being' denoted not a deity but a clever man or woman; only ideas were sacred.

In their disordered, bookish home all the girls were receiving an education richer and far more exciting and intellectual than anything available in a school or Sunday school (education in *Political Justice* was not formal but included whatever produced an idea and chain of reflections). As Aaron Burr's visit suggests, the children were surrounded by literary and political celebrities. They met, dined with, listened to and even conversed with powerful thinkers and were taught to consider social questions for themselves. A household where girls listened to Coleridge reciting *The Rime of the Ancient Mariner*, even if they were dragged to bed by Mrs Godwin in the middle of it, and where they would be taken to hear his lectures on Shakespeare at the Royal Institution, offered much to an enquiring or imaginative mind. Many years later, Claire would nostalgically portray life in Skinner Street:

> All the family worked hard, learning and studying: we all took the liveliest interest in the great questions of the day – common topics, gossiping, scandal, found no entrance in our circle for we had been brought up by Mr Godwin to think it was the greatest misfortune to be fond of the world, or worldly pleasures or of luxury or money, and that there was no greater happiness than to think well of those around us, to love them, and to delight in being useful and pleasing to them.[14]

Fanny and Mary were not close but both suffered from their relationship with their stepmother: where Mary turned her desolation outwards, openly hating Mary Jane as 'odious' and 'filthy', Fanny turned hers inwards, feeling the need, in her insecurity and reverence for Godwin, to mitigate the faults of the woman who was his wife. Both girls escaped into reading and both perhaps took their books and lunch to sit alone in the churchyard with the lost mother.

Mrs Godwin knew people compared her unfavourably with Mary Wollstonecraft, whose portrait had come from the Polygon to be rehung over the mantelpiece in her husband's corner study. It cannot have been easy to follow a genius, a dead celebrity made calm and beneficent with hindsight. Many looked askance at the upbringing she was giving the children, forgetting perhaps that Mary Wollstonecraft had not had much time to put her theories into practice. Mary made it clear she disliked her stepmother from the moment she arrived as rival for her father's love, and she blamed Mrs Godwin for the family's need to move into the city and set up as tradespeople. Since Mrs Godwin resented having to serve in the shop downstairs and become a mere shopkeeper, she often made the girls take on this unpopular and cold duty.

There were complex rivalries throughout the household: between the daughters, between the two sets of children and most subtly between the dead and living mothers. Years on, when he had become an excitable adult, the Godwins' son William wrote a novel called *Transfusion*, which suggests a curious relationship to his older sister Mary, the direct competitor for attention from their biological father. In the book a mother dies leaving two children, the trio sounding a little like Mary Wollstonecraft, himself and Mary Godwin. The boy is good, wise and deaf, the girl headstrong, imperious and rude, her insubordinate spirit deriving from her difficult father. When she insults a trusty would-be guardian, she asserts she has done no more than 'vindicate her just rights'. Following a well-worn literary path the girl falls victim to a heartless seducer while the good boy, cured of his deafness, grows solitary and unfamilial, rather like Frankenstein when he leaves his family to pursue his solitary studies. Like Victor Frankenstein and Godwin's St Leon, he finds a dark elemental secret, not Frankenstein's generation of life or St Leon's prolongation but a transfusion between lives, the beaming of a soul into another's body. Since his sister is now dying of grief at being abandoned, the brother tests his transfusing skills by entering her dying body just in time to denounce the wicked nobleman and die as both himself and his sister.

It is fiction from a later period but it may give some insight into William's perspective on the household. Fanny and Claire have disappeared and the only sibling that exists is Mary, who incarnates the sacred mother. The story reveals quite openly a sort of war of parents, the first and second Mrs Godwins. It was a war that enveloped all the children and was especially virulent during times of crisis like the one now brewing.

⟡

The press had a strong list of titles, which included the Lambs' popular *Tales from Shakespeare*, Lady Mount Cashell's *Stories of Old Daniel*, Mary Jane's translation, [*Swiss*] *Family Robinson* and Godwin's *Fables Ancient and Modern* – comically, this anonymously published work was much commended by the *Anti-Jacobin Review*, scourge of the radical Godwin a decade before – and an exemplary life of the learned Lady Jane Grey. But, despite this publishing strength and despite *apparent* profits, the Juvenile Library could not flourish. With the family's existing debts, too much was demanded of it; there was always too little capital, and schools and individuals who owed them money were often tardy. The 'monster with the great maw' swallowed up everything.[15]

Joseph Johnson, who in the beginning helped the Godwins manage their bookshop, when he saw how things were going organised a subscription to help them out. But it was insufficient both to float the business and to service the debts to which Godwin was always adding, rather in the manner of Gilbert Imlay before him.

A few months before he died in 1809 Johnson had several conversations with Godwin, probably about the money owed to him from earlier years and from the bookshop. The debts could not be hidden and on his death his heirs wished to collect. The bond for £200 which Johnson had intended for Fanny's use was to have been taken out of what Godwin owed him. But in the event the sum was simply swallowed up in the general debts of the household. So Fanny's bequest, the only money that she could have called her own, was never given to her. At the same time another of Godwin's creditors himself went bankrupt and his debts were transferred to more importunate men.

The stress of these multiple disasters told on Godwin; he had long suffered from embarrassing narcolepsy – many amusing stories were told of his falling asleep in mid sentence over dinner; now he had an attack of what he called his 'deliquium', a period of blackout or dizziness. It was a physical condition to which he would be prone for the rest of his life, one exacerbated by stress.

Following Johnson's death, the Godwins fell into deep gloom for some weeks. Then they found a new saviour.

He was Francis Place, a rich Charing Cross tailor and supporter of radical causes. He had revered *Political Justice* but, ominously, he despised those who could not manage money. He agreed to become a successor to Johnson and organise and part finance a loan of £3,000. With this Godwin would be able to pay off his debts and establish the book business on a proper footing.

Friends and admirers, including Elton Hammond, another intense enthusiast of *Political Justice,* were brought in to help (for a person whose work had fallen into disrepute, Godwin even now managed to command remarkable devotion). All advanced various sums of money to achieve the necessary subscription; Hammond borrowed £500 from his sisters while Place put in his own money, not telling his more cautious wife what he had done (he had fifteen children to support, hence perhaps his later interest in birth control).

As the months went by the plan faltered. Debts were rolled over and continued to spiral. Place accused Godwin of falsifying the initial accounts and continuing to accumulate debts. '[O]ur efforts were useless,' he concluded. In a short time 'Godwin was as much embarrassed as ever, we had also embarrassed ourselves and had been the means of risking the property of others …' Place, who had raised himself from desperate poverty, became impatient at his old friend's 'trickery' and called him feckless and mendacious: where his own interests were concerned, Godwin was 'one of the most heartless, the most callous of men. He was perfectly regardless of the mischief he might bring upon any one and quite as regardless of the feelings of others.' Had he directed his efforts prudently rather than spending time touching friends for money he would have flourished. To Place's future biographer, William Godwin became 'the prince of spongers'.[16] Even the idealistic Hammond became disillusioned (maddened by many such disappointments, he would shoot himself in 1819).

As for Godwin and Mary Jane, they believed they worked hard and borrowed where they could. They acted no differently from many of their friends in these economically volatile times.

What was happening? When Francis Place looked over the books from the business he concluded with astonishment that for ten years Godwin had been borrowing £400 from friends and that his annual expenses appeared to exceed £1,500 despite living rent free in Skinner Street.[17] It was perplexing since, although Place thought Godwin a spendthrift, most visitors noted the austerity of his household – there was little finery in furnishings and dress. Some faulted Mrs Godwin for trying to live above their means with her insistence on servants, long visits to seaside resorts and expensive schooling for her own children, but Godwin did not grudge her these. On the other side, Fanny and Mary did not cost much.

CHAPTER 9

FANNY

THREE GIRLS IN a dysfunctional household with insufficient money to go round inevitably squabbled. Alliances shifted. A little younger than Mary, Claire was in awe of her clever stepsister, while seeing her as a rival for everyone's attention except her mother's. Alternately she copied and competed, and there were many quarrels and reconciliations. Godwin noted Claire's 'baby-sullenness', a trait she shared with his wife; she thrived on the upheavals that pained the others.[1] Moody Mary bridled at her stepmother's desire to control them all, including Godwin, and she scorned Claire's need to show off.

Three years older and with an early memory of being an only and loved child, Fanny was pained by bickering; constantly she tried to soothe and make peace. She chided Mary for her moods, which she saw disturbed Godwin. Her efforts irritated her half-sister while making Claire despise her for her docility, for not joining the fray. Sometimes she became 'only Fanny' for the others.

As the famous actor John Philip Kemble, a friend of Godwin, remarked, 'Girls generally find out where to place themselves.'[2] Fanny among the Clairmonts was learning her place. Charles Lamb once labelled her 'sulky', which suggests she resisted the resentment of her stepmother. But it was no baneful sulkiness and Elizabeth Dawe, the miniaturist who was painting her portrait, perhaps as a present for her Wollstonecraft aunts, found her 'neither reserved nor sullen', and Lamb admitted that the miniature she produced was 'tolerably like'.[3]

Mary had gained through her childhood a sense of specialness which the others never achieved. It was difficult for the illegitimate children of Mary Jane Clairmont and Gilbert Imlay to compete with the daughter of Godwin and Mary Wollstonecraft, a girl who was by birth part of what an acquaintance called 'the aristocracy of genius'. Later Claire remarked that, in the Godwin household, 'if you cannot write an epic poem, or a novel that by its originality knocks all other novels on the head, you are a despicable creature not worth acknowledging'.[4] Only Mary would show she could do this.

From the time of the union of the two families, exclusive outings for Fanny ended, but quite often as the eldest she went visiting with Mrs Godwin – when she dined with Godwin's poorer sister Hannah, for example. Sometimes she accompanied both Godwins to a play considered unsuitable for the younger Mary and Claire, like Otway's bombastic tragedy *Venice Preserv'd*, or she took a walk with her step-parents to Ludgate Hill as far as the great coaching inn, the Belle Sauvage. But most trips were now inclusive, taking in all the girls and William Jr: they went as a large family group to Astley's again and to the theatre to see *Cinderella*, and they boated down the Thames from Greenwich to Richmond. Often in his diary Godwin simply noted a trip with 'MJ & 4'.

Fanny's birthdays were celebrated just like the others' and, when Godwin visited his mother and brother in Norfolk, Charles assumed he would be back for the event, still a week or so away. He added: '& we are all thinking we shall have a rainy day of Fanny's Birth Day' – a bit of forward meteorology or perhaps a slightly chilling family joke.[5] In fact the day was celebrated in some style, for the whole family, together with Godwin's disciple Tom Turner, successor to Basil Montagu, paid a visit to the Tower of London where they saw the exotic caged animals in the Royal Menagerie, started when the Holy Roman Emperor sent King Henry III a wedding gift of three leopards. They also visited the exhibition of past weaponry and armour on show to the paying public since the time of Charles II.

Within the family the girls assumed different roles and displayed different skills: Claire excelled in singing and playing, Mary in writing and cleverness, Fanny in drawing and being useful. Claire imitated her mother's volatility and histrionics. Mary responded to the Clairmont drama with coldness and contempt, while gaining Godwin's notice with her quickness; when he published a reworking of a little poem mocking English ignorance of the French, in which 'je n'entends pas' becomes in the boorish Englishman's mind a Frenchman called 'Mounseer Nongtongpas', Mary at eleven charmed her father by providing some ideas for the poem.[6]

With her patience and desire to please, Fanny often acted as scribe for her stepfather and he employed her as trusted messenger to his many creditors, even sometimes as his deputy with friends. When Tom Turner's mother died Godwin decided to dine with an important friend rather than pay the proper visit of condolence; so instead he sent Fanny to view the corpse and console Tom Turner: she was a suitable emissary for he melted 'plentifully into tears' in her presence.[7] Fanny also had to deal with the household servants and with importunate tradespeople for both her step-parents. Mary Jane gave her more household duties than the other children; she was a good deal older and such duties usually fell on the eldest girl.

When he visited Skinner Street in 1809 Aaron Burr made charming pictures of the three girls together, the 'goddesses' as he later called them.[8] On first meeting the family, he found the occasion so congenial that, although they dined at four, he stayed chatting till late at night. He told his daughter Theodosia: 'I have seen two daughters of Mary Wollstonecraft. They are very fine children (the eldest no longer a child, being now 15), but scarcely a discernible trace of the mother ...'[9] He knew her image well and would have been reminded of it by the portrait in Godwin's study. In his diary he noted that Mary did not look healthy, the lack of comment on Fanny suggesting that she herself was reasonably robust.

Aaron Burr's enthusiasm for Mary Wollstonecraft was whetted by his meeting with Fanny despite the lack of physical resemblance. Fanny was a strong presence in *Letters from Sweden* and he now requested a copy of the book from Mrs Godwin. He then set off for Scandinavia to tread in his heroine's footsteps; inevitably he would also be accompanied by the image of baby Fanny. Then he visited France, scene of Fanny's birth and desertion by her father. Before he left, the Godwins had requested that he track down in Paris a favourite former pupil of Wollstonecraft, with whom they hoped to be in touch again. Probably this lady would also remember Fanny as a baby.

On his return from the Continent in October 1811 Burr was back in

Skinner Street. He found that Fanny, Mary and Claire had matured while he was away and he enjoyed their flirtatious chatter. Perhaps they teased him about his accent – he tried shedding some of it but noted in his journal that, according to his 'learned friends' Jeremy Bentham and William Godwin, words such as 'hostile, engine, interesting' betrayed his American nationality.

When he called in the evening of Christmas Day and found only the three girls at home, he was not displeased: he had grown very fond of them and he stayed to talk. In the new year he thought he should like to give them a present. He had obtained three pairs of beautiful stockings which he intended to give them; they should appear to come from his daughter Theodosia (for whom he had kept back three other similar pairs). This was probably a politic idea since Burr had a reputation as a boisterous ladies' man, and silk stockings were rather intimate and expensive gifts for teenaged girls.

Having rolled them up nicely, he went round to Skinner Street and climbed the stairs to the schoolroom where Fanny, Mary and Claire were usually to be found. But Fanny was not there. He felt her absence, as well as the bustling presence of Mrs Godwin, and was inhibited. He came away again without presenting his stockings.

It was the day on which the Godwins were preparing for a ball in honour of the wedding of Godwin's protégé, Tom Turner, 'fils d'un bucher', as Burr noted in his journal, the use of French suggesting a remnant of rank consciousness in the American democrat.[10] Godwin had, in Turner's view, rescued him from the 'perdition' of homosexuality: when in 1803 he had developed a 'violent affection' for a man he begged his mentor, through weekly conversations, to cure him of this 'fire that consumes my soul'. The curious plea appears to have initiated a routine; as late as 1820 Maria Gisborne noted in her diary that Turner had been passing 'three hours in the evening two or three times a week' with Godwin 'for many years'. Godwin considered the young man's conversational skills more 'fluent and entertaining' than anyone else's.[11] Whether or not their animated talk had entirely negated his homosexual desires remains unclear, but now in 1812 Turner was marrying a beautiful young woman called Cornelia Boinville and all at Skinner Street had been invited to the celebrations.

On the evening of the ball Aaron Burr visited again, to see the 'three lasses' dressed in their best; 'they were extremely neat; and with taste'. Next day he came again to ask how they had all fared. He never did give his presents and at the end of his stay in London, when he was quite out of money, he was trying to sell the stockings, along with his watch and books, to help pay his fare home. He found the white ones unsaleable but disposed of the black ones for two guineas.

On other occasions 'Les goddesses' insisted he stay to tea or they pressed him into going with them to family friends or seeing sights such as the burial place and bust of Milton. Frequently he strolled alone with Fanny, the most grown up of the trio and the most eager to talk on abstract and political subjects. They may also have spoken of American politics, even about her father Gilbert Imlay, whom Burr quite likely knew: both of them had been intimately involved at different moments with the treacherous General Wilkinson, who, as well as his land speculating in Kentucky, managed to double- or treble-deal with the Spanish, Americans and French concerning the Louisiana territory.

One day Burr watched the boy William, now eight, giving his weekly lecture to his family on the model of the public lectures of Coleridge – and the hellfire sermons which Godwin used to deliver from his highchair when a child in Norfolk. Burr thought the words had been written by one of the girls, probably Mary; William delivered them from a little pulpit which had been made for him. His subject was 'The Influence of Governments on the Character of a People'. Burr was asked to judge the performance. Then, after evening tea, 'the girls sang and danced an hour'. Burr was impressed with the gaiety of the three, all lively and nicely dressed. He enjoyed the pleasant domestic scenes which mitigated his loneliness.

Like his admired Mary Wollstonecraft, Aaron Burr was much intrigued by educational methods that avoided punishment, using carrots and no sticks. He heard of an experiment in a school south of the river and went to see for himself. It was called the Lancaster School.

In 1804 the Quaker Joseph Lancaster had founded it in Borough Road, Southwark. He instructed over a thousand children in writing and reading using a 'shame not pain' approach to discipline. Children were allocated regular 'rejoicing times', as Lancaster termed their weekly races, games and excursions to villages around London. Since his demand for school books was low, Godwin was probably not keen to promote Lancaster's new mentoring model, where small groups of children were tutored by an older pupil and in which, to keep fees down, Lancaster had his books printed in a large size and cut up so that every little group could work on one page at a time.

When Aaron Burr visited the school, Lancaster was already showing signs of a progressive manic-depressive disorder that affected his financial judgement. Despite generous support – the radical Lanarkshire mill owner and reformer Robert Owen had at one time donated £1,000, William Allen, a lecturer in chemistry at the Royal Institution, another £4,000 in 1811 – Lancaster was deeply in debt. Francis Place, a long-time subscriber to Lancaster's school, despaired of him and when, in the following year, he publicly confronted him about the mismanagement of funds, he recorded how Lancaster 'quarrelled and boasted and cried as his passions alternated'. (At least, Place may have mused, he did not go on holiday in the way Godwin, his other beneficiary, tended to do when things began collapsing.)

Despite the failings of its founder, the daily routine of the school remained smooth: the pupils 'appear to be constantly running about, and are all cheerful, as if at play', Burr recorded in amazement. Having watched the boys, he moved on to the 300 girls being taught in a single room 'by one of about 14 years old, in the same mode. But this was prettier.'

The following week when Aaron Burr visited Fanny they discussed this novel educational method. She was intrigued. Perhaps the excited talk took her mind off her domestic activities. Normally she made the tea just right for her sensitive visitor. 'It is only Fan. I can trust,' he noted, while avoiding Claire's strong tea – she may have copied her stepfather who drank 'gunpowder tea, intensely strong', then fell fast asleep. But on this evening Fanny failed him as well and made it too strong; he had insomnia till past four in the morning. Yet he was back next day at Skinner Street with a letter to be copied by one of the girls.

The talk about the Lancaster School made Fanny want to see for herself. Burr agreed to take her. On the chosen day he was busy in the morning preparing for his return to America, and he arrived at Skinner Street by two. Since it would be a long excursion they would miss dinner, so Fanny packed up a picnic for them both consisting of oysters and bread and butter with some porter or beer to drink. As for other English people, for Fanny these oysters were a treat, but Burr thought all European oysters had a copper taste which he did not like; tactfully he said nothing.

The day was blustery and they felt chilly on their hour-long walk, especially near the river. At the school they were received politely by the female principal, the male director and the young head of the girls' school. For two hours they were shown round, given time to ask questions and see the children at work and play. Fanny and Aaron Burr were charmed and impressed, especially with the way in which the children seemed so happy and cheerful, yet to be learning so much. They were particularly struck by an African boy who had been at the school only five months and had learnt not only the English language but also the rudiments of writing and arithmetic.

Despite the weather, the day in Southwark was a success. Burr saw Fanny back to Skinner Street and went home; he returned next day to visit Mrs Godwin and the girls in their upstairs rooms.

What is clear from Aaron Burr's letters and journals perhaps more than from any other source is the amiability of the three girls together now they were in their teens. When he called, they were often sitting or reading, studying or sewing upstairs alone in the schoolroom or having their breakfast and tea without the parents. Throughout his stay he enjoyed their company and found pleasure in walking and talking with them, especially with Fanny, whose intellectual and social interests emerge from his records. Burr left England on 26 March 1812 and wrote of his last visit to Skinner Street, 'That family does really love me.'[12]

❧

The following year Robert Owen, earlier benefactor with Francis Place of the Lancaster School, also visited Skinner Street; like Aaron Burr he came often, staying for breakfast, dinner and tea and talking excitedly about social reform. Although he agreed with Godwin in deploring a strong central government, his socialist or at least social collective ideal was rather at odds with his friend's individualist anarchist one, and the two men argued a good deal. Owen believed that, in part, improvement might most usefully be brought about from the top downwards: his vision needed an authoritarian leader and its implementation the resources of capitalists. Godwin distrusted both as agents of transformation. There were also personal differences between the two men: in the last analysis Owen was a prosperous humanitarian industrialist, Godwin a debt-ridden idealist.

Now nearly nineteen, Fanny was fascinated with ideas about social justice and redistribution of wealth, and about the education that might help bring them about. Owen provoked her thinking. Inspired by what she had seen at the Lancaster School, she listened attentively to his arguments; she left no account of her conclusions at this time but her later involvement with his theories and social analysis suggests that he always piqued her interest and made an impression – even a level-headed man like Francis Place had taken to Owen at once, describing him as 'a man of kind manners and good intentions, of an imperturbable temper, and an enthusiastic desire to promote the happiness of mankind'.[13] Owen was also said to be something of a ladies' man – the fact that he spent long periods away from his wife and was even rumoured to have joined Francis Place in supporting birth control fuelled the perception.

Owen further attracted Fanny as an admirer of her mother. In believing day schools desirable for the masses, he was closer to Mary Wollstonecraft than to Godwin, who distrusted any collaborative endeavour. And his devotion to Wollstonecraft went beyond her ideas – he even imagined her alive, intimately involved with himself and his utopian plans.

❦

The 'girls' were growing up in a swirl of ideas that were both theoretical and immediate. Books, especially those of Godwin and Mary Wollstonecraft, became as real to them as memory and experience. Each was impressed by the fabled past, represented by the portrait in the study which spoke of a calmer, more intellectual time than the present, one that appeared less sordid, money-grubbing and debt-ridden. They were overshadowed by this past which gave them a sense that they were living in less heroic times.

In fact Mary Wollstonecraft had been constantly in debt, and her short life with Godwin had been partly financed by Tom Wedgwood and Joseph Johnson. But this was an aspect of the past that did not emerge either from Godwin's *Memoirs* or from Mary Wollstonecraft's letters. So the problem of money and debts seemed to the girls to belong only to the present and, for Mary in particular, to be associated primarily with the reign of the second Mrs Godwin, who had taken them all away from the life of the mind and into the disasters of trade.

All felt the influence of Mary Wollstonecraft. Mary received her mother's intellectual inheritance, early on assuming she too could succeed as an author; with no blood connection, Claire considered her own spiritedness made her a worthy successor of the unconventional feminist (she also felt the written legacy and in time became as wonderful a letter writer as her heroine). Mary Wollstonecraft had claimed that pity was her prevailing passion; Fanny might have said the same of herself.

Together Fanny, Mary and Claire discussed feminist ideas, the need for a woman to reason, to go beyond contingency and wifeliness, to gain self-esteem and make herself an independent being, relying on herself alone. Although she idealised her mother, Fanny could not find that her intellectual theories provided much inner solace. Although Mrs Godwin might sideline her, she was the only one of the younger generation who had known Mary Wollstonecraft as a mother, had been her 'Fannikin'. So the iconic figure became for her a loving parent and an admirable woman rather than a celebrated feminist; she was the author less of *The Rights of Woman* than of *Letters from Sweden*, the book that united her with Fanny.

When Mary and Claire mouthed progressive views of female independence and rights, then, Fanny argued that a woman might yearn for a purely domestic existence. She remembered her early years of closeness, finding them described so movingly in *Letters*; she could not imagine a preferable situation for a woman, or more important or enjoyable duties than nurturing a child. Judging from his portraits of ideal women in *St Leon* and *Fleetwood*, here her views were not far from Godwin's.

And it was Godwin as live man and embodiment of still-vibrant ideas who dominated the present household, however bustling and irritable Mary Jane might appear. To Fanny he was a wonderful, overbearing presence for whose artistic powers she had the greatest respect. With its huge esteem for literary achievement Skinner Street had never been an easy place in which to think well of oneself artistically or intellectually; there were too many egos around, too many visiting celebrities competing for expression and influence. For Fanny, Godwin stood above them all. In different ways both she and Mary wanted him to herself — or rather they wanted to have him without his wife. While Mary tried to emulate her father and Claire often defied him, Fanny served him with an enthusiasm that was both intellectual and emotional.

She wished to support his genius. *Caleb Williams* and *St Leon* had been wonderful novels; she wanted him to write more and to help him in his projects by nurturing him, by ministering to his comfort. Sometimes when Mrs Godwin and Mary or Claire were away for their health – Mary Jane insisted on an annual trip to escape the filthy London air – Fanny stayed with her stepfather alone, looking after him, keeping the house running, writing out his letters and going on errands. One summer Mary Jane went away for a month to Margate with Mary; Fanny remained at home with Godwin. He reported, 'Fanny conducts herself delightfully, and I am what you call comfortable …' When it was suggested that Fanny join the others at the seaside, she vigorously opposed the idea: 'this cook is very silly … you cannot imagine how many things I have to do,' she declared. Godwin accepted her care: 'Fanny is quite ferocious and impassioned against the journey to Margate. Her motive is a kind one.'[14]

And yet she must also have glimpsed what so many friends and new acquaintances saw in Godwin: a shabby, rather absurd and shuffling figure, bereft of the dignity he continued to claim and unworthy of present homage. For, acting as scribe and messenger, she knew all about his financial dealings, especially with Francis Place, and was fully aware of the cringing, boastful, self-pitying modes in which he cajoled and begged for his family. When Mary Wollstonecraft had died a good friend had written to the widower, 'you are a hero whose dignified province it is to teach by example how great miseries are to be endured with unshaken fortitude'.[15] But times were altered, and the bold philosopher and teacher jostled the timid, selfish man: 'Shall I be torn to pieces & destroyed, merely because I am not a young man, & because I employed my youth in endeavouring with my pen to promote the welfare of my species?' he exclaimed to Place, even as he insisted that his 'integrity' adhered always to him.[16] '*Integrity*', snorted Place.

❧

This outburst of self-pity occurred in 1813, when Place finally gave up trying to help. By the beginning of September of that year Godwin could neither pay nor borrow further and the household was near collapse. As in 1800, when he had gone to Ireland in part to escape demanding creditors, now again Godwin decided on a respite out of town; he wanted, he said, to regain 'strength & spring of mind'. Presumably Fanny did not find fault with this response for she had to convey it to the offended Place – if she did

1. Mary Wollstonecraft, Fanny's mother; she died when Fanny was three.

2. Signature on a letter by Gilbert Imlay, Fanny's father, who deserted her soon after her birth in 1794.

3. William Godwin, who married Mary Wollstonecraft just before she died; he became Fanny's stepfather and guardian.

4. The Polygon, Somers Town, where Fanny spent some of her happy early childhood with her mother and William Godwin.

5. St Pancras Churchyard, showing Mary Wollstonecraft's grave, marked by a square pillar between the trees. Both Fanny and her half-sister Mary spent much time there as children.

6. Skinner Street in central London where Fanny spent most of her life: on the left is the bookshop run by Godwin and his second wife.

7. Charles Clairmont, son of the second Mrs Godwin and Fanny's half-brother; he trained for the book business in Skinner Street but left home as soon as he could.

8. Mary, Fanny's half-sister, who never knew her mother Mary Wollstonecraft. Mary became the lover and, later, wife of Percy Bysshe Shelley.

9. Claire Clairmont, daughter of the second Mrs Godwin; Fanny's stepsister. Claire was possibly Shelley's lover and certainly Byron's mistress.

10. Aaron Burr: former American vice president; he visited the Godwins during his exile in Europe and often talked with Fanny.

11. Francis Place, one of the many philanthropists who tried to rescue the Godwins from debts incurred in their book business.

12. A caricature of the idealist industrialist, Robert Owen: 'A Peep into the City of London Tavern'; Owen discussed politics and progressive education with Fanny.

disapprove, she kept her view to herself for she followed Godwin's line in telling Place that the holiday was a 'duty' – and pointing out that it was only costing just over ten shillings.

Clearly Fanny had become deeply implicated in Godwin's dealings with creditors, especially Francis Place, but it is unlikely that the younger Mary and Claire knew so much about them or their father's painful reliance on benefactors. The next 'saviour' would, however, impact on them all. For it was during this near catastrophic time that Percy Bysshe Shelley, heir to a fortune, came fully into Godwin's view. He would minister to the older man's need both for homage and for money.

CHAPTER 10

SHELLEY

IN 1809 SIXTEEN-YEAR-OLD Percy Bysshe Shelley, a strange, excitable, even violent Eton schoolboy, visited his younger sisters in Mrs Fenning's School on Clapham Common. It was attended by thirteen-year-old Harriet Westbrook, daughter of a retired owner of a coffee house and wine business. John Westbrook could afford the fashionable boarding school for his youngest daughter – as well as his handsome house near Park Lane – for he had done well in life; he was pleased now to see Harriet mixing with children from the landed gentry: the Shelley girls were the daughters of an MP, Timothy Shelley, of Field Place, Sussex, and granddaughters of the wealthy baronet, Sir Bysshe. The Shelley sisters admired Harriet with her fine figure, pretty face, elegant clothes, and cheerful temper.

Young Percy Bysshe was given to showing off; on this occasion he spilt port wine on the headmistress's tablecloth and had to be calmed down. He was in love with his cousin Harriet Grove, who was visiting the school with him. For a while afterwards she seemed receptive but later grew cool. Shelley threatened suicide, toyed with laudanum, then found he admired his sisters' pretty schoolmate – her hair 'a poet's dream'. He turned to her for comfort. He sent her *St Irvyne*, a Gothic thriller he had just published. She felt flattered. This was his second novel and it revealed in embryo many of Shelley's lifelong obsessions.

It tells of a passionate young man, Wulfstein, who, sceptical and despairing,

takes up with a robber band. He falls in love with their fair captive, Megalena, and to gain her kills the robber leader who had befriended him. A
free thinker, Wulfstein believes sexual gratification rational and restraint 'the
imbecility of nature'. His love is 'like the blaze of the meteor at midnight',
an image of passionate transience that haunted Shelley throughout his life.
After his own career of debauchery Wulfstein decides that Megalena is a
fashionable and boring lady, not the celestial model of perfection his warm
imagination once assumed. But, while possession may leave a man cold,
it apparently increases the ardent, uncontrollable passions of woman to
madness, as it does with Megalena. Although no longer her admirer, Wulfstein is persuaded by her to murder his new love, another lady passionately
devoted to him. At the conclusion of the novel all die, the irredeemably
wicked going to hell and the others growing pious. Throughout the tale the
characters act histrionically, hurling themselves around in body and spirit.
Harriet was impressed with the novel but too young and inexperienced to
see that its author might have complicated desires. She may, however, have
noticed its Godwinian view of marriage as 'but a chain' which binds the
body but 'leaves the soul unfettered'.

As his Gothic tale suggests, Shelley had been less sheltered in experience and imagination. With his father, beautiful mother, four younger and
pliable sisters, and a very much younger brother, he had spent his privileged
life as heir apparent in a Sussex mansion within extensive hunting grounds.
The Duke of Norfolk, his father's political patron, was a frequent visitor,
and nearby lived his grandfather Sir Bysshe, famous for being worth at least
£120,000, a fortune helped through elopement with two heiresses, one
sixteen. He had produced nine children, the eldest of whom was Shelley's
father Timothy. Sir Bysshe intended his money to glorify his family and
remain intact through the generations. Very early in life his grandson had
other ideas.

From Oxford, which he entered in October 1810, Shelley corresponded
with Harriet Westbrook, even dedicating 'A Poetical Essay on the Existing
State of Things' to her; holding increasingly radical opinions, he also
continued to argue with his father over politics and religion.[1] Proud of
his literary son, Timothy Shelley could be a little sceptical in religion, but
in politics felt the world should be accepted largely as it was, especially
since, unlike Percy Bysshe, he had experienced the turbulent 1790s with its

revolution in France and unrest in England. Shelley felt both positions inadequate. His mother was alarmed at his radical views: she 'fancies me on the High Road to Pandemonium, she fancies I want to make a deistical coterie of all my little sisters', he wrote with satisfaction.[2] He had once got them to join hands to be electrified in a scientific experiment – their white dresses had been stained black; now he believed his twelve-year-old sister Hellen would be a 'divine little scion of infidelity if I could get hold of her'. He already knew his powers.

He also knew his position in life. Although careless with and of money, Shelley expected it to be forthcoming and, when not actually escaping creditors, he lived well. He ate out and went to plays, and he ran up tailors' bills for fine clothes, rich silk pantaloons, striped waistcoats and a 'Superfine' blue coat with a velvet collar and gilt buttons, all of which he wore with the negligence of habit and privilege. When he published he expected good paper and when he ordered a carriage he assumed it would be well upholstered and decorated. He was not greedy or acquisitive, was generous with money when he had it, but the power of primogeniture dominated his mind as thoroughly as it did any patriarch's: he was heir to £6,000 a year from entailed estates of £200,000 and knew it; if he cared to alienate some of it, that was his right, but that he was owed much was always clear to him.

He had teamed up with a serious and admiring student intended for the law, Thomas Jefferson Hogg, son of a Yorkshire barrister. Idealistic but more conventional than his friend, Hogg accepted Shelley's emerging creed that money and persons must be communal and all opinions challenged. At Eton Shelley had been much influenced by an elderly part-time master, Dr James Lind, who featured as the first of his sage-like father figures. Possibly Lind introduced Shelley to sceptical writings, including those of William Godwin, or Shelley may have come to the incendiary works himself.[3]

Employing Godwin's rationalism, Shelley and Hogg now published a pamphlet with the inflammatory title *The Necessity of Atheism*; this they sent to bishops and heads of colleges. Its views were rather different from those in *St Irvyne*, where the villain ends in the clutches of the devil, for it argued that belief in God and the devil required reason and proof, both of which were lacking. Expulsion was inevitable and welcome: it showed the power of free thought. The two men immediately skipped off to London. Shelley's father muttered about his son's 'sallies of Folly and Madness'.

Timothy followed Shelley to expostulate but the young man might have quoted the Noble Youth's words in Jane Austen's *Love & Freindship*: 'No! Never shall it be said that I obliged my Father.' Hogg, however, lacked the secure inheritance of his friend; he soon 'obliged' his father and left for York to study law. Alone, Shelley turned more and more to Harriet and her receptive sister. Eliza Westbrook was thirteen years Harriet's senior and, living at their parents' house, she mothered her young sister. Perhaps she encouraged the attentions of this heir of a baronetcy and fortune – Shelley later said this was the case – but she and their father were also wary, given his antagonistic relationship with Timothy, and Shelley and Harriet needed no one's encouragement to fall in love. She was beautiful, laughing, biddable and a good listener; he was entertaining, hectically charming, intense, and charismatic.

Harriet and Eliza Westbrook flattered Shelley with their progress in free thinking. Harriet quickly lost her initial horror of 'Atheism' and after a few months of Shelleyan education the girl who had once wanted to marry a clergyman could declare, 'my soul is no longer shackled with such idle fears' as the devil and punishment – although under Shelley's Gothic imaginings she grew 'petrified' of goblins.[4] Her expensive school with its coaching in feminine accomplishments became a 'prison' which, said Shelley, she might escape through love. She – or Eliza – had sense enough to see that the love he preached was different for men and women, and, when Shelley sent her Godwin's books, Harriet, with her sister's help, countered with *Adeline Mowbray* by Amelia Opie, who had based her novel loosely on what she had heard of Mary Wollstonecraft's sad experiences outside wedlock. Sympathetic to its subject, it yet showed that free love for a woman, however theoretically fulfilling, in present society brought misery and death: the heroine regrets 'the hour when, with the hasty and immature judgment of eighteen ... I dared to think and act contrary to ... the reverend experience of ages'.[5] Free love was not practical as things stood – indeed Godwin, who twice made women pregnant outside marriage, was now saying the same thing, although Shelley ignored such backsliding. He was still reading *Political Justice* in the first, 1793 version.

Even as he beckoned Harriet towards him, Shelley yearned for community not coupledom. He always intended to include her sister in any schemes of life. Although highly sexual – he feared he would be driven to 'impurity & vice' if he did not have regular sex with someone he loved – Shelley yet could reveal a distaste for simple, fleshly, unvisionary sex. As well as routine gratification he longed for experience beyond the body, something which might perhaps be glimpsed through communal loving, through non-possessive relating. While drawing in Harriet and her sister, he was also writing to a thirty-year-old schoolteacher, Elizabeth Hitchener, in Sussex. His letters were enthusiastic, self-revealing, even passionate, and under their influence Miss Hitchener, radical in politics but less so in relationships, came to suppose that she, rather than the schoolgirl Harriet, was the object of his love. Shelley's ideas were more advanced: he assumed that in time all of them, including Hogg, would form the nucleus of a liberal and libertarian radical community of like-minded spirits sharing minds and bodies.

Secular utopian communities had been imagined by the previous generation, caught up in the rage for emigration to unspoilt, primitive parts of America. The Romantic poets Southey and Coleridge, for example, had, in their youth, planned a Pantisocracy of men and women supporting each other in revolutionary fraternity and living equally off the soil. Under the influence of Fanny's father Gilbert Imlay, whose only novel, *The Emigrants,* painted a seductive picture of what life might be in unconstrained rural America, they first decided on Kentucky, but then changed it to the Susquehanna region. Nothing came of the plan, except an unhappy marriage for Coleridge, and only the more commercial and authoritarian communities such as Robert Owen's New Lanark had been successfully put into practice.

The bloody course of the utopian French Revolution had for a time put paid to most dreams of egalitarian society. So Shelley was something of an anachronism in the new more prosaic and conventional early nineteenth century: he still believed such experiments should be tried and could work. (In different form they would surface again after the late 1820s with Fourier and his cooperative 'phalanxes'; the transcendentalist Brook Farm in Massachusetts; the millennial Oneida communities with their stress on sex as free, social and spiritual as well as biological; with the Saint-Simonians and their short-lived community of communal property and equal rights; with Robert Owen's equally short-lived American utopia of New Harmony and its anti-slavery offshoot, Frances Wright's Nashoba.)

By August 1811, his head full of utopian visions, Shelley had proposed marriage to Harriet: 'Her father has persecuted her in a most horrible way, & endeavours to compel her to go to school.' He added, 'resistance was the answer'. To Hogg, who, like Miss Hitchener, thought he had been his friend's main confidant and soulmate, Shelley declared that Harriet threw herself on his 'protection'. 'If I were free I were yours,' he told Hogg. A 'kind of ineffable sickening disgust' seized him when he thought of marriage – but it was necessary to free Harriet – and the union would be another rebuff to his father and his upper-class attitudes: Timothy could forgive liaisons and bastards but not a misalliance.

The pair eloped to Scotland and were married in Edinburgh on 29 August. Shelley responded to paternal outrage by deprecating 'any anger on your part': 'perhaps also I may succeed in pointing out its inutility, & inadequacy to the happiness of any one whom it may concern,' he wrote. But Timothy's anger was not useless – he held the purse strings and from now on would use this weapon against his recalcitrant son.

The wedding dashed Elizabeth Hitchener's hopes, but Shelley reassured her that he had acted because of Harriet's infatuation with himself: '*still* thou are dearest to me'. Miss Hitchener must come and join the household, be part of their 'little circle' of kindred spirits.[6]

Harriet was just sixteen, and nineteen-year-old Shelley, with his Eton and Oxford education, was inevitably a mentor-husband. Under his tutoring she now read works of history, philosophy and politics. Soon she embarked on Latin, then would move on to Greek. She was being prepared as helper in Shelley's grandiose work of liberating humanity from intellectual error. After six months she had made such progress in her husband's opinions that, despite her sheltered upbringing, she declared, 'yet did I know that all was not as it ought to be; I looked with a fearful eye upon the vices of the great & thought to myself 'twas better even to be a beggar, or to be obliged to gain my bread with my needle than to be the inhabitant of those great houses when misery & famine howl around'.[7]

The vocabulary she used was mimicking Shelley's but the views were not uncommon among liberal-minded people. The Revolutionary and Napoleonic Wars had dragged on for eighteen years and England in 1811 was at low ebb, the unpopular conflict at stalemate. An invasion was still possible, so the army was stationed all over the country: it was both expensive and disruptive. The murdering revolutionaries had been the bogeymen for the British in the 1790s; now the devil was the imperialist Napoleon; anxiety had become less ideological than nationalist. Yet there was unease. King George III had just been declared permanently mad and the government was about to be headed by his son as Prince Regent, a dissolute man, famed for his bloated body, extravagance, gambling, adulteries and vicious treatment of a discarded wife. He would celebrate his new office by turning his back on the liberal views he had supposedly once held when out of power. The aristocratic elite of London was increasingly censured by a more austere and principled middle class, while the gap between rich and poor widened as landowners benefited from the high agricultural prices of the war years; in the cities poor men were hanged as Luddites for smashing the machinery that was taking their jobs and reducing their families to starvation.

Shelley's analysis, which he communicated to his young wife, was, then, mainstream enough for the liberal section of the population. But his emerging solution of universal rational change was more typical of radical English thought of twenty years earlier when Godwin's had been a revelatory and inspiring voice, when there was still all to play for politically and when English idealism had not been dented by events across the Channel.

❧

Like Elizabeth Hitchener, Harriet made rather less progress than Shelley could have wished in the radicalism of private life. Despite the arguments put forward for non-possessive affection, her husband alone engrossed her and she could not share herself. Enthralled by his friend, Hogg tended to follow him in love. Shelley had once urged him to court his sister Elizabeth, who closely resembled Shelley in appearance, but Elizabeth had been unimpressed with Hogg or the idea. Now, with little experience of sex but with a decidedly voluptuous imagination, Hogg, a heavy, intense man, arrived to join the newly married couple. Astonished at Harriet's beauty and charm, he fell in love.

They all moved to York and when Shelley went south to raise money and bring back Harriet's sister to live with them, Hogg seized the moment to importune Harriet. She fended him off and, when Shelley returned, he was told of the event and her dislike. His response was anxious and confused. It was what he wanted, yet surely Hogg had done wrong in imposing himself. Here even the first edition of *Political Justice* was useful since it stated that any sort of intercourse between two people 'must be regulated ... by the unforced consent of either party'. Yet Shelley remained worried. Had he and Hogg been ideologically mistaken, he wondered, or was it a case of simple jealousy? Meanwhile, the two fathers corresponded miserably about the complicated ménage.

The quarrel with Hogg was quickly resolved, but the emotions it raised continued to disturb Shelley – indeed they came to envelop more than himself and his wife, for about this time he even accused his mother of adultery with a music master. He poured out his intense sexual feelings to Elizabeth Hitchener in a stream of intimate letters. More practically, since Eliza Westbrook had brought some money with her, he decided that he, Harriet and Eliza should all secretly leave Hogg in York and head for the Lake District. The region attracted Shelley as home of the *once*-radical older generation of Romantic poets, Southey, Wordsworth, and Coleridge. Left behind, Hogg sublimated his feelings into fiction. *Memoirs of Prince Alexy Haimatoff* presented a Shelleyan Hogg irresistible to the women in the story, all of whom resembled Harriet. (When he read the book Shelley admired its melodramatic qualities but thought that it vulgarised the idea of free love into the 'intercourse of brutal appetite'.[8])

Harriet settled happily into a cottage near Keswick and learnt her Latin while her sister read Tom Paine, so she could edit his writings for the working classes; she also kept house for them all – Shelley liked clean clothes and hated dirt. To the women the ménage seemed pleasantly studious and domestic. But they were poor – now and in other periods of penury none of them considered they might do paid work – and they were running up debts.

Although he had initiated the move, Shelley was restless without Hogg; he disliked being 'tranquillized' in domesticity. Usually he found a reason to move – persecution, debts or a mission – but there was also an inner compulsion not to be rooted, to be always having to go elsewhere. This time he was helped by the bluff Catholic Duke of Norfolk on his nearby estate. Wanting to mend the rift in his old friend's family, the duke managed to persuade Timothy to resume support of £200 a year to stop his son 'cheating strangers'. As leader of the Catholics in the House of Lords and supporter of the downtrodden Irish Catholics, the duke also fed Shelley's interest in

Ireland, already revealed at Oxford when he wrote in support of a radical Irish journalist persecuted by the government. Needless to say the young man was not much interested in Catholicism.

But before he could act in the cause of Ireland he had an acquaintance to make. Through the duke Shelley at last met Robert Southey, one of his favourite poets. The two men were at once wary of each other. The older one, at thirty-seven, saw a youth with erroneous radical ideas which he would grow out of with age – as he himself had done. Although he rather warmed to Southey at first, Shelley ultimately saw a man 'corrupted by the world, contaminated by Custom', now prostituting his talents.

Mrs Southey and Mrs Coleridge dismayed Shelley. Years before they had been intended for the Pantisocratic commune on the banks of the Susquehanna. Now, however, they had become merely domestic wives, lacking their husbands' intellectual interests. Shelley was appalled: he had no wish for Harriet to become a maker of biscuits and cakes, especially not the rich buttery ones he was forced to eat at Mrs Southey's tea table.

According to Hogg, years later, when Shelley had abandoned Harriet, Southey hinted to him that one wife was really as good as another, that a maker of biscuits could be lived with as companionably as any other woman. It was not a notion to appeal to an idealistic, erotically charged young man.

⁂

Since schooldays Shelley had been mouthing the opinions of Godwin's *Political Justice*. For the past few years there had been silence on radical causes; so he assumed Godwin was dead. Formerly a huge admirer of *Political Justice*, Southey had moved decisively from its theories, but he knew Godwin was still alive and living in London. When he heard the news Shelley felt 'inconceivable emotions'. Here would be no apostate.

On 3 January 1812 Godwin received a letter addressed to him as the one man who could restore a young writer's faith in the radical generation of the 1790s. Godwin was, the letter declared, 'a luminary too dazzling for the darkness which surrounds him'. Used to enthusiastic disciples, the older man replied cautiously. To appeal further, when he wrote again, Shelley summarised his life in mythic mode, detailing his progress from Gothic to Godwin – *Political Justice* had made him 'a wiser and a better man' – and turning his father into an avenging tyrant who had tried to filch his son's patrimony. In time Timothy would even become Shelley's 'dead life', a torturing form 'Masked in grey hairs and wrinkles' who wound his son in his hellish arms and dragged him 'down, down, down!'[9]

As the head of a family himself, Godwin suspected the tale somewhat slanted – although in the *Memoirs* he had followed Mary Wollstonecraft in calling her father a 'despot' – and he was uneasy at the way Shelley referred back to the old version of *Political Justice* with its diatribes against marriage and convention. Also, while Shelley claimed he would try for Godwinian 'sobriety of spirit', he was in fact displaying an alarming degree of arrogance: 'I have not heard without benefit that Newton was a modest man,' he would write.[10] To Godwin he must have seemed raw and callow, full of restless intellectual ambition.

Yet, despite noting the conceit, when he learnt of his new disciple's social position, financial prospects and enthusiastic desire to help him, Godwin was tempted. Shelley had accepted the point in all versions of the revolutionary book, that money and property should go where they were needed, that the rich should give and the poor demand by right. Mrs Godwin was equally excited; she wrote to Lady Mount Cashell that Shelley was 'a young man who will one day have a large fortune and who is a great admirer of Mr. Godwin'.[11]

Soon Shelley was Godwin's 'lasting friend, who, according to the course of nature, may contribute to the comforts of my closing days'. The letter containing these resonant words took three months to catch up with the peripatetic Shelley, but when it did its recipient replied grandly that he would indeed 'regard it as my greatest glory, should I be judged worthy to solace your declining years'. A later letter promised the Godwins a house when Shelley came of age and into his inheritance. It was all they could have wished. Shelley was planning to settle in Wales, primarily because this had been the home of Godwin's hero Fleetwood; the Godwins should join him once he and Harriet were settled.[12]

Before he could appreciate his effect on the impecunious older man, Shelley had dashed to Dublin with Harriet and Eliza Westbrook, intent on liberating Ireland from the English – and Catholicism. Staying in elegant lodgings in Sackville Street, he and Harriet distributed the pamphlets and broadsides he had written and printed exhorting the Irish to sobriety and courage: 'Awake! – arise! – or be forever fallen,' he wrote, echoing Milton's peremptory devil in *Paradise Lost*. 'We throw [the pamphlets] out of window and give them to men that we pass in the streets,' recorded Harriet, adding with an un-Shelleyan sense of the ridiculous: 'for myself I am ready to die of laughter when it is done and Percy looks so grave'.[13]

By now Shelley was imagining – in complete opposition to Godwinian doctrine – an association of philanthropists, a sort of Masonic organisation of ardent men who would begin changing the world without waiting for the labouring classes to catch up: ties of liberality and virtue would unite atheist, Muslim and Christian in charity and fraternity.

Soon he lost faith in the timid, self-serving Irish; he now thought again that utopia should begin privately, in a personal 'paradise' of devoted repub-licans. Harriet and Eliza were conforming to everything he desired, even accepting his conversion to vegetarianism and exchanging their diet of chicken and lamb for apples and cabbage – or almost so since a later letter had Harriet remaining 'slightly animal till spring'. It was heady discipleship for a dogmatic young man and Shelley was eager to extend it to include Elizabeth Hitchener, who had rhapsodically called herself Portia when asked by Shelley to choose a new name. Harriet and Eliza were good women but Miss Hitchener would bring an intellectual robustness to the group. In classical times Portia was the daughter of the younger Cato and the wife of Brutus, assassin of Julius Caesar, that is, the daughter of one republican icon and wife of another. Shelley's acceptance of the name for Miss Hitchener suggests that this was the kind of woman he was expecting. She was, he told Godwin, a self-made republican; she would be their 'better genius' for 'Great responsibility is the consequence of high powers'.[14]

The society of like-minded spirits should be in Elan Valley in Wales, where Shelley had lodged the year before when lonely and dreaming of Harriet. He would use his inheritance to make a remote radical commune, a new primitivistic family of brothers and sisters who would share everything from chairs, glasses and plates to money and inheritance – and each other; they would think high thoughts and till the soil. The dream echoed South-ey's and Coleridge's Pantisocracy but with a more dedicated leader; also it would be located in Britain rather than Gilbert Imlay's American outback. Shelley found a large house in the valley and they all moved in. He had recently raised £500. More he was sure would be coming from his father.

He had presumed too much. Timothy Shelley had been appalled at his son's recent attempt to persuade his little sister Hellen to join them ('if you were with me ... you might run & skip read write think just as you liked', he had written clandestinely to her). So no further money was forthcoming from him or anyone else for the perfect community. The house had to be given up and 'Paradise' postponed. Although she had been severely ill there Harriet would always yearn for this Edenic retreat.

They moved to Lynmouth in Devon, settling in a pleasant sprawling cottage with a splendid sea view called Hooper's Lodging – even without money Shelley, who referred to the 'poverty and humbleness' of the house, rarely lived below the level of a gentleman. He had begun a long visionary, political poem *Queen Mab*, using the rhythm of Southey's epic *Thalaba*; it would describe how the soul of Ianthe (an idealised Harriet) would be carried into space among the stars to view the earth from her ethereal form; she would be instructed by Queen Mab in Shelleyan doctrine, understanding the tyranny of war and governments and learning that man, not inherently evil and selfish, is, however, corrupted from birth. The poem would have extensive philosophical and historical annotation, so Shelley was reading widely. Among the books he discovered at this time was *The Empire of the Nairs*, a romance by James Lawrence describing a society of free love and female choice in distant India: 'Perfectly and decidedly do I subscribe to the truth of the principles which it is designed to establish,' he wrote. He also sent to London for Mary Wollstonecraft's *Rights of Woman*, which had in part inspired Lawrence's romantic fantasy.

Waiting for Elizabeth Hitchener, Shelley felt expansive. He dispatched an invitation to Skinner Street for Godwin's stepdaughter Fanny to join them. He was intrigued by the idea of a daughter of Mary Wollstonecraft, a woman who, he knew, had herself suggested various unconventional ways of living – as a trio with the married painter Fuseli and again with the departing Imlay and his new mistress. Fanny could travel down with Miss Hitchener from London, then return in the autumn when they would all come to town. For Godwin and Fanny he described his projected commune in less libertarian terms than he used to the others; he did not intend actually to plough the field himself after all, nor Harriet to cook and clean, and there would be no untrammelled sex: '[N]ow, a ploughboy can with difficulty acquire refinement of intellect, & promiscuous sexual intercourse under the present system of thinking would inevitably lead to consequences the most injurious to the happiness of mankind,' he wrote.[15] For the moment he was accepting the sexual modification of *Political Justice* – but he had forgotten his own admiration of the ploughboy Robert Burns, who had exhibited considerable 'refinement of intellect'.

Even thus toned down the prospect did not attract Godwin, who declined on Fanny's behalf (she was older than Harriet but Godwin did not suggest she correspond directly with the Shelleys about the invitation). He had not met Shelley yet, not 'seen his face', he said, and could not send Fanny to strangers. How curious, remarked the (partially) liberated Harriet, since Shelley had been pouring out his heart to Godwin for many months: Shelley could hardly be termed a stranger. It was an invitation which, to Fanny's chagrin, would never be repeated. In the years to come she must sometimes have recalled it and perhaps regretted Godwin's quick refusal.

↦

In mid July, just before Harriet's seventeenth birthday, Elizabeth Hitchener gave up her laboriously established school, defied 'impotent malice' and set out for Lynmouth, much against her publican father's warning that she would lose income and reputation by this rash act; in Sussex it was said she was going to join Shelley's harem. She had no fears: she had his love and, knowing the Field Place family, she expected the young man to be rich as well as charismatic. She was welcomed enthusiastically into the family.

Having declined the offer to send Fanny to join the commune, Godwin, deeply in debt, thought he himself should try to make face-to-face contact. He would take a trip to Lynmouth and meet Shelley at last. He wrote at the end of August, then set out in early September. After an appalling sea voyage of fifty-one hours, he arrived in Lynmouth only to find that his potential patron and the three women had moved away in the previous month, leaving Shelley's books as security for arrears of rent. Godwin had wasted an expensive journey. He did, however, learn the good news that the Shelleys would be in London within a fortnight.

In fact, having come too often to the attention of the authorities with his habit of sending off inflammatory pamphlets in bottles, paper boats and fire balloons, he and the women had all gone off to Tremadoc in North Wales, where Shelley found a new mission: a scheme to hold back the sea from an estuary and create agricultural land for a model village.

Even before the move to Tremadoc there were strains in the ménage. The idealism with which Shelley had clothed Miss Hitchener had disappeared soon after her arrival. She had proved insufficiently 'intellectual' for his taste, too much infatuated with himself, perhaps too sexually demanding. He was also acutely aware of her ugliness – she was too tall and dark. Once his 'Portia', she dwindled into 'Bessy' – Harriet had never approved the unusual name. Soon she became 'the Brown Demon' – 'an artful, superficial, ugly, hermaphroditical beast of a woman'.[16] Harriet disliked being treated as her pupil and Elizabeth Hitchener hated being pushed to the background when they mixed in genteel society. They would go to London to raise money for the embankment scheme and Miss Hitchener would not return to Wales with them.

She felt betrayed and bitter at Shelley's 'barbarity': rejected after four months following such lengthy persuasion. Back in Sussex she found herself a subject of mockery and scandal as a cast-off mistress. Shelley offered her an annuity of £100, but it was paid only once – and was cancelled out by a loan of the same amount she had earlier made to Shelley.[17] 'We were entirely deceived in her character,' Harriet declared. 'She built all her hopes upon being able to separate me from my dearly loved Percy.'[18] Home in Kent Miss Hitchener presented a miserable spectacle, close to 'insanity', according to one onlooker.

Harriet and Eliza Westbrook remained fixed, however. Eliza still kept house though she annoyed Shelley with her talk of nerves and the lengthy combing of her black hair. Having watched Miss Hitchener come and go, Harriet felt no anxiety that her extraordinary husband would ever turn his righteous fury on her; she was still very much in love, accepting Shelley's fads and incessant removings as the price to pay for the privilege of loving him. In his novel *Nightmare Abbey* (1818) their new friend, the satirist Thomas Love Peacock, pictured her in Marionetta: 'her life was all music and sunshine … She loved Scythrop [Shelley], she hardly knew why'.[19] By now she was aware that she was pregnant.

CHAPTER 11

FANNY

WITH THE EXCEPTION of Godwin's protégés such as Turner and a student named Proctor Patrickson, whose studies at Cambridge Godwin was helping to support, not many young men called regularly at Skinner Street. Shelley is the first who seems to have made a deep impression on the girls. Later, after the catastrophe of the elopement, Mrs Godwin reported that all three had been infatuated with him when they first saw him; romantic, charismatic, fascinating and as histrionic as Claire, he excited them all by turns and together, allowing them to live in his exotic realm of noble feelings, high emotions and social possibilities.

If Mrs Godwin is right, the seeds were sown early, before any of them had set eyes on him, when Godwin read out Shelley's long self-fashioning letters by way of overture; they presented him less as a privileged scion of the gentry than as a radical knight errant. Fanny had experience of responding intensely through the written word: it was the way she most knew her own mother.

When Godwin had first replied to the would-be disciple, he had offered him the glamour not only of his own radical past but also of the coming generation: 'You cannot imagine how much all the females of my family, Mrs. G. and three daughters, are interested in your letters and your history.' Indeed he seemed to revel in a notional connection between Shelley and his girls. Long before they met him Godwin was writing that they thrilled to see 'the well-known hand' and were 'on the tiptoe' to know what was in the letters.[1] In the process of his tortuous financial negotiations and thinking primarily of what Shelley might do for them all, he raised expectations in Fanny, Mary and Claire, not diminished when they learnt that Shelley had rescued Harriet Westbrook from 'domestic oppression'.

Despite the long overture of letters and promises, neither money nor man materialised. Over the months Godwin flattered Shelley by arguing philosophy with him, edging him away from the immature political adventures in Ireland and Wales, the militancy of overt political action, and into a wiser, more intellectual discipleship which included his seeing Godwin as the best of causes on which to lavish his wealth. Finally, after a full ten months of dedicated letter-writing, on 4 October 1812 the Shelleys, now without Miss Hitchener, appeared in Skinner Street.

The first encounter over dinner started well. Ignoring Godwin's squat, unprepossessing appearance, Shelley saw the author of *Political Justice,* embodiment of the radical 1790s, while Harriet found a 'Family Man'. In Mrs Godwin she initially discerned 'great sweetness' and 'magnanimity'.

The Godwins intended to charm. After dinner Shelley and Harriet were taken into Godwin's study, where they contemplated the picture of Mary Wollstonecraft. A proud Godwin told Shelley that the absent daughter Mary resembled this 'most lovely woman' – he did not add that in many ways her features were a lighter version of his own for he knew the pull of the voluptuous and by now iconic Mary Wollstonecraft for a young man like Shelley. Then they discussed philosophy – and Godwin's pressing financial needs. Harriet was enthusiastic: '[W]e love them all,' she wrote.

The first meeting was deemed a success and after it the Shelleys visited daily, even determining to stay in London for the sake of being near Skinner Street. But first impressions were soon modified. Harriet speedily changed her mind about Mrs Godwin. Indeed she came to consider her so disagreeable that for a time she refused to visit Skinner Street at all. In less than a year she was writing to her friend, 'We have not seen much of Godwin, for his wife is so dreadfully disagreeable that I could not bear the idea of seeing her. Mr. S. has done that away, tho', by telling G. that I could not bear the society of his darling wife. Poor man, we are not the only people, who find her troublesome.'[2]

Godwin, meanwhile, was so anxious for money that he hinted to Shelley that it might be best if he simply made peace with his father. This conventional idea, together with his opposition to the young man's idealistic schemes, made him seem 'old and unimpassioned' to Shelley – he even wanted him to join the moderate Whig Party in Parliament. At the same time Godwin constantly proclaimed his own intellectual status. According to Harriet he expected 'such universal homage from all persons younger than himself, that it is very disagreeable to be in company with him'.[3] In her turn Mrs Godwin soon thought both Harriet and Shelley conceited and unreliable.

But each side needed the other, and on several occasions Fanny was taken to dine with the Shelleys in their hotel, Lewis's in St James's Street. All played their parts and Fanny and her stepmother took every opportunity of conveying to Shelley the difficult message that Godwin was at once a great and a needy man, wanting respect, 'a little ready money' and 'immense Capital'.

Perhaps at this point they were too importunate for Shelley's taste and too eager to stop him returning to Wales not simply to avoid his throwing money into a greedy scheme but also to prevent him living there in an expensive house. Or perhaps he was too entangled in Tremadoc to have anything immediate to offer the Godwins, and so felt uncomfortable. Otherwise it is difficult to explain what happened next.

On 13 November the Godwins had been invited to dine with the Shelleys at Lewis's hotel, where they were to meet the solicitor dealing with Shelley's financial affairs.[4] Shelley had been unsuccessful in raising money for the Tremadoc scheme and, still under-age, could not easily obtain large sums for any other purpose either. But something might be done and the Godwins were hopeful.

When they arrived, however, they found their hosts had left for Wales that morning – it seems they had planned this for some time without mentioning it. Godwin was in no position to complain at the unpredictable act. However, when he spoke again to Francis Place about his debts, he did not mention the erratic behaviour; he had been placating Place with Shelley's promises and he knew Place did not like Shelley.

The first of the girls in the Godwin household under Shelley's spell was Fanny. On the initial visit both Mary and Claire were away, and only she was at home. Harriet saw in Fanny, the daughter of that 'dear Mary Wolstoncroft', a girl 'very plain, but very sensible. The beauty of her mind fully overbalances the plainness of her countenance'.[5] It was the judgement of a pretty girl on someone with dowdy clothes. Fanny's appearance was usually mentioned in relation to Mary's beauty and was an aspect of herself with which she must have become very familiar during her teen years; however, the Godwin ménage, with its stress on intellectual accomplishment and inner resources, was probably as comfortable an environment as there could be for a girl not a beauty to grow up in. Although it was hard to appreciate it, plainness had some advantages: the plain girl was less on show, could be more watchful and observant. People noticed how thoughtful Fanny was.

Shelley may have expected more flamboyance in a child of the passionate encounter of Gilbert Imlay and Mary Wollstonecraft, the girl he knew through *Letters from Sweden,* Godwin's *Memoirs* and the private love letters to Imlay. Yet Fanny with her long brown hair, bluish eyes and good figure pleased him. She was honest and open, and engaging; she held firm opinions and rewarded attention with affection.

In her turn Fanny appreciated the fact that Shelley admired both her mother and stepfather, that he talked alone and volubly to her in his high-pitched, unstable voice. Shelley was the intellectual Godwin had taught her to revere, a young embodiment of those views which her stepfather had once so thrillingly held and lived himself. For the Shelley she first met was not primarily a poet but a reformer and political thinker like her mother and Godwin. He was an idealist who spoke about the coming bright world, what people might be when transfigured, and his ideas 'almost acquired the intensity of sensations'. His 'right angled originality' caught her vividly, along with his restless charm; his animation was infectious.[6] No wonder she was dazzled.

Later she noted that, with all his vitality and volubility, Shelley rarely laughed. He knew this himself: when he intended to laugh he found he was grinning sardonically, worse than a 'Cheshire cat'. He often harped on death – was his pre-Lewis Carroll Cheshire Cat a jocular version of the grinning death's head or his own grinning devil-as-self? He once wrote in a notebook, 'I fear that I am hardly human.'[7]

Probably with his overwhelming presence – even Godwin admitted that Shelley was 'so beautiful', a word Claire also used for his dark blue eyes and marble forehead – and with his particular bantering, eighteen-year-old

Fanny did indeed begin to fall in love.[8] He had a devoted, winning way with women who were easily attracted to him. Mrs Godwin claimed that he 'paid immense attentions' to Fanny and Fanny returned his love, but Mrs Godwin was not known for strict truth.

Perhaps to Fanny Shelley was an object less of sexual than of sentimental desire. Having learnt where sexual passion had taken her mother, she reverenced the sentimental affections above all – benevolence, kindness and sympathy; where other girls of her age devoured romantic fiction she was reading newspapers and pamphlets about the poor who were suffering in these harsh years of the new century. And Shelley, though highly sexualised, spoke often of his ideal love beyond the sexual, something closer to what subsisted between loving uninhibited sisters. At the same time, Fanny read the poetry of Wordsworth and Coleridge and her passions were stirred by the Romantic writings that stressed individual emotion and the ecstatic moment.

Whatever her burgeoning feelings for Shelley, to his annoyance Fanny was aware of the social divide between them. For Percy Bysshe Shelley was not only an eager devotee of Godwin – and no doubt 'as raffish in his appearance as I would wish every Disciple of Godwin to be' in Jane Austen's words[9] – but also a privileged, rather swaggering gentleman from a world of grand salons and estates; if his clothes were usually rumpled they were also fashionable and cost a lot. The Shelleys were staying at a fancy hotel, and with their expensive appearance together they made a fine show in drab Skinner Street, where there was little spare money for female finery or lavish furnishings. The girls dressed plainly in dark colours. Years later Mary's friend Christina Baxter, when asked about the Shelleys, whom she met in Skinner Street, above all remembered Harriet's 'beautiful blue silk dress'. Fanny was similarly impressed and spoke of seventeen-year-old Harriet as a fine lady.

The social assumption irritated Shelley. 'How is Harriet a *fine lady*?' he retorted, 'You indirectly accuse her ... of this offence – to me the most unpardonable of all.' He urged her simple habits and unassuming manner. Fanny remained unconvinced. She saw that Shelley and Harriet expected services and attention the Godwin family did not. Shelley was and looked like a patrician, and his wife was a lady. Also he often traded on his status and was quick to condemn the unwashed and uneducated: he was peremptory even with his egalitarianism.

In fact he was uneasy with his status. In theory he wanted all people to be equal: '*I* have no taste for displaying genealogies, nor do I wish to seem more important than I am,' he had written to Miss Hitchener's poorer, working-class father while blaming him for thinking only of '*profit*' and distrusting 'those who happen to be borne to more wealth & name than yourself'. When his social position was hinted at, Shelley responded, 'You remind me of what I hate despise & shudder at, what willingly I would not, & the part from which I can emancipate myself from, in this detestable coil of primaeval prejudice, that will I free myself from – Have I not foresworn all this, am I not I [a] worshipper of equality —.'[10] The incoherence of his remarks suggested how disturbing he found the situation.

When the Shelleys suddenly decamped to Wales without warning the Godwins, Fanny at first feared writing – unmarried young ladies were not supposed simply to correspond with young men. But Shelley reassured her: despite being 'one of those formidable & long clawed animals called a *Man*', he was inoffensive and lived on vegetables. He did not bite and could therefore decently 'obtrude' himself on her. Yet he did not need to bite to make an effect and Fanny had some reason to fear the emotions he had aroused by his presence and would continue to arouse with his intimate flirtatious letters.

Like Godwin she was hurt at his going and scolded him for his rudeness; he had left 'in haste and coldness' without bidding adieu to any of them. He accepted her criticism: his abrupt removal must indeed have appeared 'insensible & unfeeling … an ill return for all the kind greetings we had received at your house'.[11] Fanny would have sympathized with him and Harriet had she known their conflicted motives and pain, he told her. He explained neither.

CHAPTER 12

SHELLEY

SOON SHELLEY WAS disillusioned with the Tremadoc drainage scheme. Its promoters now seemed exploitative and selfish. When in the Lake District, he believed he had been attacked by an assailant who hit him and left him unconscious. Here again in Wales there was an intruder, who came twice during the night in a fierce storm and shot at Shelley through a window. He fired back. Pacifism was never instinctive with him: it was a creed not a need and he frequently gave the impression of barely controlling a violent nature. He was usually armed with pistols, as on this occasion.

Were the attackers real or hallucinatory? Other people heard the disturbance in the Lake District and there is some basis for believing it happened. In Tremadoc too the attacker could have existed, sent by one of the many local gentlemen he had offended with his criticism of their dealings with labourers. Or he might have been someone dispatched to find incriminating papers in the house, then disturbed in the act.[1]

Or on both occasions he could have been a figment of Shelley's mind – Hogg and Peacock (and later Harriet) thought this the case. Shelley was in an excited and excitable state, taking large quantities of laudanum for his headaches. He feared the results of alcohol but worried little about the effect of this powerful opium-based drug and he took it throughout his adult life. Later he drew the Tremadoc assassin as the devil with horns, though, since he saw the devil as a human projection, this did not render him unreal. In his poems the devil would become a kind of satirical alter ego. Or, since he was often entranced by his own reflection in pools, rivers and mirrors, did he see his own face in the window, destroyed when he fired? Mary later transmuted the event into a scene in *Frankenstein* where the Creature looks through the inn window at his creator after murdering his wife.

Real or imagined – and the shopkeepers to whom Shelley owed money thought it a ruse – the effect was the same: he and his entourage left Tremadoc and continued their manic travelling. (Shelley's egalitarianism coexisted with a patrician unconcern for the small tradesmen who paid for his comforts.) He would now be heroic in word rather than deed. Political change should be brought about less by direct political action than by inspirational writing.

Still expecting an agreement with Timothy Shelley and an influx of money, he now installed himself, Harriet and Eliza Westbrook in an expensive suite at Cooke's hotel in Albemarle Street, London, and ordered a fine carriage from Thomas Charters. Hogg was soon in attendance, especially on the very pregnant Harriet, encouraged again by Shelley. When she saw him, Eliza managed a faint smile; after a greater initial effort at cordiality, Harriet once more found her husband's friend intolerable.

Shelley began his new phase of radicalism by printing the completed *Queen Mab*. The lengthy poem was blatantly radical. Some of its views, such as the destructive power of capitalism and commerce, were respectable among liberals; others, such as its advocacy of drinking only pure water and eating only vegetables (suggested even for carnivorous animals), were considered cranky. Inevitably it was difficult to find a publisher, but probably Godwin here stepped in and introduced Shelley to his bookseller Thomas Hookham (there were two Hookhams in the firm but Shelley usually dealt with Thomas, the more amenable). Hookham agreed to print 250 copies at the author's expense. Seventy of them were distributed privately once Shelley understood that the poem with its abject slavish kings and religion's puerile God was unsuitable for general release. Harriet was impressed with its daring; the work 'must not be published under pain of death', she wrote, 'because it is too much against every existing establishment'.[2]

In good Godwinian style *Queen Mab* urged freedom from old beliefs through mental effort and imagined a pacific utopia in which people would share life's good things and be free from injustice, materialism and religion; the many would not 'faint with toil/ That few may know the cares and woe of sloth'. However in Canto VI it went rather beyond Godwin in insisting on a more magical transfiguration, as well as on the usual Shelleyan group of special people dedicated to this transfiguration: 'some eminent in virtue' with 'truth' on their 'pure lips' would 'bind the scorpion falsehood with a wreath/ Of ever-living flame'. A mystical non-Christian utopia must have its charismatic leader and Shelley struck everyone he met with his intensity and glittering eyes.

Despite Godwin's change of heart on marriage, one of Shelley's foot-notes echoed the first edition of *Political Justice*: 'A husband and wife ought to continue so long united as they love each other; any law which should bind them to cohabitation for one moment after the decay of their affection would be a most intolerable tyranny … Constancy has nothing virtuous in itself'; the 'welfare of their mutual offspring' should not take precedence over individual happiness. Harriet, now seventeen and close to her time, was unconcerned, for the dedication, though not much about her as a person, was full of Shelley's love:

> Harriet! … thou wert my purer mind;
> Thou wert the inspiration of my song;
> Thine are these early wilding flowers,
> Though garlanded by me.

❦

On 23 June 1813 Harriet gave birth to a daughter whom Shelley named Ianthe after the heroine of *Queen Mab*. He wrote a sonnet to the baby in which he saw 'some feeble lineaments of her/ Who bore thy weight beneath her spotless bosom.'[3]

Perhaps Eliza aided Harriet's decision not to use this bosom for its natural purpose but to take a wet nurse, as was common but not invari-able among women of her class. Shelley's heroine Mary Wollstonecraft had written lovingly of her own breastfeeding of Fanny and had described a mother with 'a bosom bursting with the nutriment' her 'cherished child' desired.[4] She had suckled baby Fanny for a year; during the time she had been immensely desolate but the experience of breastfeeding so comforted her that she dreaded weaning the child.

Shelley had strict views on what women should be as mothers and lovers, and years later Peacock blamed some of his disenchantment with Harriet on her decision not to breastfeed. At the same time Shelley believed birth itself a coming into sickness and in *Queen Mab* the newborn baby is a 'stranger soul' 'bound/Ere it has life'. It is ruined almost at once by its surroundings, especially by its parents and nurses. He, Shelley, might be 'pure' but Harriet was less so and he absolutely hated the wet nurse: surely the baby was sucking poison from her. On one occasion he snatched Ianthe away and held her to his own breast as if he, rather than any woman, could give the proper sustenance.[5] Although observing the quarrels she caused, Peacock thought him fond of the baby; Hogg said Ianthe appeared neither to give 'gratification' nor to excite 'interest' in her father.[6]

Shelley's hatred of the wet nurse expanded to include the person who had hired her: Harriet's sister Eliza Westbrook.

She had been organising their household over the past months and naturally took over much of the childcare from Harriet. But despite her usefulness, like the wet nurse and Miss Hitchener, Eliza now became for Shelley a demon, a 'loathsome worm'. The adjective was a favourite one used for physical and emotional repulsion – the verbal equivalent of the paroxysms of fury for which Shelley had been famous since schooldays. 'I certainly hate her with all my heart and soul,' he wrote, and 'I sometimes feel faint with the fatigue of checking the overflowings of my unbounded abhorrence for this miserable wretch.' He was disgusted when she caressed little Ianthe, 'in whom I may hereafter find the consolation of sympathy'.[7] He grew desperate to expel Eliza Westbrook from his household.

A hostile critic, the American writer Mark Twain, surmised that Shelley's new hatred had less to do with the baby and more with Eliza's efforts to modify a connection he had recently made in the Boinville family.

⤶

This had come about through Godwin, who introduced Shelley to Mrs Harriet Boinville, a lady from a progressive, well-heeled family with income from West Indian plantations. Her husband, aide-de-camp to the revolutionary General de Lafayette, had been killed during the invasion of Russia three months earlier, though she would remain ignorant of this until the autumn of the following year. Mrs Boinville was staying in Pimlico near her musical younger sister, Mrs Cornelia Newton, a mother of five. Hogg mocked their circle of libertarian friends as 'two or three sentimental young butchers' and an 'eminently philosophical tinker' who 'sighed, turned up their eyes, retailed philosophy, such as it was, and swore by William Godwin and *Political Justice*'; Shelley, however, was enchanted with them.[8] On a visit to Vauxhall in July 1813, just after the birth of Ianthe, Hogg noted that a 'mundane critic' might have observed that there was 'a most desperate flirtation' between Cornelia Newton and Shelley, who enjoyed working his charm on susceptible older women.[9] The Newtons were vegetarians and rumoured to practise 'nakedism'; they were also associated with 'Nairism' following *The Empire of the Nairs* – Lawrence was a friend of Mrs Boinville's – though free love remained more fantasy than reality.

Mrs Boinville returned from Pimlico to Bracknell near Windsor; Shelley soon followed – Bracknell would become his 'happy home', for the moment away from Harriet, her sister, the baby and her wet nurse. Knowing Shelley's wealthy background, Mrs Boinville even agreed to stand surety for a debt.

As in Wales, Shelley's expected money failed to materialise and to economise, and continue near Mrs Boinville, he moved his family to Bracknell. Mrs Boinville had a beautiful daughter of eighteen, another Cornelia, married to Godwin's protégé Tom Turner – the Godwin girls had been to their wedding two years before, when they had impressed Aaron Burr with their nice clothes. Soon Shelley was learning Italian with the sympathetic Cornelia, living a few miles away at Binfield.

Her name was a bonus for, like Portia, it was a worthy republican one. The most famous Cornelia was the daughter of Scipio Africanus and mother of the Gracchi: two radical and reforming noblemen. Perhaps this modern melancholy Cornelia was neglected by her bisexual husband, who was away in London at the time. Shelley was more attentive, finding in Cornelia 'female excellence' (as well as beauty), something closer than Harriet to the ideal female who tantalised him through life. As a result this was both the happiest time he had experienced and, considering the ties that bound him, a period of 'struggles & privations, which almost withered me to idiotism'. Friends drew a picture of a man so nervy, agitated and susceptible he was close to breakdown. As with Miss Hitchener, Shelley was etching his pattern of longing and revulsion while Harriet continued to dream of a stable, secure life together on the Welsh farm.

Mrs Boinville enjoyed Shelley's vivacious talk 'of twenty different subjects', proud that he had 'resolved to leave off rambling' in favour of their 'homespun pleasures'.[10] But it was not the persuasive talk of the older woman that had won him. Five days after Mrs Boinville wrote these words Shelley informed Hogg that Harriet had left with the baby to stay with her sister; by now he was less troubled by this decision and the loss of his wife's 'dewy eyes' than infatuated with Cornelia's 'dewy looks' and 'gentle words'; they stirred 'poison' in his breast and he lamented 'the chains that bind this ruined soul'. Into his notebook he wrote the erotic Latin description which Claire read a few months later during the elopement to France: 'she held me in her arms in bed, and I nearly died from delirium and delight'.[11] The presence of a 'cultivated' woman made him think his effort to cultivate Harriet 'a gross & despicable superstition'. Yet, still, one 'revolting duty' remained: 'to continue to deceive my wife' – in other words to continue sleeping with Harriet, with the risk of making her pregnant.[12]

He could not, however, deceive Mrs Boinville for long and, in April 1814, noticing the growing intimacy between Shelley and Cornelia, she asked him to leave Bracknell. A little later she warned her son-in-law Tom Turner of what was going on; jealously he whisked his wife off to Devon. Faced with Shelley's later public adultery, Cornelia's mother would prove conventional – she wrote him a 'cold & even sarcastice [sic]' letter: free thinking in the Boinville set was confined to conversation and sentiment.[13] She was also irritated that he had not paid the debt she had underwritten. Later she would summarise Shelley to Mrs Godwin: 'as regards genius Mr. Shelley has more of it than anyone that has ever existed' but 'it is marred by his intense self conceit which makes him despise every one who does not think like him'.[14]

❧

With Ianthe only a few months old, Harriet found herself again pregnant by Shelley; perhaps this child would be a boy, so ensuring the succession and making Percy Bysshe's borrowing easier. He had come of age and could give post-obit bonds (loans which would be paid off at exorbitant interest when he controlled his inheritance). He had to ensure that any son by Harriet could inherit his estate and legal liabilities, so needed to make watertight the Scottish marriage. The best way was through a second English wedding. Godwin supported the idea and accompanied Shelley when he went to get the licence. Knowing the problems in his daughter's life, Mr Westbrook was pleased to witness the ceremony which occurred on 23 March 1814 in St George's, Hanover Square, notorious for its minimal residence requirements. Whatever its financial purpose, for Harriet the marriage was a renewal of vows; Peacock thought it signalled that there was 'no estrangement, no shadow of a thought of separation' between the pair.

In fact Shelley by now saw himself and Harriet as 'a dead & living body ... linked together in loathsome & horrible communion'.[15] Here he echoed the poet Milton who, in his pamphlet in favour of divorce, had imaged an unhappy union as 'a living soul bound to a dead corpse', as well as *The Empire of the Nairs* in which the heroine is actually bound to a dead man; years later Shelley would use a similar image for his final marriage.

Once Cornelia had gone and Harriet had returned with the baby but without her hated though useful sister Eliza Westbrook, Bracknell became less appealing. Shelley visited London and saw the Godwins often. Soon he was lodging in Fleet Street nearby. Weary of waiting for him to return and worn out with a new pregnancy and a small child to look after, Harriet joined Eliza to stay with relatives in Bath. Matters had deteriorated between her and her husband, but she had no inkling that there was anyone other than William Godwin and his ideas keeping Shelley in London.

❧

Much later Shelley denied he had ever loved Harriet. In one more fictional twist he told Fanny's childhood friend Henry Reveley that he had married her because he thought himself dying and, since Harriet was nursing him, he wanted her to be supported by his family as his widow. As for the decline of the marriage, the fault, Shelley said, lay with the conventional Harriet and her grasping father − but most of all with her demonic sister Eliza Westbrook, a vampire and a perfect ghoul with 'great powers for evil'. The reason for her evil machinations was that, like Elizabeth Hitchener, she was in love with Shelley but could not have him.[16] The image of the vampire, still lacking its definitive expression by Byron and Polidori a few years later, comes from one of Shelley's favourite poems, Southey's *Thalaba,* where the female vampire with all the 'loathsomeness of death' leaves her grave to wander and prey on mortals until struck through with an heroic masculine lance.

If it is unwise to interpret Shelley's major poetry in a straightforward autobiographical way, it is fair to see him using occasional verse to express his feelings, especially since Mary later claimed his private passions inspired his work. He was a poor letter writer and uninterested in catching the movement of his mind in prose. Sometimes his verse jottings and his finished poetry seem closer to his emotions. One poem in particular, originally written in April or May, suggests that the movement from Harriet was not without some pain to him – this despite the fact that *Political Justice* encouraged it by declaring that early marriage was often a seemingly 'irretrievable mistake' that ought to be dismissed 'as soon as it is detected'. In April 1814 Shelley urged himself forward:

Pause not! The time is past! Every voice cries, Away!
Tempt not with one last tear thy friend's ungentle mood:
Thy lover's eye, so glazed and cold, dares not entreat thy stay:
Duty and dereliction guide thee back to solitude.

The home with Harriet had become 'sad and silent', a 'desolated hearth' and he had lost his 'peace'; there remained only 'the light of one sweet smile' – and this was not hers.[17]

PART III

CHAPTER 13

FANNY

IN MIDSUMMER MRS Godwin went off for her annual break from Skinner Street, this time to Southend on the Essex coast. She was away for almost six weeks, leaving Fanny and Godwin alone in the house. Godwin made one uncomfortable visit to his wife by barge; afterwards he settled back down to his companionable and peaceable existence with Fanny.

Then Mrs Godwin came back. In so long a stretch Fanny may have got used to the calmness of the house: it would be difficult to adapt at once to the overwhelming and disruptive presence. However, to Mrs Godwin's eye, she displayed something that had nothing to do with her stepmother's reappearance: a new moodiness which she ascribed directly to Shelley's effect.

She believed she saw an erotic interest on Fanny's part. When Shelley visited the Godwins again, he began, she reported, to pay 'immense attentions' to Fanny. Claire (in later life) believed he was in love with Fanny and that Fanny was in love with him, though holding back because of his wife. This is a summary of Mrs Godwin's letter to Lady Mount Cashell:

after a time [she] saw things, though she could hardly say what
– glances, sighing, gazing. Frances from being cheerful, grew dull
and heavy. The indications were too slight to justify Mrs. Godwin in
supposing that Shelley was in love with Frances – he, with such a lovely
wife and living on such affectionate terms with her – but she feared that

Frances might unconsciously to herself, receive a deep impression in his favour. Accordingly, she sent Frances on a visit to her aunts in Dublin.[1]

Shelley, Mrs Godwin said, grew hostile to her once Fanny was removed. He had liked her before then, she thought.

Some of this may be imaginary: Fanny went to Wales rather than Ireland and Godwin's diary shows that Shelley on his return to London did not come at once to Skinner Street despite having received eleven letters from his mentor. Yet there is no reason to suppose that Fanny, the eldest daughter of his admired Mary Wollstonecraft and an intelligent amiable young woman, could not have impressed and attracted Shelley. Later Claire claimed that he had addressed Fanny before Mary 'and that F declined him'. Whether or not it came to such a head, it is certainly possible that Fanny herself felt moved by his appreciation and attention, that she was in love with him but held back from expressing her inappropriate feelings. Shelley liked to see himself as the passive lover – he made the point with both Harriet and Mary; perhaps Fanny was not forthright enough.

Her mother and sister Mary had strong sexual feelings and Fanny need not have been very different. Shelley's talk and writings had an erotic quality, and in later months Fanny showed herself the most receptive to his intense poetry and its melancholy yearning. Claire called him 'the Exotic' and he wrote of himself as a sort of 'sensitive plant', always desiring yet never satisfied; in the early part of 1814 he seemed constantly and promiscuously aroused – as his enthusiasm for the two Cornelias suggests.

So, was Fanny in love with Shelley? The question cannot of course be answered directly but may be illuminated by the way she interacted with him and Godwin, by the assumptions she held and were held about her.

⚛

Both Godwin and Shelley insisted on the Enlightenment idea that environment made people what they were; hence society could be changed and improved by changing the environment and a person's experience, especially in childhood. Yet both were fascinated by the opposite, by the fatality of heredity, appearance and temperament – and they seemed particularly interested in this in relation to women.

When his daughter Mary was less than three weeks old, Godwin asked a neighbouring doctor named Nicholson to make a phrenological examination. Both he and Mary Wollstonecraft had been fascinated by the determinism of cranial and facial structure, although it fitted ill with their environmental theories. The baby cried throughout the examination, yet Nicholson could declare she had 'quick sensibility' and 'considerable memory and intelligence'.[2]

The curious act was repudiated in abstract – years later Godwin called phrenology quackery, a dangerous system of fatalism.[3] Nonetheless he and Shelley tended to see a fatalism in others' lives, a determined shape to character and destiny.

There were other ambivalences. The following year, when he was worrying over elements of *Political Justice*, Godwin repudiated the 'doctrine of the equality of intellectual beings as they are born into the world'.[4] His new view fed into his habit of judging through comparison, contrast, listing and hierarchising, as if people were elements in a single series. In 1811 he expressed his pride in Mary by comparing her directly with Fanny: his 'own daughter' was 'considerably superior in capacity to the one her mother had before'. Mary was 'singularly bold, somewhat imperious and active of mind. Her desire of knowledge is great and her perseverance in every thing she undertakes, almost invincible'. Fanny, so lively in her early years, was at seventeen 'of a quiet modest unshowy disposition'. She was 'somewhat given to indolence (which is her greatest fault)' but she was sober and observant and had considerable 'faculty of memory'; she was also 'disposed to exercise her own thoughts and follow her own judgment'. Of Mary he remarked, she is 'very pretty'; scarred by smallpox, Fanny was 'in general prepossessing'.[5]

Did his chilly analysis indicate his expectations and did Fanny feel them? Did she come to accept her inferiority in capacity and appearance? If so it might influence the quality and expectations of her love.

Shelley, too, compared and contrasted women; he had just judged Cornelia Turner superior to Harriet. Always he sought for the ideal, for ideal beauty, ideal womanhood, to be found in the next place, in the next stage, the next woman. As much as any lover of the orthodox God he had a sense of transcendence, an ideal presence within and beyond himself, never quite captured through any embodiment, however much he hierarchised and sought. He wanted to get to the bottom of *men's* minds – of Godwin's and later Byron's;

since they were men like himself it was part of the prime purpose of fashioning his own mind. But, as a highly sexual man, he looked for his external ideal constantly in beautiful and poetical young *women* (although he also had a penchant for older mother substitutes in life and imagination, from Mary Wollstonecraft to Mrs Newton, Mrs Boinville and later Lady Mount Cashell). In his poetry the lover of the ideal young woman was the Poet, an oddly bisexual hero, even in ordinary terms the 'maniac', the idealistic character portrayed in his later poem 'Julian and Maddalo', whose 'unconnected exclamations of … agony will perhaps be found a sufficient comment for the text of every heart'.[6] The male agony was the common disappointment since everyone (every woman) was fated to disappoint every man in time; the difference between ideal and real would always push Shelley onwards. On his way he may momentarily have looked lovingly on Fanny, eldest child of the radical Mary Wollstonecraft, romantically conceived and born during the French Revolution.

She shared with Shelley an idealising tenor of mind, but, where his idealism was ultimately unworldly, hers tended to settle firmly on individuals in the world who themselves looked beyond the world. In their fiction and poetry Godwin and Shelley both portrayed ideal women who suffered profoundly through the actions of their exceptional, amazing – or mad – men. These men had none of the contingency of the women who loved them; for all the passion they inspired and claimed to feel, they were distinct and alone, unconstrained and unconditioned. Shelley thought that he himself was both Everyman and also separate and singular, quite unlike anyone else.

With her admiration and veneration for Godwin, Fanny believed in the spiritual value of genius. In her conception it was not celebrity and had little to do with the glamorous arrogance that Byron saw in the most spectacular man of the age, Napoleon – and others saw in Byron and Shelley. It had more to do with a kind of moral and spiritual seriousness and a transcendence of the ordinary.

In some ways Fanny was a little out of her time, suited more perhaps to the eighteenth century or to the coming Victorian era with its re-emphasis on controlled virtues than with the Regency and its extreme postures and attitudes. The Napoleonic era, which made Byron believe he lived 'in gigantic and exaggerated times', did not suit her temperament. But, in her apprehension of genius, she was a thorough Romantic.

The word 'genius' was sometimes used in the modern manner to indicate a person of extraordinary imaginative powers. In 1797 Godwin was still fighting to keep alive the old concept – something close to acquired rather than innate capacity, a spirit of prying curiosity not divine election. He feared that a more supernatural notion would be socially pernicious, leading either to over-confidence or to despair. Yet his sense of his own value and what was owed to him as a superior being was not far from the Romantic idea: if his theory was recalcitrant, his practice was in tune.

In 1792 Mary Wollstonecraft used 'genius' to mean the distinctive natural aptitude of any individual but, when she wrote 'On Poetry' in 1797, one of her last pieces, she came closer to the modern definition. Here the Poet is a 'man of strong feelings' who gives us an image of his mind when conversing with himself alone. She derided modern poets who took their art from books not nature and who wrote works of elegance not genius. Although she had no concept of the Shelleyan poet who was not an imitator of books or of nature, she was, in this essay, preparing the way for her daughter's reception of genius. (Years later Everina Wollstonecraft would again bring the two senses together when in a letter she referred to Mary Wollstonecraft's novel *Mary, a Fiction* as the first fruit of her 'genius', then described Shelley as 'certainly a man of Genius and great feeling' adding 'but the effects of both were perverted by some unhappy flightings of mind that led him to cause much unhappiness to his connections'.[7])

Like Harriet, Fanny never considered herself or expected to become a genius. But both wished to be worthy of genius. In Fanny's early years the supreme quality was possessed by her dead mother and Godwin, whom she loved as her father and as a great man. Hence her grief when his wife or Mary disturbed him with their dramas, or when, as so often, he himself failed to live up to his intellectually heroic image. Shelley too had the spark of genius (like Wordsworth and Coleridge, whom she also admired): both he and Godwin were 'poets' and, in her later years, the twin poles of Fanny's life. Godwin and Shelley believed that genius should be morally worthy, but they tended to find that moral worth in themselves whatever they happened to do: they assumed that their abilities permitted them to act outside convention and ordinary restraint.

Before he met Mary Wollstonecraft, Godwin already believed in the power of imaginative writers to change society for the better through changing people's thoughts and habits. However, in the first edition of *Political Justice* he had not addressed the imagination or considered how it worked in artists and those they influenced. But through experience with Mary Wollstonecraft and his children and through conversations with Coleridge he had come to feel that the imagination was a more active force than he had once assumed. Shelley would describe the power of poets definitively in a famous formula: 'Poets are the unacknowledged legislators of the world', but Godwin had expressed the sentiment long before – a poet is 'the legislator of generations and the moral instructor of the World'.[8] Fanny had imbibed this opinion that the artist was 'the author to others of the highest wisdom, pleasure, virtue and glory'.

Harriet was astonished that Shelley should raise money primarily for Godwin while ignoring her and their child's needs, but Fanny accepted that Shelley had pledged himself to the older man for life. Such a pledge was stronger than a conventional marriage vow – or even parenthood, at least for a man – Godwin, a gifted writer and thinker, was worthy of everyone's support, whatever he demanded of them. 'I consider the question of any serious pecuniary assistance from one man to another as almost the most inviolable and sacred of all subjects,' he had written.[9] Fanny had imbibed this opinion; it was a bulwark against any competing vision of the shabbiness and shame of her stepfather's continual begging and borrowing.

When she contemplated Godwin's books, then wrote out his tetchy, demanding letters, she was separating the genius from the man. She could do the same with Shelley, especially once she came to care about his poetry. She had been present when his first letters arrived giving the melodramatic version of his villainous father and persecuted youth, and she had witnessed the Godwins' scepticism. Shelley could talk in visionary rapture while seeming to act as selfishly as Godwin. As a genius, however, he was worthy of the highest esteem: what he did must be right on some higher level.

As she had seen in Godwin the spirit of great philosophy, so she saw in the 'beautiful' Shelley a transcendent being whose greatness existed in the aesthetic realm, in visionary art. In this apprehension Fanny was rather closer in understanding how Shelley saw himself and what his poetry struggled to express than her sister Mary ever would be. If the man was perhaps careless of lives, the Poet comprehended them in the profoundest way: the Poet 'beholds the future in the present, and his thoughts are the germs of the flower and the fruit of latest time'.[10] As a result, where Godwin disliked the 'drunken, reeling, mystical Pythia form', Fanny believed that Shelley's poetry had the highest value. Imaginative dependence on such writing became true freedom. At the same time, there was an abjection in this submission. The feminine self-effacement that *Fleetwood*, *St Leon* and Shelley's later *Alastor* all beautifully displayed was life-enhancing but also self-sacrificial.

The radical generation of the 1790s had imagined the independent woman such as Mary Wollstonecraft freeing herself from orthodox religion and its demands. She existed in place of the pious lady or the contingent girl who for centuries had stood prettily waiting to be chosen as a wife. Now Fanny was on the cusp of two new developments. One was the re-domesticated woman who, unlike her eighteenth-century counterpart, was also morally superior, guardian of the purified home from which she would not wish to stir; this woman was thoughtful and cared for her family as much as her God. The other development was the cult of creative genius, which held immense fascination for women. After the failure of the French Revolution and Enlightenment hopes of social progress, British and German theorists such as Friedrich Schiller had turned to art for regeneration; secular artistic texts became patterns for life and pathways to the divine. Shelley the poet – Coleridge's magus from 'Kubla Khan' with 'flashing eyes' and 'floating hair' – became sacred along with his poems.

Charlotte Brontë portrayed Jane Eyre yearning for her 'Master' but Mr Rochester's appeal was not as artist and intellectual. Brontë still told the Cinderella story. In George Eliot's Dorothea, however, there exists a woman who wants to fulfil herself by serving a male intellect. She desires not just to serve but also to achieve an expanded vision for herself through another person rather than through religion. Henry James took up the amalgam of yearning and serving woman: in *Portrait of a Lady* Isabel Archer thinks that, giving all she has to a man she believes a conduit to the civilising and spiritualising arts, she will find a richer life for herself.

Contemplating Goethe, some contemporary German women also displayed Fanny's mingled erotic and aesthetic fascination, the effort to poeticise the world and find a means for self-development through the Romantic transcendence of the Poet. The 55-year-old wife of his publisher told Goethe, whom she had never met, that she had been devoted to him 'ever since the first spark of your genius fell into my ever so receptive heart ... what is more natural than to love the most charming poet and philosopher – never have I uttered your name without a quickening of my pulse and secret longings'.[11]

Bettine von Arnim expressed similar adoring sentiments in her fictionalised treatment. She wanted to come to knowledge through longing: 'Passion is the single key to the world ... And thus I feel that I have just been born into the spirit through love to [Goethe] ...' She imagined how she would serve him 'like a cool wind in the summer heat, give him fresh water, warm and care for him in the winter'.[12] And she recorded of another poet: 'It certainly seems to me with Hölderlin as though a divine power had overwhelmed him with its floods. It was Language sweeping along in its overpowering rapid stream that flooded his senses, drowning them in its waves ... with what he says of Poetry and Language he seems near unveiling the divine mystery ...' Poets 'soar as eagles of intellect'; through them others catch a glimpse of the Divine.[13]

Fanny's attitude to the genius of Godwin or Shelley is similar. She may have loved Shelley in the sexual emotional sense of the word but her love was also bound up with this most feminine of idealisms. She wanted a hero; she wanted through Shelley to be inducted into a richer life. When years later she yearned for physical rescue from the vibrant Shelley, as her aunts had yearned for rescue from her vibrant mother two decades earlier, she also desired to share and contemplate his mental riches. She wanted to tell him 'every thing'.

So there is no clear answer to the question whether Fanny loved Shelley in any straightforward sexual sense – if sex is ever quite straightforward. She was certainly inspired by him, fascinated, and a little overwhelmed. And she responded to him with many of the complex needs of a disrupted life.

❧

However she loved, the meeting and immediate mutual infatuation of Shelley and Mary, occurring just before she herself left Skinner Street for Wales, would have been a painful blow to her heart.

Ah, sister, Desolation is a delicate thing:
It walks not on the Earth, it floats not on the air,

But treads with lulling footstep, and fans with silent wing
The tender hopes which in their hearts the best and gentlest bear,
Who, soothed to false repose by the fanning plumes above,
And the music-stirring motion of its soft and busy feet,
Dream visions of aerial joy, and call the monster Love,
And wake, and find the shadow Pain ... [14]

CHAPTER 14

MARY

'THE LOVE OF a daughter is one of the deepest and strongest, as it is the purest passion of which our natures are capable,' wrote Mary in one of the many works in which she would portray intense father–daughter relationships.[1] Several friends noted her deep, even passionate devotion to Godwin; she deplored having to share him with the hated stepmother, perhaps the main trait she had in common with her half-sister Fanny. In her later fiction she repeatedly described an exclusive and intense love between a father and daughter, undisturbed by any other relationship of child or wife.

Despite Fanny's best efforts to keep the peace for Godwin's sake, Mary and her stepmother constantly squabbled. Mrs Godwin grumbled of ill health while Mary's own state declined under the strain of resentment and family strife. When she was thirteen, her eczema flared up frighteningly. Possibly such a pale girl might be tubercular. A worried Godwin consulted doctors but he also suspected the psychosomatic nature of many of his daughter's ailments. He was irritated at her hostile adolescent moods, the 'unfavourable appearances', as he called them, and responded to them with coldness and withdrawal: 'His strictness was undeviating,' wrote Mary later; sometimes he tried to tolerate self-pity and resentment in those not too close to him, like his pupils, but he had little patience with these emotions in his own children. His wife complained of Mary's aggression, while Mary hated her stepmother's combination of violent temper and sentimentality. Her own remarkable mother had been volatile and demanding, but for Mary she existed primarily in the calm, radiant portrait in her father's study.

When her symptoms persisted it was thought Mary might benefit from a period of sea bathing, a prescribed remedy for many ailments at the time – the sick person was to dip into the cold sea before breakfast and also drink sea water. So, with her son William in tow, Mrs Godwin combined her own desire for a holiday with the need for Mary to consult a doctor in the resort of Ramsgate. She and William stayed a month, then left Mary alone in Miss Petman's boarding school on the High Street for another period of six months.

Mary's lonely time away did not improve her condition, her attitude to her stepmother or the 'unfavourable appearances'. When she returned to London in the middle of a perishing cold December Godwin wrote to Shelley, 'I have again and again been hopeless concerning the children ... Seeds of intellect and knowledge, seeds of moral judgment and conduct, I have sown, but the soil for a long time seemed "ungrateful to the tiller's care". It was not so.' Either he wanted to impress his new correspondent or he was out of touch with his family, for tensions continued unabated in Skinner Street. If Mary could go somewhere health-giving without expense, both she and those left behind might be better off.

Godwin had friends near Dundee in Scotland, a family of radical Dissenters who, while not following him into atheism, continued to share his belief in community of property. They were well off from a canvas-making business and they owned a roomy house on bracing, windy Tayside. The Baxters responded warmly to his suggestion that Mary visit for an extended period; five months was mentioned, though if her temper did not agree she could be shipped back earlier, Godwin wrote. She would benefit from the country and sea air and be taken in as one of the family. Recently apprenticed to a bookseller in Edinburgh, her stepbrother Charles Clairmont would be relatively close and could visit Mary. No one should put themselves out for his daughter, Godwin told the Baxters; Mary should be brought up as a 'philosopher, even like a cynic'. By this he meant that she should disdain luxuries and be self-sufficient. He hoped they would encourage her to work harder.

On 7 June 1812 Fanny, Claire and Godwin, without his wife, went to Downes's Wharf to see Mary off on the boat; they stayed an hour on board with her until the boat sailed for Scotland. She was fourteen, facing a journey of nearly a week alone – as Godwin remarked in a letter to the Baxters next day, she would probably 'arrive more dead than alive, as she is extremely subject to sea-sickness'.[2] The money she had hidden in her stays was stolen on the voyage and she arrived in Scotland penniless.

At once she saw she would like the place and the Baxters: both their daughters and their stern intellectual neighbour and son-in-law David Booth. The Baxter house, about four miles from Dundee, was largish but not grand, and looked out on the austere Tay estuary. With her sophisticated London background, Mary never felt inferior to the six Baxter children, who included Isabella, soon her best friend – it helped that one of Isabella's heroines was Mary Wollstonecraft. All the Dundee family treated her with respect.

The stay in Scotland was a success and, after a brief visit to Skinner Street, Mary returned to experience again that warm, stable, middle-class family life that neither Fanny nor Claire would ever know in their child-hood. This time she stayed for ten months, returning home after a voyage of ten days at the end of March 1814. She arrived in a cold London just before Napoleon surrendered to the allies and was exiled to Elba. The capital was about to erupt in celebrations. Godwin allowed his family to watch the fire-works while he looked sourly on: the old discredited order was returning to Europe and, for all his backsliding, he would not welcome it. His family was outside the common life of patriotic songs and shows.

Mary had matured in Scotland. Still devoted to her father she had learnt to distance herself from him in a way her half-sister had yet to do. He still loomed large in her vision but with so long an absence he had probably shrunk a little in stature and intellect from what she remembered. She had by now a keen sense of her own worth, and it was no wonder that she was envied, admired and copied, certainly by Claire and probably to a lesser extent by the older Fanny. She had returned with a more interesting ward-robe than the one she had taken with her: she now wore a tartan frock made fashionable throughout the country by the rage for Walter Scott's Romantic ballads.

In character she was less inward and insecure than Fanny and less vola-tile, impulsive and resilient than Claire. Or rather her insecurity had a lofty quality about it; she had become an almost formidable presence. Living in the glare not only of her famous parents but of a house of watchers and critics, she had even before she left developed a sense of tense significance now enhanced by her months among the admiring Baxters. Later a friend described her as witty, social and animated in company but mournful when alone. Coming from a voluble household, she was articulate and secure in opinion, but not garrulous; she had a developed sense of privacy. Knowing what was owed to her, she could, when it was not provided, be resentful and peevish.

In appearance she was a little short, slender, with graceful movements and attitudes. She was very pale with grey-hazel eyes, thin chiselled nose and large forehead. An observer of the grown Mary declared she was like a 'picture by Titian' and noted her control, even her coldness. Later she would be described as 'the beauty-daughter', for the comparison with Fanny had grown into a cliché. Probably it affected them both, for the same observer, the actor Kemble, added that he actually did not think Mary a beauty but that 'she rather thinks herself one, and yet there is something about her that would pass for such'.[3] As Harriet saw Fanny's face redeemed by her intelligence, so Edward Trelawny saw Mary redeemed 'by having bright and intelligent eyes'.[4] She also had very fine, light golden-brown hair which hung in natural gauzy waves. Shelley was always attracted by lustrous female hair – he had been so with Harriet's.

By now he had rescued quite a number of young women from their families and secure lives and he had recently been casting his eyes on the gentle Cornelia Turner – and, if Mrs Godwin is to be believed, on Fanny as well. He could hardly be expected to resist a girl of sixteen called Mary Wollstonecraft Godwin, a girl touted by her father as both clever and beautiful, without an obvious republican name, it is true, but with *two* republican parents – indeed Mary Wollstonecraft's power was such that she shed a republican aura over even this common appellation. Her father had conveniently written that a man should 'assiduously cultivate the intercourse of that woman whose accomplishments' strike him in the most powerful manner – beside that attraction, 'sensual intercourse' was 'a very trivial object'.[5]

Godwin should have been prepared; he may even have had intimations that men were noticing his daughter's charms. The recently bereaved David Booth from Dundee visited London about the time Shelley reappeared and it is possible he came to ask for Mary's hand. If so, it was refused, and he turned to her Scottish friend Isabella Baxter, who accepted him despite his church's prohibition of marriage to a sister-in-law. If there was such a proposal, it should have emphasised to Godwin the attraction of his nubile daughter. She had no money but in her father's eyes she had an intellectual legacy that counted for much, and in the eyes of most young men rather more on her own account to recommend her. It is curious, then, that Godwin did not consider what would seem likely to many onlookers – perhaps including Fanny, who, even more than Claire, had become used to attention focusing on her half-sister.

Between her two Scottish trips Mary was in the same house with Shelley but she was tired and probably stayed upstairs. On 5 May 1814, however, they certainly met. The result was almost inevitable. After this date Shelley visited Skinner Street regularly for the rest of the month. Since the girls had to take turns alone in the shop on the ground floor, Mary had ample opportunities to see him by herself whilst her stepmother was upholding more genteel standards upstairs. Godwin, on whom it would be assumed he had come to call, continued to prescribe periods of silence in the house when he should be disturbed by no one. Fanny, who would have seen the infatuation growing and probably tried to intervene or at least warn Godwin, left for Wales at the end of the month.

CHAPTER 15

FANNY

ON 23 MAY 1814, a day when Shelley was visiting Skinner Street, Fanny set out for Pentredevy in Wales, an event important enough for Godwin to record it in his diary. She went after a period of moodiness and after having seen Mary's inflammatory effect on Shelley.

Her destination is unclear. There is no town or hamlet with the exact name of Pentredevy listed in atlases for Wales. Most likely the name refers to a house, and there is a Pentredavies farm near Llandeilo, not far from Laugharne in South Wales.

Laugharne is an ancient township of cottages and Georgian houses guarded by a ruined castle overlooking Carmarthen Bay. It had been important in Mary Wollstonecraft's life. She had liked the scenery when she lived there but not her family's reason for decamping so far from London – to avoid creditors. She also disliked the fact that, before her mother died, her father Edward had begun an affair with Lydia Woods, a girl about her own age from Laugharne whom, as soon as his first wife was dead, he married in 1783. The couple spent the rest of their lives in South Wales, living in Market Street, Laugharne, a hand-to-mouth existence helped by gifts from Edward's daughters and their portion of the rent from the Primrose Street houses.

In 1803 Edward Wollstonecraft died and by autumn 1805 Lydia's financial situation was desperate. She begged Godwin and Johnson to forward her share of the Primrose Street rents, owed on top of the £100 stock which her stepson James, executor of her husband's will, had asked them to remit. Godwin, who had received £50 from James half a year earlier when he had been about to embark for Jamaica, perhaps saw his brother-in-law's sudden death as a chance to delay payment. Harassed by her dead husband's creditors, Lydia had reason to complain but restrained herself, wishing instead for some information on Godwin's daughter: writing her letter exactly eight years after the death of Mary Wollstonecraft, Lydia was still unaware of the girl's name. By accident she had heard two years ago that 'she was a delightful child'.[1]

Everina, Eliza and Mary Wollstonecraft had all been in Laugharne as girls, and, when governessing nearby in Pembroke, Eliza Bishop had frequently seen her father and his second wife; she had even tried to help them with small handouts from her own meagre salary. She had had more dealings with Lydia than her disapproving sister Mary and in later life found her 'truely a well meaning woman … willing to do the little she can do to lessen the debts'. For their father was as incorrigible a debtor as Godwin was, and a drunkard as well, and Lydia's life in Laugharne cannot have been easy at any stage.

Contrary to Mary Wollstonecraft's dismissal of her as a kind of upper servant, Lydia was not socially much below the Wollstonecrafts: her father was an alderman, her nephew a draper, her niece a schoolmistress like Eliza and Everina, and her sister Charlotte, the wife of a Bristol gentleman called Joseph Howell, a well-off tobacco manufacturer in Laugharne. Everina kept in contact with Charlotte throughout her life – she may have been a friend from their days as girls in Laugharne. Years later they were discussing erecting a tomb for Edward and Lydia Wollstonecraft. Mary, another of Lydia's sisters, married a clergyman Walter Price from Llanarthney, whose brother married the only daughter of the owner of Pentredavies. Here at last is something close to the name of Fanny's destination. Since Mrs Godwin's version of her holiday in the summer of 1814 translated Wales into Dublin, the error probably came from the fact that one purpose in her travels was to meet her Wollstonecraft aunts and step-grandmother Lydia Wollstonecraft. Mrs Godwin had trouble with the truth but there seems little point to this particular variation. Carmarthenshire in South Wales seems a good place for relatives from London and Dublin to come together, and the Towy Valley where the villages and farms lie was on the Gloucester to Brecon coach route.[2]

Fresh from the excitement and anguish of Shelley and Skinner Street,

Fanny was in a vulnerable, sensitive condition. So, if this was the moment when she and her aunts talked over her future and when they offered her a home and work as a teacher in their school, the offer cannot have been very welcome. Aunt Eliza Bishop was still generally mentioned with affection but over the disappointing years aunt Everina had only grown sourer, enough to put off a shy girl like Fanny. Although her niece Mary admitted she could be amusing and witty, she also described her aunt in old age as 'never a favourite with any one – & now she is the most intolerable of God's creatures ... I know no punishment so great as spending an hour in her Company' (a pity since Everina always liked Mary).[3] Neither aunt had Fanny's high regard for the Godwins, which would make conversation difficult. And if Fanny was indeed suffering from disappointed love, anything that took her away from where Shelley was must have been painful.

Nonetheless, if she spent any time with Eliza Bishop she would have encountered her aunt's keen appreciation of natural beauty. The sights and sounds of the Welsh coast and mountains where she had spent part of her youth always moved Eliza and they had been her main solace when as a miserable governess back in Wales she had been close to despair after the breach with her sister Mary soon after Fanny's birth. Although she had read about her amazing infancy among the fjords and cascades, Fanny was too young to remember Norway and Sweden, and almost all her subsequent life had been in dingy London. Wales was therefore a revelation.

Like all the children of Skinner Street, she had been taught to respond to nature. She would have come prepared for deep impressions, her emotions heightened through the last weeks of closeness to Shelley. He had recently come from Wales where the land around Elan Valley and Tremadoc had enchanted him, so much so that he often reverted to his hope of a utopian commune in this wild country. Mary too had been full of the wide rivers and open spaces of Scotland when she returned from Dundee. Certainly Fanny delighted in the hills, valleys, cliffs and rushing streams. Claire would later remind her of her impressions when she too escaped Skinner Street for the dramatic landscape of Lynmouth in Devon. Her sense that Fanny would understand her descriptions because of her memory of Wales suggests that she visited her grandparents' old dwelling-place of Laugharne, also near the meeting of two rivers; as in Lynmouth, the tidal waters of the Bristol Channel flowed by beached fishing boats.

Mary and Claire were probably too preoccupied to write to Fanny or to receive her descriptions of her emotions and her response to the new scenery, but Godwin wrote a letter to her in Pentredevy on 28 June, the day after he learnt of the momentous event that had just occurred at his dead wife's grave.

CHAPTER 16

MARY

ON 8 JUNE 1814 Hogg recorded a visit he and Shelley made to Skinner Street. Godwin was not at home but they waited for him in his study where his overwrought companion kept absent-mindedly asking Hogg where Godwin was, while pacing up and down the room. Then the door was slightly opened and a 'thrilling voice called "Shelley!" A thrilling voice answered, "Mary!" and he darted out of the room.' Hogg glimpsed a girl: 'very young … fair and fair-haired, pale indeed, and with a piercing look, wearing a frock of tartan'. Asking later who she was, Hogg was told 'the daughter of Godwin and Mary'. When he came to London Peacock remarked about Shelley: 'Nothing that I ever read in tale or history could present a more striking image of a sudden, violent, irresistible, uncontrollable passion, than that under which I found him labouring.'[1]

Shelley now took lodgings in Hatton Garden close to Skinner Street. Perhaps more in awe of the Mary who had returned from Scotland than of the girl who had left, Claire was content to be a third in the unfolding drama. To allay any suspicions of the older people, she accompanied Mary and Shelley on their outings as they walked through the streets of Islington and in the gardens in Charterhouse Square. There, according to an observant gardener's wife, Shelley and Mary sat whispering in an arbour while Claire strolled off alone.

As a trio they went to St Pancras' churchyard to sit by Mary Wollstonecraft's tomb. Again Claire sauntered off; Mary and Shelley 'wished to talk on philosophical subjects'. For Shelley, Mary was clothed in the 'radiance undefiled' of her mother's 'departing glory', while Mary saw in Shelley something of what her mother had seen in Gilbert Imlay and described for her heroine in her last novel *Maria*: an embodiment of the passionate hero Saint-Preux created by Rousseau in *La Nouvelle Héloïse*. 'There was something in the character of Saint-Preux, in his abrogation of self, and in the worship he paid to Love, that coincided with Shelley's own disposition,' she would later write.[2]

Claire was little use as chaperone. On 26 June she and Mary went with Shelley to Mary Wollstonecraft's grave and, while Claire, as usual, walked off, Shelley opened 'with the ardour of love, his whole heart' and Mary in turn declared her passion for him. Shelley now embarked on yet another version of his early years in which his tyrannical father had planned to have him incarcerated in a madhouse, from which he was saved only by the aid of the good Dr Lind. All his life had been preparation for this moment, he said.

Although her rejection of Hogg pointed to the contrary, Shelley hinted at Harriet's infidelity, while descanting on the insignificance of marriage as an institution. Mary too chose at this point to revere the radical side of her mother's and father's thought. Probably by now she had read Godwin's *Memoirs* of Mary Wollstonecraft and so knew she had been conceived out of wedlock; she had as little interest as Shelley in the 1805 preface to *Fleetwood*, which declared that men should not trample on the institutions of their country, however prejudicial they seemed. Shelley described to Hogg the 'sublime & rapturous moment' when he realised that Mary shared his views and had not suffered the 'corrupting contamination of vulgar superstitions'. The ecstatic point when she 'confessed herself mine, who had so long been her's in secret cannot be painted to mortal imaginations'.

Perhaps this meant a simple verbal pledge, a vow that she would become Shelley's lover in future. Or perhaps, more romantically, the pair consummated their love the next day either near Mary Wollstonecraft's grave shaded by willows – or, in the lurid imagination of Mrs Godwin, on the tomb itself. This was the kind of wedding Shelley approved, under the heavens with no banns or ceremony. The date, 27 June, was, he declared, his true birthday. The life which in April still depended on Harriet now depended on Mary. He wanted from her, as he had wanted from Harriet, companionship, intellectual love and sex.

To Shelley Mary was original, lovely, wild, sublime, gentle and tender – though he also allowed her 'ardent indignation & hatred'. 'I do not think that there is an excellence at which human nature can arrive, that she does not indisputably possess,' he told Hogg. He began by feeling inferior – she was the daughter of two people he revered – but soon discovered there was no gap between them; they were identical. Mary was the living illustration of her parents' works and also a dream of himself – the nearest to his soul. When he spoke of her he felt 'an egoist expatiating upon his own perfections'.[3]

Shelley afterwards told Hogg that Mary, like Harriet, had declared love first, although Mary said that Shelley unfolded his heart to her, which suggests his was the initiative. Harriet snatched and ran with the idea of her rival's unfeminine forwardness: 'Mary was determined to seduce him. She is to blame. She heated his imagination by talking of her mother, and going to her grave with him every day, till at last she told him she was dying in love for him.'[4] Then, according to Harriet, Shelley thought of his wife and begged Mary to get the better of a passion as degrading to him as to herself. But Mary told him she would die if he rejected her. Harriet preferred to blame the woman.

Assuming that Godwin would appreciate the frankness that had marked his earlier dealings with the world, Shelley intended at once to tell him what had happened: that he now loved Godwin's sixteen-year-old daughter better than he loved his own wife and child. He chose an inopportune moment.

ぴ

During the early part of 1814 Godwin had felt disappointed in Shelley; he was beginning to suspect he was one of those causes the young man embraced, then threw aside. Recently, however, the creditors had thought up a plan. A money broker would auction a post-obit bond on the Shelley inheritance, while the Shelley family would be pressed to come to an agreement with Percy Bysshe; he would then be free to support Godwin. The plan was accepted and Godwin was led to believe that he would soon receive £3,000, the amount Francis Place had once tried to raise in the mistaken notion that it would refloat Godwin's business and family.

Shelley took some part in the transactions but left Godwin and the lawyers to do most of the work. Then the lenders grew anxious and the money, so tantalisingly near, was not delivered. Meanwhile the Godwins had to be on their best behaviour with Shelley, needing to secure the money before he took it in his head to dash off to Wales again with Harriet, or so they feared. During this crucial time Shelley often stayed for several nights in Skinner Street with Mary and Claire. But, with his head full of money-lenders and post-obits, Godwin thought little of it, except that his pretty daughter could help keep Shelley in the fold. When he and his wife had believed Fanny in danger, she had been dispatched to Wales; perhaps Mary and Claire still appeared children in their eyes.

However, on 27 June, the day following the declaration of passion and before the loan was finalised, Shelley informed Godwin that he loved his daughter. He saw no purpose to secrecy since *Political Justice* was so eloquent against any 'species of disguise' and so thoroughly opposed marriage. He ignored the fact that Godwin had changed his mind on the matter.

No longer the man of 1793, Godwin was aghast; the idea was 'madness'. But, unable to forbid Shelley the house before the loan was secured, he told him only to call less often. When he related the event to others Godwin changed the sequence, so that the loan came through *before* he learnt of Shelley's infatuation with his daughter.[5] It can only be surmised what he wrote to Fanny in Wales on 28 June.

In early July the financial transaction was complete, although Godwin did not yet know it had raised only £2,593 in cash, sold on a huge post-obit of £8,000. Shelley came to celebrate over dinner in Skinner Street. Now he told Godwin he could advance only £1,120, keeping the rest for his own needs. Godwin was horrified; he was transfixed when he learnt for what some of the remainder would be used: Shelley would end his marriage with Harriet and go with Mary to Switzerland, which Godwin had described so rhapsodically in *Fleetwood*. He asked Godwin not only for his approval but also for useful contacts abroad.

Instead of a generous patron, Godwin now saw a spoiled youth who thought he could take whatever he wanted, someone closer to Mark Twain's caricature of a man 'stung into repurifying himself by deserting [Harriet] and his child and entering into scandalous relations with a school-girl acquaintance of his'.[6] Yet, furious though he was, Godwin remained financially dependent on Shelley: he had to be patient. He explained yet again that he had revised the views on marriage and filial respect expressed in the first version of *Political Justice*. His ideas had always been appropriate for a society closer to perfection than that of contemporary England; as things were, marriage should be endured and parents obeyed. He had never advocated *individual* flouting of the law or of convention.

Shelley was unrepentant and, once he received his (depleted) share of the money on 19 July, Godwin became sterner. After writing to Hookham to discover why her husband was not communicating with her, Harriet had returned to London to weep in Skinner Street – and tell Godwin of earlier events in Bracknell. Godwin now refused to let Shelley enter the house but he visited Harriet; it was perhaps on his advice that she wrote to Mary begging her to persuade Shelley to conquer his passion and return to his wife. She and Claire then visited Harriet's home in Chapel Street, where Claire heard Mary agree not to see Shelley again. Echoing Mary Wollstonecraft's sentiments to the departing Imlay, pregnant Harriet pleaded that even animals stay by their kind when they are bearing their young. In the crisis Godwin at last thought to send his daughter out of harm's way, but he much misjudged his power.

A short interval of peace followed as Mary stayed in the schoolroom. Godwin thought he had stopped the lovers communicating. But, enjoying the excitement, Claire was acting as messenger, slipping in and out of the house with letters. Godwin got wind of her activity and ended it but the correspondence continued through the bookshop porter, whom Shelley bribed.

Upstairs in Skinner Street Mary pored over a copy of her lover's *Queen Mab*. The notes were full of Godwin and the books Godwin had recommended to Shelley. Reading them, Mary could see that, however much her father rumbled and fulminated from the room below, Shelley was Godwin's heir and double, an embodiment of the idealised father, so different from the shabby sponge he had become for many. In responding to Shelley she was coming as close as possible to having for herself the man whose exclusive love she had always craved. In his first letter to Godwin Shelley had written 'I am young: you have gone before me.' Years later Mary looked back on Godwin: 'Until I knew Shelley I may justly say that he was my God – & I remember many childish instances of the excess of attachment I bore for him.'[7]

From another angle, her predicament was more Byronic than Shelleyan. On the fly-leaf of *Queen Mab* Mary wrote out Byron's poem 'To Thyrza', in which a poet laments the loss of his beloved whose heart was allied to his. Shelley was her 'Dearest and only love'; if she could not be his, she would never be another's: 'I have pledged myself to thee and sacred is the gift,' she wrote, a suggestion perhaps that the physical as opposed to the spiritual consummation was still to come.[8]

Violent acts followed violent emotions. According to Mrs Godwin, once, while Godwin was out, an hysterical Shelley burst into Skinner Street. He pushed the portly Mrs Godwin aside, then dashed up to the schoolroom. Arriving behind him, she found him urging a suicide pact: Mary should swallow the laudanum he had brought and he would shoot himself – he was brandishing his small pistol. The lovers would be united in death.[9] It was not fearful: 'There's not one atom of yon earth/ But once was living man,' he had written in Queen Mab.

By now Claire was screaming and Mary was crying, promising everlasting fidelity if Shelley would calm down and retreat. With Marshall's help, Mrs Godwin and Mary succeeded in restraining him; he went home, leaving the laudanum behind.

The event has a ring of fiction, though whether Mrs Godwin's in the telling or Shelley's in the acting remains unclear. Shelley had written novels in which men moved passionately from one woman to another, finding aspects of themselves in each, then provoked suicide. He especially admired Charles Brockden Brown's Ormond, where the hero is a man of lofty talents who believes marriage absurd because of 'the incurable imperfection of the female character'. Yet he loves the beautiful Helena, who produces in him a 'trance of the senses rather than an illumination of the soul'. Then he meets the intellectual Constantia, educated by her worthy father; she stimulates his mind and he turns in horror from Helena's 'voluptuous blandishments'; he tells her of his new love and Helena kills herself with laudanum.[10] In life, according to Peacock, Shelley himself carried a bottle of laudanum, declaring: 'I never part from this.' Probably true, since he was a lifelong laudanum user if not quite an addict.

Shortly after the schoolroom episode Shelley's landlord came to Skinner Street with news that his tenant had taken an overdose. Godwin hurried over and found a doctor in attendance. Between them the two men brought Shelley round and kept him awake through the night.

The cavalier attitude to suicide which Shelley took in these episodes was quite at odds with the horrified, majority view in Britain. Most people knew that a proven suicide could attract gruesome penalties. At worst the body could be staked, covered in quicklime and buried at crossroads at night, so that public footsteps would keep down the malignant ghost. Parliament forbade this practice only in 1823. At best the corpse could be refused burial in consecrated ground, instead lying isolated in the north corner of a churchyard at right angles to worthier graves.

But in more literary circles another view was possible. Indeed a suicidal posture had been quite modish in the later 1770s and 1780s, when Goethe made his hero Werther commit suicide in sentimental style after writing a series of yearning letters; these, Godwin had once declared, were equalled in intensity only by the letters Mary Wollstonecraft had written to the faithless Imlay while making her own two attempts on her life.

Godwin's acceptance of suicide was rational rather than emotional, and he was much blamed for it. In *Political Justice* he had written that it was probably not right to kill oneself to avoid pain and disgrace but that suicide was no sin or crime: 'The difficulty is to decide in any instance whether the recourse to a voluntary death can overbalance the usefulness I may exert in twenty or thirty years of additional life.'[11] Later, in a long, unpublished letter to an editor, he reiterated the right to suicide: 'Soberly and impartially speaking, the power over my life with which nature has endowed me, is a talent committed to my discretion ... the being that made us has with equal clearness, endowed us with the empire over our own life or death.' Mary Wollstonecraft, when rescued, declared her suicide attempt 'one of the calmest acts of reason'.[12]

Shelley was more theatrical than rational. He threatened suicide frequently though never seriously enough to succeed – as Peacock noted when he made his fictional Shelley in *Nightmare Abbey* intend to kill himself with 'a pint of port and a pistol' at exactly seven twenty-five on Thursday; then prevent himself by ordering his butler to put his watch back. It is an affectionate portrait, perhaps because Peacock too felt suicidal at times.

Godwin was in an ignoble position. He continued to need Shelley's money but he also needed to save his daughter. He had to keep her from the fate that he felt sure would be hers if she agreed to Shelley's plan. Towards the end of July he therefore wrote to Shelley urging his feelings as an aggrieved father. The infatuation for Mary was a 'caprice and momentary impulse'; Harriet was an innocent and worthy wife. Blaming Shelley for entering his house as a 'benefactor' only to leave 'an endless poison to corrode my soul', he begged him to spare the 'fair and spotless fame of my young child'. The letter was more in the mode of sentimental and Gothic romance than of the rational *Political Justice* or *Queen Mab*.[13] Shelley was unimpressed. Since Godwin was treating him and Mary with 'cruelty & injustice' he considered they had the right to disregard everything except 'the happiness of each other'.[14]

This 'happiness' required that they ignore Godwin's feelings and simply elope. So, three years after absconding with sixteen-year-old Harriet, Shelley left for the Continent with another sixteen-year-old girl. Mary went with Shelley knowing there could be no chance of marriage – Shelley was securely married to Harriet and he was the father of her daughter and prospective father of their second child. But his physical and emotional presence impressed her too deeply for restraint. Her sister Fanny had felt it; now it was her turn.

When infatuated with Cornelia Turner, Shelley feared he had destroyed Harriet's love for him – his heart was 'most worthy of thy hate', he had written. He painted a picture of himself as a gasping youth, his cheek 'pale with anguish', eye dim and limbs 'trembling'. The image would become common in his poetry. He was even more in anguish now. When he remembered the time, Peacock noted his friend's struggle against violent passion and the physical and mental effect it had: Shelley's mind was wracked, his eyes, and his hair and dress in disarray. Since he liked Harriet, Peacock remonstrated on her behalf. Shelley replied, 'Every one who knows me must know that the partner of my life should be one who can feel poetry and understand philosophy. Harriet is a noble animal, but she can do neither.'[15] Harriet, who had been educating herself in Latin and free thinking but who also liked nice clothes and carriages, could never equal the clever daughter of Godwin and Mary Wollstonecraft.

CHAPTER 17

FANNY

IN 1811 CHARLES Clairmont had cut his leading strings to Skinner Street when he went as a publisher's apprentice to the distinguished Edinburgh firm of Constable's. It was expensive training but the Godwins believed it a good investment since Charles would one day manage successfully the business that had defeated them.

When in August 1813 Archibald Constable offered to extend his appointment, Godwin swiftly communicated his despair at the prospect – melodramatically he predicted Mrs Godwin's death from overwork should Charles decide not to return and help in the bookshop. Charles yielded, though probably more out of consideration for his stepfather than his mother – her death, he later explained to Shelley, 'would be no more than the sorrow occasioned by the loss of a common acquaintance'.[1]

He came back to London late in January 1814, very much the young man where his stepsister Fanny, a year older, was still treated as a child. Soon Godwin reported back to Edinburgh his disappointment: his stepson was 'not yet a master tradesman'.[2] But he and his wife continued to hope for great things – in the meantime Charles was a new way of raising loans, this time against the young man's prospects.

The day after the elopement of Mary, Shelley and Claire, Charles was deputed to write to Fanny in Wales and ask her to return. She was a useful presence, and both Godwin and his wife depended on her help. Left to himself he might have told her the news directly but, writing on Godwin's instructions, he was more discreet. Godwin wanted to keep the elopement out of the public eye. This was for his own reputation and to avoid the ridicule it would bring on him; he also hoped that matters might still be mended. (Of course the news did seep out: Mrs Godwin suspected the clerks in the shop or perhaps Harriet was spreading it about.)

Two weeks after the letter was sent, Fanny was in Skinner Street. Godwin was relieved and wrote out her name in his diary, which usually featured only her initials. She returned with intricate emotions. Two people she dearly loved, Mary and Shelley, had run off together without her; they had even taken Claire along. It would have been strange if she had not felt jealous at the choice and envious of the adventure on which they had all embarked, however foolhardy and selfish she thought it. '[H]er emotion was deep when she heard of the sad fate of the two girls; she cannot get over it,' commented Mrs Godwin.[3]

Wanting so much to be wanted, Fanny must have been pained at their neglect – they had not even left a note for her. Harriet had called at Skinner Street with the letter from Shelley inviting her to join the commune in Switzerland. It strengthened Fanny's sense of exclusion – the earlier (rejected) invitation to her had never been renewed. It all drew attention to her own blank future. The only knight errant who had appeared at Skinner Street within her brief life – Mary called him the 'Elfin Knight' while he named himself the 'knight of the shield of shadow' – had left without her.

As the only young woman in the house Fanny bore the brunt of the Godwins' disappointment. Godwin told his old love, Maria Gisborne, that his wife was 'a being of the most irritable disposition possible' and that she suffered 'the keenest anguish on account of this misfortune, of which M[ary] is the sole cause ... she regards M. as the greatest enemy she has in the world.' As the sister of her 'greatest enemy' Fanny felt acutely the effects of the 'irritable disposition'. Mrs Godwin tried to comfort herself by blaming others and by forming interpretations that removed all culpability from her own child: in her version a couple of wicked runaways had snatched away her innocent daughter. Meanwhile Godwin withdrew into his study and consoled himself by expecting that both 'unworthy children' would return after their adventure and 'seek the protection and aid of their father'.

Miseries accumulated. Proctor Patrickson, Godwin's protégé at

Cambridge, had been depressed in the alien university world; he did well in his studies but was lonely and felt people mocked him for his poverty. Just before Shelley and Mary eloped Patrickson had asked Godwin for more money. But, when Godwin replied on the day after the elopement, he told Patrickson he could help no more – he himself was too plagued by debts and anxiety. On 8 August Patrickson came to London and dined at Skinner Street for the last time. He returned to Cambridge; on the following day he shot himself. Godwin's influence had left him with no 'hope of future happiness', while happiness in life was impossible without a 'respectable settlement'. Aware of her mother's two suicide attempts, Fanny heard the news with added horror when she arrived back in London.

The gloomy atmosphere had already oppressed ten-year-old William. On the day when Patrickson was committing suicide, he decided he could bear the house in Skinner Street no longer and ran away. He was found two mind-racking days later. He said he felt ridiculed at school.

To cap everything, just as the Godwins had feared, the public, who had been harsh on the author of *Political Justice* ever since he had written his frank life of his first wife, were gleeful when they heard of the elopement. It was put about – in part by Harriet – that the old radical had sold his daughters to Shelley, charging £700 for Claire and £800 for Mary. If people knew that Godwin was still trying to get money out of Shelley, substance would be given to the rumours. He therefore demanded of Shelley that in any transaction his name should never be used: this was no time for Godwinian frankness. Indeed, the second edition of *Political Justice* had conceded that 'sincerity … is a duty, only for reasons of utility'.[4]

Fanny's spirits sank with such cumulative woes. Godwin later remarked that her mind was always unsettled after Mary's elopement. She had lost two people she deeply cared for, one of whom she may have loved with passion. Although she did not spend the rest of her life depressed, it remains true that the remarks on her occasional melancholy start here.

❧

Godwin made things worse by imposing his own attitudes on the household. Contrary to his expectation, Mary and Claire did not seek his protection when they returned from the Continent, and he remained adamant about not receiving either his daughter or Shelley at Skinner Street. Despite needing them to pry money out of Shelley, Fanny and Charles were to have nothing whatever to do with the runaways. As Crabb Robinson later remarked, 'when integrity is so hard to preserve under poverty we ought not to expect moral delicacy and refinement'.[5]

Godwin's instructions irritated Charles. He found the atmosphere at home so bad that, far from wanting to rescue the book business, as his parents had fondly hoped, he desired simply to escape. 'Any refuge would be more acceptable to [him,] however menial,' than Godwin's house.[6] He even thought of emigrating to the West Indies. For a woman, such acts and attitudes were impossible. Fanny had known no independence from Skinner Street and the Godwins, and her position was far more difficult both emotionally and financially. She had, of course, the aunts in Ireland – and their home had always been considered a refuge for her when she wanted to take it. But it had never seemed a compelling prospect, or else she might have persuaded Godwin – and certainly his wife – to let her go there before now.

In any case the elopement of Mary with a married man put a new complexion on things. Soon enough the scandal reached the Wollstonecraft aunts in Dublin and, echoing their sister's scandalous doings fifteen years earlier, it was a further blow to their hard-won respectability. Surely theirs was, as Everina put it, an 'ill-fated family'.[7] So, for the first time, they wavered in their intention of taking their niece. Years later, when she became a teacher in Vienna, Claire too would be dogged by the scandal of these years: she observed of working women, 'what a handle for mischief against them' any shady rumour 'puts into the power of the society by whom they gain their bread'.[8] Eliza Bishop thoroughly upset Mrs Godwin by suggesting that, to keep Fanny untainted, Claire should not be allowed to come back to live in Skinner Street. Mary Jane bristled at the idea and forwarded the letter to Shelley to show him the damage he had done, less to Fanny than to Claire. Shelley responded that he was not sorry to have 'withdrawn one victim from the tyranny of prejudice'.[9] Mrs Godwin must have marvelled at his use of the word 'victim'.

Fanny understood the seriousness of her aunts' anxieties; she also knew the Godwins could not keep her indefinitely. Although she had always taken a very full share of domestic duties both in the house and in the business,

Mrs Godwin, anguished at the loss of Claire, declared her a financial burden. The unpaid legacy which her mother's friend Joseph Johnson had intended for her and which Godwin had never paid had long been forgotten.

What could she do? Francis Place had thought that Godwin might make 'his grown up girls maintain themselves', though he did not say how. Excluding what her aunts might offer, Fanny's options were few. Despite lacking much formal schooling, her education was enough for a governess or companion in a middle-class home. But, with her reserved nature and her mother's warnings about the horror of such a dependent state ringing in her ears – her first book, *Thoughts on the Education of Daughters*, vividly depicted the emotional repression required of clever women in service in unsympathetic households – Fanny may have shied away from these options.

Very possibly they were not open to her – it would have been a daring family that would take a girl called Godwin or Wollstonecraft into their house just now. The *Memoirs* had announced the scandal of her birth as the illegitimate daughter of the notorious feminist and London was agog with the new scandal of Shelley's libertine affair with her two sisters. Her aunts' anxieties suggested the effect. To top it all, Mary Wollstonecraft's name was being invoked in yet another disgrace in Ireland: when the Godwins' friend Lady Mount Cashell called at Skinner Street just after the elopement, she was on her way to Italy with a lover, abandoning a brood of children; like her sister Mary King's earlier scandalous conduct, hers was by many ascribed to her year under the tutelage of Mary Wollstonecraft. The connection was made the clearer when Lady Mount Cashell, in her new vagabond life, assumed the name of Mrs Mason from Wollstonecraft's *Original Stories* for children, the kind of fare the Godwins were producing and selling in their shop. And of course Lady Mount Cashell was one of their authors.

Beyond Fanny's financial predicament was her emotional one. On one side was Godwin, the man who had dominated her life and treated her kindly, and on the other the sister she had mothered and the man who in one way or another had stirred her passions. Whatever she did, whomever she helped and obeyed, she would be resented by some of those she loved.

CHAPTER 18

HARRIET

DESPITE THE IMMENSE shock of discovering her husband enthralled by another woman, when Shelley returned from the Continent Harriet wished to keep the connection warm. From Mrs Boinville she had heard of his attentions to Cornelia and Mrs Godwin may have added her suspicions about Fanny. Harriet hoped that her husband was simply going through a phase of acute susceptibility to women. She had seen his wild mood swings with Miss Hitchener and her sister Eliza Westbrook, his enthusiasms and violent disillusionment. He might yet return. She still loved him.

Like the Godwins trusting that the trio would disperse when they reached England, she was disappointed to find them taking lodgings together. But Shelley chose a place, 56 Margaret Street, close to the Westbrooks' house in Chapel Street; intercourse between them would be easy. Hoping to reclaim her husband, she tried to be amenable and sent books and clothes when he asked.

His publisher Thomas Hookham continued to disapprove of Shelley's abandonment of Harriet; nonetheless, when they met at her Chapel Street home the two men made up their quarrel. Soon Hookham was dining regularly with Shelley and Mary, though Mary never took to the 'nasty little man' and the relationship with Shelley remained uneasy: he would, they discovered, later betray them. Like Fanny in Skinner Street, Hookham must have felt torn between warring parties.

Harriet's emotions vacillated. Sometimes she wrote lovingly to Shelley, anxious about his health; her care gave her proprietorial feelings, for she knew his fads and needs so intimately. In the beginning she tried to be circumspect where Mary was concerned, knowing her husband's scorn of female jealousy. But as she lost hope she lashed out at Mary and especially Godwin, seeing them both in league against her; then she withdrew, anxiously fearing that she would lose Shelley irrevocably.

In his turn he upbraided her for not being 'above the world'. He was, he considered, being kind to her despite his 'violent and lasting passion for another'. Mary was 'the noblest and the most excellent of human beings' and, if Harriet could not accept this, their 'intimacy', such as it was, had to end. Near the time of her confinement, Harriet was finding it hard to dwindle quite so quickly from being a wife. There were moments when she utterly despaired.

Shelley's efforts at borrowing for the upkeep of his household, pregnant Mary and Claire, as well as for Godwin required that he keep his complicated relations secret. Harriet was instructed not to go near a solicitor. When he learnt that she had, he exploded: 'I was an idiot to expect greatness or generosity from you.' She was 'enslaved to the vilest superstitions' and was lost to him. Stunned, Harriet replied that she had only asked advice, but she could not resist deflecting her hurt into anger at Mary.

Shelley was incensed: 'Your contumelious language toward Mary is … impotent & mean … I consider it an insult that you address such Cant to me.' When he next wrote he was forthright: 'I am united to another; you are no longer my wife. Perhaps I have done you injury, but surely most innocently & unintentionally, in having commenced any connexion with you.' With sudden mood change, he expressed insouciant confidence that she *would* have an easy birth and no problems – despite the fact that her first one had been extremely painful. He then declared he was 'in want of stockings, hanks, & Mrs. W's posthumous works'.[1] These, he may have forgotten, included Mary Wollstonecraft's letters detailing her long abandonment by Fanny's father Gilbert Imlay and her consequent suicide attempts.

Harriet sent the stockings and handkerchiefs but not the books. (He must have obtained them from somewhere else – probably Hookham's circulating library – because soon he was reading aloud to Mary and Claire from these desolate volumes.)

Like Mary Wollstonecraft before her, Harriet felt she should live for her 'sweet Infant' despite her 'deepest wounds'. Since Eliza Westbrook had taken the delicate Ianthe to the sea resort of Southampton for her health, Harriet was now alone in London with her disapproving father. Her mind took a Gothic turn. Godwin was the wicked enchanter of an innocent victim: 'Mr. Shelley has become profligate and sensual, owing entirely to Godwin's *Political Justice*' and its 'false doctrines', she wrote. Unconsciously she echoed Shelley's own ghoulish metaphors: 'the man I once loved is dead. This is a vampire.' Shelley noted the change and revised his ideas for a commune: on his continental trip he had still thought it might include Harriet in some subordinate capacity. Now it could not: it would consist of himself, Hogg, Mary and Claire. Harriet was not able to express 'the sublimist virtue'.

At low ebb on 30 November 1814 Harriet prematurely brought 'an other infant into this woful world'. It was a son, the heir of the Shelley line. In her weakened state she may have exaggerated Shelley's callousness when she reported: 'He said he was glad it was a boy, because he would make money cheaper.' The baby, named Charles Bysshe, had Shelley's features and Harriet echoed Mary Wollstonecraft's lament over Fanny, who reminded her mother of the absconding Gilbert Imlay: 'what a dreadful trial it is to bring children into the world so utterly helpless as he is, with no kind father's care'.

The moody post-partum weeks plunged her into self-pity: 'life is scarcely worth having ... At nineteen I could descend a willing victim to the tomb. How I wish those dear children had never been born. They stay my fleeting spirit, when it would be in another state.' Shelley had introduced her to Enlightenment thought, including Godwin's acceptance of suicide as an individual's decision rather than a sin, and in their early married months he, and especially she, had talked glibly or gravely of death. They even carried around poison so that suicide was always within reach: 'Is it wrong, do you think, to put an end to one's sorrows?' Harriet now asked; was there 'another world' where she could find peace?[2]

On hearing through Hookham of the birth of Charles Bysshe, Mary confided to her journal, 'S[helley] writes a number of circular letters of this event which ought to be ushered in with ringing of bells, &c. for it is the son of his *wife*.'[3] She felt only bitterness against Harriet; she was sorrier for her heavily pregnant and uncomfortable self.

CHAPTER 19

FANNY

FANNY, SO SUSCEPTIBLE to pity, also withheld it from Harriet. Despite their present shared isolation, the first impression of difference remained. She needed to hold firmly to the idea that Harriet was causing pain to Shelley, Mary and ultimately Godwin. If she expressed any sympathy for their enemies, Mary would accuse her of being censorious about her and Shelley. She must not think of the pregnant Harriet's plight as deserted mother, very like Mary Wollstonecraft. So the two women never made contact or provided the comfort both needed.

When Harriet made public the fact that Shelley was still raising money for Godwin, Mary retorted that she was trying to 'ruin Papa'. Fanny could not follow her sister and Claire into calling Harriet 'detestable'; yet she never accepted that Harriet and her children had a higher claim than Godwin to Shelley's money. It would have been strange had she thought otherwise: even Shelley, who was disappointed at Godwin's cold shouldering, still revered the author of *Political Justice* and expected everyone else to accept his claims.

Fanny understood Godwin's position. She knew the world suspected that he had been complicit in the elopement; many thought he had actually ensnared a young gentleman of fortune who could not now extricate himself. With his business based on children's books and his need to write for money, Godwin could not afford further tarnishing of his already disreputable name – he could not be seen to condone the actions of Shelley and

Mary. At the same time he was desperate for Shelley's funds. So, on the one hand he enforced social exclusion on Shelley, the thief of his daughter, and on the other ignored it so he could make demands on Shelley as his patron. This he often did through Fanny.

Whatever her initial attitude to their going, Fanny now felt nothing but compassion for Mary and Claire. Her mother had portrayed the miseries of ardent young women unprotected by marriage. In the eyes of the world her sisters were 'ruined' and Mary, she soon knew, was pregnant. In the *Memoirs* Godwin had remarked that 'the rules of polished society condemn an unmarried woman', while Mary Wollstonecraft noted that woman's reputation was confined to 'a single virtue – chastity'. Mary's situation was unenviable.

Determined to be the peacemaker, when she could Fanny ran errands for everyone and, like Godwin, both her sister and Shelley airily demanded tasks of her. Following their return she visited Mary in their first lodgings at 56 Margaret Street, then, after the end of September, in 5 Church Terrace, St Pancras, near where she and her mother had once lived before the move to the Polygon. She came round as often as she felt able, especially when Mary was ailing. Godwin pained her by raging at her for being loyal to his daughter, threatening not to speak to her if she visited the runaways again. She might have echoed Crabb Robinson when he remarked: 'Godwin is frequently very indelicate in forcing one to say or hear said things very offensive to one's feelings (viz. speaking against friends of mine); … Godwin had so often hurt my feelings that nothing but my great respect for him made me keep up the acquaintance.'[1] At the same time Fanny knew that Mary, Claire and Shelley despised her for her lack of courage in standing up to her stepfather and thought her pathetic when she heeded his threats. They mocked what for her were heroic and painful attempts to serve them while remaining true to Godwin in spirit.

Her situation was not helped by equivocation. When Mary, Shelley and Claire were still in Margaret Street, Fanny and her stepmother went round to their lodgings – Mary Jane was desperate to see her daughter. Godwin agreed to their going and yet his prohibition had to be respected; so the two women walked past the window but refrained from knocking. They wanted to see and be seen. They had their wish but, when Shelley ran out, they refused to talk to him and rushed on. Hookham, who was dining with them, left early. Perhaps he was put off by all this family turmoil. Over the next months the two sides would spend much time spying on each other through windows: sometimes it was Fanny who looked in on Mary, Shelley and Claire; at others Claire and Shelley spied on the Godwins.

The bolder Charles was less worried than his stepsister about Godwin's anger or his mother's tirades. Having heard of Mrs Godwin and Fanny's encounter, he waited until nightfall, then went round to Margaret Street. He threw pebbles at the window, caught their attention, and went in. He found Shelley writing to Godwin, Mary in bed and Claire reading the notes to *Queen Mab*; he so much enjoyed the evening that he stayed till three in the morning, listening to the story of their travels. In his turn he gave them news from Skinner Street, telling them of a plan to get Claire away and place her in a convent – Charles may have inherited his mother's imaginative flair for it is hard to imagine the atheist Godwin putting anyone in such a place. More likely, if they could pay for it, the Godwins considered some sort of parlour-boarder arrangement at a school, a respectable situation for a young woman alone. Years before, Mary Wollstonecraft had lodged her married but separated sister Eliza Bishop like this while considering what next to do with her. Meanwhile, to repudiate any part in these clandestine meet-ings – or near meetings – with his stepchildren, Godwin wrote to Shelley to break off all contact; when Shelley, Mary and Claire tried to visit Skinner Street he refused them entry.

Once Shelley was known to be in London creditors endeavoured to learn his address. Hence he hid it from Harriet, who he assumed would want to betray him. He was heavily in debt and the carriage maker Charters in particular was pursuing him with his bill (he was never paid).

Towards the end of October Fanny learnt that bailiffs had discovered Shelley's whereabouts from the Hookhams. She faced a dilemma. She feared both to disobey Godwin by going to tell Shelley and Mary what threatened them and to stay away, so leaving Shelley in danger of arrest. After delib-erating a while she wrote a letter of vague warning and decided to take it round herself.

She arrived in Church Terrace unclear to the end what she would do. Over the weeks of emotional tugging, upbraidings and conflicting demands, her nerves had been jangled. She felt torn and abused. As Godwin would much later admit: 'duty kept her with us: but I am afraid her affections were with them'. She was experiencing the emotional tug acutely just at this moment. She found it hard to breathe.

For a while she stood on open ground close by the lodgings, trying to settle her edgy spirits. She was aware that Shelley and her sisters were dining together inside and would jump up as soon as they knew she was close by. After some time she plucked up courage and sent a small boy to them with her note. Creditors were closing in on them, it said – the coach maker, the unpaid landladies and moneylenders.

On receiving the message, Shelley and Claire dashed down. When she saw them Fanny began to run off, but Claire snatched at her to stop her escaping. It seemed a joke to Claire but Fanny screamed out. Claire let her go and she fled.

The event is worth reading in Claire's journal, not so much for the facts as for the raw emotions clear in all of them, and for a sense of the contempt Claire felt for the lonely older girl left at home to cope with the pain she and Mary had caused:

> Dine at six – When the cloth was removed the servant enters with a letter which a little boy said a lady waiting in the opposite field [h]ad sent him with. It was from Fanny Shelley & I hasten to the field – I catch hold of her – She foolishly screams & runs away – She escapes – Shelley & I hasten to Skinner St. We watch through the window we see Papa, Mama, & Charles – [2]

It is difficult to interpret the events without Fanny's voice. Was it conflicted thoughts of Godwin and Shelley that struck her and made her scream? Or did she feel a momentary thrill at being at last wanted by them or – and this seems most likely – at being close to Shelley again after so long and tumultuous a time? Nobody stopped to wonder. Nor did they concern themselves with where she could have gone when she ran off. Evidently she did not feel able to face the Godwins at once.

They needed more detail. So, following the warning, Claire and Shelley wrote to Charles. Perhaps he would know something else. Then Claire walked round to Skinner Street to deliver the note and ask for a meeting.

Reluctantly Charles agreed to see his sister, although he did not like her coming to the house. So they conversed outside. She asked him directly about Fanny's warning. He knew nothing about the matter, he said; Fanny was obviously being overdramatic.

They had to be sure; so, when Claire rejoined Shelley, they both wrote to ask Fanny for more reliable information. It was decided that next day Mary and Claire should both go to Skinner Street to speak to her, without Shelley being present. They needed to get to her and not let Godwin know.

In the early morning the two girls waited outside their old home for the shutters to open, assuming correctly that only Fanny would be up in the early hours, the most domestic and busy of the family. Mrs Godwin in particular was noted for staying in bed late in the mornings.

While the Godwins slept on, Fanny opened the door and was forced to confront her sisters, however much this meeting disobeyed her stepfather. A few minutes' talk apprised Mary and Claire of what Charles had kept secret: that the Hookhams had betrayed them. They believed Fanny – they saw how difficult she found it not to tell the truth. They related the news to Shelley, who, when he heard it, threatened to tear the Hookhams' hearts out by the roots with irony and sarcasm. He quickly calmed down – as much as Godwin needed him he needed Thomas Hookham, who so often dealt with moneylenders for him.

Fanny, useful on this occasion, was not always reliable, they found. Shelley in particular was shocked at the way she could be manipulated by the Godwins. He was especially furious at Mrs Godwin's manner of employing her to pull Claire away from him, something he had no intention of allowing. The approaches were made when they themselves were at a low ebb, without money or squabbling together or ailing in different ways. Either Fanny or Charles must have relayed their sorry state to Skinner Street and the Godwins took advantage.

On the first occasion Fanny was deputed to write to Claire requesting a meeting without Mary. Charles would deliver the letter and the encounter could take place in their old friend Marshall's lodgings. To this Claire agreed without consulting Shelley. Mary was contemptuous of Fanny's role and said she probably would not be 'allowed' to come since it was raining. However Fanny braved the rain and did meet Claire. Even in their most impoverished moments Shelley and Mary seemed able to command a carriage when necessary; Fanny walked almost everywhere and frequently got soaking wet on behalf of others.

The meeting with Claire took place at Marshall's at 11.30 in the morning. Claire and Fanny talked for nearly three and a half hours – so long indeed that Mary began to imagine her stepsister had been lured to Skinner Street there and then. But, when she sent a message to Marshall's to find out what was happening, the reply came back that Claire intended to return to their lodgings. She was not to be dispatched so easily.

While the meeting was clearly at Mrs Godwin's behest, it was also a good moment for Fanny and Claire to be together. They had not been close in childhood – they were simply too different – but they now had something in common. Claire knew that Mary did not much care to have her around and Fanny, whose return the Godwins had asked for when she had been on vacation in Wales, felt unwanted in Skinner Street. Both young women saw themselves as waifs, not quite belonging to any family. The same might be said of Patrickson, whose death Fanny now told Claire about. It was a shocking thing and could in part be ascribed to the elopement – or at least its baneful effect on Godwin.

They spoke also of their different futures, what they wanted, hoped for or expected. Fanny told Claire what she had been doing in Wales when they all eloped in the summer, but Claire did not record her words, and Fanny's diary, if she kept one – as seems likely in the scribbling Godwin household – does not survive. But the holiday had clearly been an important time in her life and plans, and when Claire mentioned the conversation to Mary, she too noted it in her journal. Most likely Fanny spoke of her reluctance to go to live with her aunts and begin on a life of schoolteaching but her sense of having few other choices. If so, this dilemma was something with which both her sisters could sympathise. After their talk Claire walked Fanny back through the rainy streets almost to her old house but kept out of sight of her mother. She was not yet ready to go home.

Three weeks later the Godwins made another attempt to get Claire away. News of her ongoing discontent in the Shelley ménage had reached Skinner Street: Fanny should write asking for a further meeting, this time on the Blackfriars Road. She would bring a message to Claire that her mother was dying and wanted to see her. Since three days before the message was sent Mrs Godwin attended a performance of *Macbeth,* one of her favourite

Shakespeare plays, this seems unlikely — and Lamb called her 'the liar par excellence'.[3] Yet it is hard to imagine Fanny lending herself to a direct false-hood, and Crabb Robinson remarked that Mary Jane was sometimes very poorly that winter — perhaps for a short time she convinced Fanny that her illness was more than tactical.

Claire replied that she could not come to Blackfriars Road but that Fanny could visit their lodgings — probably a ruse to allow Mary to overhear the conversation. Fanny agreed and came but, obeying Godwin, refused to see Mary. Her sister scorned her for allowing herself to be so patently used by their stepmother.

Whether or not believing the news of her mother's illness, Claire found Fanny persuasive. She felt one too many when Shelley and Mary were about, and sensed Mary's irritation. Mrs Godwin's appeal came at an apposite moment. Besides which, Claire had run out of clothes. Fanny dutifully went to Skinner Street to fetch some. Perhaps her fresh clothes reminded Claire of her easier life and, when Fanny returned home, Claire went with her before Shelley could stop her. From Skinner Street she wrote to Mary and Shelley that she was content to be with the Godwins and did not know when she would come back to them.

Mary's relief was short lived. Mrs Godwin was not dying and Skinner Street was in its usual uproar about money; the atmosphere did not appeal to Claire any more than it had to young William the year before. It was not the haven she had momentarily imagined. Meanwhile she ensured her stay either at Skinner Street or elsewhere as a paying guest would not be long by informing her parents that, wherever she was, she must be able 'in all situ-ations openly [to] proclaim and earnestly support a total contempt for the laws and institutions of society, and that no restraint should be imposed on her correspondence and intercourse with those from whom she was sepa-rated'.[4] Within two days of her arrival in Skinner Street Shelley escorted Claire back to their lodgings.

Fanny's part in this incident drove a wedge between her and Shelley. When it came to her dealings with the Godwins, he now felt he knew on what side she would be and he could not trust her.

Fanny had other reasons for gloom. She was spending long hours reading reports of the suffering unemployed. Her mother's 'prevailing passion' of pity was strong in her and she saw misery wherever she turned. The wartime government had run up a huge public debt which had to be serviced by various methods of taxation, much of which fell on the middling and lower ranks more heavily than on the rich. With Napoleon's exile to Elba the streets of London had filled with old and wounded soldiers. Fanny's heart bled for them all. Hearing of her anxieties Claire tartly remarked that the lachrymose hero of Henry Mackenzie's *Man of Feeling* 'would have just suited Fanny for a husband'.[5] For so many people she was most vibrantly alive in her mother's writings – it was only one step further for Claire to imagine her marrying a character from a novel.

Godwin's crises continued; once again he was sure he was facing bankruptcy. Despite the earlier help from Shelley, the debts to Place and his fellow creditors were still outstanding and he had involved them all in other borrowing through his manic playing off of creditors against each other. So dire were matters that he was even thinking of selling the bookshop stock, a last resort since it would mean the end of the business on which he still hoped to rely. On top of this the owners of his house were at last demanding rent (in fact Godwin avoided paying anything for almost another decade). In this tetchy atmosphere Mary wrote Godwin what he termed a 'cold & indelicate' letter. It arrived in Skinner Street like a hurled weapon, and Fanny witnessed the effect. As so often she felt the brunt of the ensuing quarrel as Godwin renewed his threat, that if she had any further contact with Mary he would never speak to her again. She was crushed.

When Mary heard her reaction she mocked both sides: 'a blessed degree of liberty this!'[6] Why had Fanny not the courage and loyalty to stand up for her sister? Fanny, Mary thought, sided with the Godwins against her. Having with the help of her lover taken her own spirited stand against her father and stepmother, she could not see why Fanny failed to oppose Godwin's threats – and especially their stepmother's. Like Shelley irritably demanding why labouring men suffered patiently and shrank into their 'cellars, holes, and cells', Mary did not comprehend what she had never quite had to endure. She felt, too, some jealousy towards the daughter who, unlike herself, continued to be approved by her father.

Despite the bad-tempered rhetoric on both sides and despite Mary's continued banishment, Shelley did in fact come to Godwin's rescue: to fend off the major creditors he was allowed to call at Skinner Street so he could arrange costly post-obits on the estate he would inherit. Francis Place was brought in to help find a buyer. According to the unreliable Mrs Godwin, the aim was to take a bet on the death of Shelley's father, a man 'upwards of 60' (it would have been a poor bet since Timothy lived to over ninety). Godwin was promised £1,200 when all was arranged.

Godwin accepted Shelley's help without thanks: he was still the man who had stolen his daughters. In any case the sum was nowhere near enough to rescue him. *Political Justice* had declared that gratitude 'can be no part either of justice or virtue'. Despite the largesse Fanny was still forbidden to deal with Shelley and her sister.

One incident added to Mary's scorn for Fanny. In a moment of sentiment, she sent her sister a friendly token, a lock of her hair. It was not delivered with discretion and, when Mrs Godwin heard of the gift, she was furious. More rigid about the prohibitions on contact when it came to Mary than to her own daughter, she forbade Fanny to come downstairs to dinner as punishment for receiving the lock. Fanny was by now a woman of twenty.

Charles Clairmont, who freely dined with Shelley and his stepsister, relayed the event to Mary. Both she and Claire saw themselves as unconventional spirited women in the manner of Mary Wollstonecraft, and, on hearing of her sister's obedience, she snapped: 'Fanny of course behaves slavishly on the occasion.'[7] Mary depended on Fanny for errands, news and sympathy but was contemptuous of her docility. She thought her sister dull and secretive; sometimes she hated her. She forgot that Fanny had had a great deal more of their stepmother than she had. Apart from the recent time with Shelley, Mary had spent much of 1810 and 1811 in Scotland and had also had periods in boarding school. Fanny had very rarely been away from the Godwins. But Mary was lashing out at them all. Her own life was uneasy and she had no pity to spare for others.

CHAPTER 20

MARY

THE HOSTILITY OF Skinner Street was primarily due to Mrs Godwin, Mary thought. Shelley supported her view for he disliked Godwin's wife as much as Harriet had done. Mary shuddered at the very idea of her stepmother; she made the life of her 'poor father' a misery. She might have added 'and Fanny's life too'.

Despite his coldness and bouts of fury, Godwin still existed in his daughter's mind as a loving father manipulated into abandoning his child by a cruel and plaguing wife. Without this infernal woman he would 'follow the obvious bent of his affections & be reconciled,' she was sure.[1] As Harriet blamed Godwin for corrupting Shelley, so Mary found comfort in seeing her stepmother as the source of her father's failings. 'Oh, my beloved father!' a heroine exclaimed in her novel of father–daughter love, 'Indeed you made me miserable beyond all words, but how truly did I even then forgive you, and how entirely did you possess my whole heart.'[2] There are not often second heroines in the stories she wrote and Mary rarely stopped to consider how her stepmother had felt at the loss of her daughter Claire, which she always laid at Mary's door.

The pure and celestial felicity Mary and Shelley assumed would be theirs when they returned to England from Switzerland had been swiftly interrupted by bailiffs; reality was a procession of dreary lodgings taken to escape their creditors. Nonetheless the Shelley camp was unrepentant. Money might be tight but their self-engrossed life had desultory pleasures, and all were young. They studied together Godwin's *Political Justice,* reminding themselves of the author's more radical phase; they marvelled at his apostasy: 'I confess to you that I have been shocked & staggered by Godwin's cold injustice,' Shelley told Mary.[3] Dire though things were, Shelley occasionally hired a carriage for Mary; visited and was visited; bought prints and books in Holborn, though most were obtained from Hookhams' circulating library; went to the theatre with Mary and Claire; once even stayed a night with Mary at a hotel when the lodgings seemed too dingy. Sailing paper boats on a pond near Primrose Hill was free – it was always one of his favourite pastimes.

Having been warned by Charles Clairmont of the plan to kidnap Claire, Shelley ensured she was never alone. Far from wanting to diminish his household, he imagined adding to it two of his sisters now boarding in Hackney and forbidden to see their brother. Shelley believed they could benefit from joining his family, where they would be rescued from prejudice and taught liberal principles. He sent Mary and Claire with letters hoping to establish connections with them so that he could convert them to atheism and communal living. But they were reluctant to be rescued.

By the end of October such schemes had to be postponed. When Fanny warned Shelley that bailiffs knew of their lodgings, there was no option but for him to go into hiding, leaving Mary and Claire to plague each other alone. The girls were so poor they had insufficient money for decent food; occasionally they had to make do with cakes from Peacock's mother in Southampton Buildings.

Shelley would be on the run for just over a fortnight, during which he felt 'almost degraded to the level of the vulgar & impure'.[4] He could see Mary openly only on Sunday, when debtors were beyond the law; at other times the pair met in coffee houses, in St Paul's Cathedral where they could sit down, or in Gray's Inn gardens where they had to walk about. Mary hated waiting alone in public places and feared lingering in dangerous parks. Or they met, or perhaps only exchanged secret letters, at Southampton Buildings, where Shelley lodged some of his time.

Mary's spirits sank with his absence. She was worried that it might portend the inconstancy Harriet experienced once her husband was away from her. She begged Shelley to think of her all the time, noticing that, while she felt she could write to him throughout the day, he was away taking long walks. Could he not keep her in mind every minute? She sank further when she discovered he was communicating more with Claire than with herself; she was 'a poor widowed deserted thing no one cares for'. Was she, after all, just one in the series of Shelley's girls, valued mainly for her famous parentage, having in Harriet's bitter words to Peacock no attraction except 'that her name was Mary, and not only Mary, but Mary Wollstonecraft'?[5]

As she sank down with Shelley's absence, so she swung up when he returned. While together, the pair spent happy times in bed: their 'Love in idleness' glossed by a disgruntled Claire as a 'Very philosophical Way of spending the day – To sleep & talk – why this is merely vegetating'.[6]

By early November Shelley had managed to organise a loan for about £500 with the help of Hookham and Peacock, and he could openly join Mary and Claire again. They moved to better lodgings: 2 Nelson Square, Blackfriars Road, south of the Thames.

But nothing much improved. They were all sickly and discontented. Mary's pregnancy was troublesome and she was often tired and fretful. Hogg, back studying law, called on them often.

Shelley was always preoccupied with his health – he had even rewritten his robust childhood as a series of illnesses. With a keen sense of the body's decay, he imagined parts of himself stretched, shaken, rubbed or weakened. He noted his various agitations and fevers, at one moment believing himself afflicted with elephantiasis, at another suspecting consumption. He had hysterical attacks, spasms, and problems with his kidneys and bladder. He consulted doctors and mused much on death; frequently he told people he expected soon to die. And while alive he assumed he suffered intensely: in his *Defence of Poetry* he would write that the Poet 'is more delicately organized than other men, and sensible to pain and pleasure, both his own and that of others, in a degree unknown to them'. The pain could be physical as well as mental.[7]

Mary felt both sorts. Her pregnancy made her sick and she often stayed in bed. Claire's presence was becoming intolerable. After their return from the Continent she had expected her stepsister to leave her and Shelley alone. But her lover's enthusiasm prevented this: Claire remained essential to his idea of the commune of like-minded people who would 'resist the coalition of the enemies of liberty'.[8] When Mary went to bed early the pair stayed up late planning an association of philosophical seekers unbound by conventions, a 'world of perfection' in Claire's term. Under Shelley's prompting Claire read Lawrence's *Empire of the Nairs* and grew excited by its explosive ideas of free love and polyandry, and – more significantly – its condoning of incest. In the eyes of the world she and Mary were sisters and Shelley the master of both.

Claire engaged spiritedly with Shelley's Gothic imagination. She continued to excite him as she had on the Continent, encouraging his fascination with abnormal mental states and the heightened vision that might come from them. He responded intensely to her thrills and fears, intrigued by her mingling of foolhardiness and agitation. She stirred both him and herself with her nightmares and sensational reading – Lewis's *The Monk* and *Tales of Wonder and Delight* or Hogg's *Prince Alexy Haimatoff*. When Shelley read aloud from the *Ancient Mariner* and Wordsworth's 'Mad Mother' with her coal-black hair and wild eyes, only Claire stayed up to listen, then talk by the fire until one in the morning.

She could always be worked on by a frightening story – Shelley had not had so susceptible an audience for his macabre fancies since he left his little sisters in Field Place.

Once he told her a tale of soldiers having skin cut from their backs, then said it was 'the witching time of night'. He asked if she could feel the silence tingling in her ears, the mysterious feeling of the supernatural. What she certainly felt was the overwhelming presence of Shelley who, she said, 'looks beyond all passing strange – a look of impressive deep & melancholy awe'. '[T]ake your eyes off,' Claire cried, then ran up to bed and put her candle on the chest of drawers. Then she looked at her pillow in the middle of her bed, turned her head to the window, then back, and found the pillow no longer there but on the chair. Panic-stricken, she ran downstairs and burst into the bedroom where Shelley was bending over Mary to kiss her goodnight, intending to stay up reading. Claire's face was white and 'distorted most unnaturally by horrible dismay' and 'the lineaments of terror'.

She asked Shelley if he had been in her room and touched her pillow. If not, had she experienced something supernatural? Presumably suspecting the erotic nature of her reaction, Shelley told her what perhaps she did not know for sure until now, that Mary was pregnant. The news checked 'her violence'. In Claire's account Shelley 'gives the most horrible description of my counte-tenance [sic] – I did not feel in the way he thinks I did – '.

Shelley and Claire then left Mary and went into the parlour, where they sat by the fire exciting each other through the rest of the night. Just before morning Claire again perceived the strange expression on Shelley's face which she interpreted as 'a mixture of deep sadness & conscious power over her'. She shrieked and writhed on the floor until Shelley sent up for Mary and together they calmed her down.[9] After a couple more episodes of this sort Mary recorded in her diary: 'Shelley and Claire sit up late and for a wonder do not frighten themselves.'

A week after the pillow event, Shelley blamed a presumably importunate Claire for being incapable of friendship. 'How hateful it is to quarrel – to say a thousand unkind things – meaning none – things produced by the bitterness of disappointment,' confided Claire to her diary. Perhaps at this point Shelley also told her of his resolve to content himself for the moment 'with one great affection'. Whatever he said of Mary, he soon felt he had been too severe on Claire and came to apologise. '[H]ow I like good kind explaining people,' she exclaimed. But she continued to feel distressed and recorded in her journal, 'I weep yet never know why – I sigh yet feel no pain'. That night she once again walked in her sleep, then groaned for over one and a half hours before Shelley responded. He had to give her his place in the bed with Mary. In the morning the pillow in Claire's room was found to have moved again. Shelley could no longer take such happenings quite seriously – perhaps it had got sleepy and fallen down on its back, he joked.[10]

The pair continued to exchange notes, in one of which Shelley declared he was unhappy. 'God in heaven,' Claire exclaimed, 'what has he to be unhappy about!'[11] Later she tried to erase the entries which recorded the intimate talks between herself and Shelley with Mary absent.

Claire continued fretful and gloomy; 'she is very sullen with Shelley', Mary noted.[12] Her feelings were becoming too obvious, as were her efforts to attract Shelley with what Mary called her witchcraft. It was during this time that she chose the name of Claire, quite likely after the histrionic and ambivalently sexual second heroine of Rousseau's *Nouvelle Héloïse*. If so, she accepted the lovers Mary and Shelley as Rousseau's central pair, Julie and Saint-Preux; the second heroine Claire was there to love and torment them both. It was not a vision Mary shared. Twenty years earlier, her mother Mary

Wollstonecraft had herself been much influenced by Rousseau's book, but she imagined herself in the role of Julie and made no room for a Claire.

When her stepsister hurriedly returned from her short stay in Skinner Street, Mary kept to herself her reactions to both sisters. But Shelley, who had been furious at her going, admitted he had suffered from 'disquieting dreams' while she was away. The pair were, Mary feared, locked together. They spent the day after Claire's return 'hopping about the town' together; a few days later they were out buying dresses for Claire. On one occasion they managed to get themselves locked in Kensington Gardens – going out 'as usual', as Mary expressed it in her journal – while she stayed home nursing her ill health and edgy feelings. When she herself felt a little better, Claire on cue fell ill; when she recovered and found Mary and Shelley reading together, Claire grew petulant. She came out of her mood only when Shelley spent time talking her round.

Whenever Shelley's attention strayed, Claire complained that he treated her unkindly and Mary had to console her to bring peace to the household. Even Shelley occasionally grew tired of the demands and noted Claire's frivolous interruptions of any interesting talk.[13]

<hr />

On 5 January 1815 Shelley's grandfather Sir Bysshe died at eighty-three. Anticipating an income, they all moved to spacious lodgings in 41 Hans Place; a month later they moved again to new apartments at 1 Hans Place. Hogg was a frequent visitor to both addresses. Probably shocked at the comings and goings of so many entangled young people, one pregnant and unmarried, landladies were unfriendly and, in Mary's view, determined to fleece them. The winter was cold and they continued in bad health. It was difficult to get good fresh vegetables in London, and Shelley's spartan vegetarian regime told on them all, especially the pregnant Mary, who was continually unwell; Claire sometimes had a liver complaint for which she was bled, on one occasion by Shelley. He himself consulted doctors for his various ailments.

Mary felt cross with everyone – with Fanny for not taking sides more forcefully, with Harriet for still being Shelley's wife, and with Shelley and Claire for making her suffer. Two years earlier Shelley had been confused over Hogg's approaches to Harriet, but that was because she had not wanted them; in principle, he wished Hogg to love the women he loved. And again Hogg was only too willing. With Shelley and Claire gadding about town together, Mary began to find some solace in his visits. The pages of her diary entries for these weeks have been torn out, so the probable efforts at full communal living are obscured.

Initially Mary had been no keener than her predecessor to share herself with this unattractive, persistent man, who was altogether too reverent towards the established order for a daughter of Godwin. Claire later recorded that Mary, like Harriet, was reluctant to have sex with Hogg and cried bitterly at the idea. In fact Mary's own record is more ambiguous and suggests that, although not quite ready when he declared love on New Year's Day 1815, she was becoming increasingly flirtatious and responsive to him. The pair read Ovid's erotic poetry together, talked about sex in general and in particular of the sexual consummation that might occur after Mary's baby was born. Hogg would teach her Italian – always an erotically charged pursuit in their circle. Occasionally she had strange dreams about him. When she expected Shelley and Claire to be out till late she asked Hogg to come 'and console a solitary lady', while declaring she did not wish to persuade him to do what he ought not; a few days later she sent him a lock of her hair.

But the devotion of Hogg, though momentarily welcome, was no recompense for Shelley and Claire's mutual absorption. Her anxiety about Shelley remained the context of anything and everything: her life hung 'on the beam of his eye', she told Hogg; her 'whole soul' was 'entirely wrapt up in him'.[14]

In a weakened state, on 22 February, several weeks before her time, Mary gave birth to an undersized girl. Shelley noted that the baby was not expected to live. Despite past disagreements Mary now wanted the soothing presence of her sister. Shelley sent for Fanny at once.

When his message arrived in Skinner Street, Godwin and Mary Jane were away, and their absence allowed Fanny to dash over to their lodgings and stay with Mary. She felt fellowship with the precarious tiny baby. Later, after the Godwins returned, Charles arrived with baby linen from Mrs

Godwin. Godwin appears to have winked at this activity on behalf of his first grandchild. Fanny stayed the night and left the next day.

The condition of the delicate baby cannot have been helped by the move her parents and Claire made ten days after her birth to new lodgings in 13 Arabella Row, Pimlico, some distance away. (A year and a half earlier Shelley had trundled Ianthe back and forward to the Lake District and Scotland from Bracknell when she was only two months old, but Ianthe, though appearing fragile, must have been a more robust child.) The move was designed in part to give Shelley more room for the commune which, now he had retrieved Claire, he hoped to put into practice – without Harriet and always without Fanny. It was in Pimlico, four days after the move, that Mary woke to find the baby dead. It had always been weak but the death was a shock. Mary was distraught; she wanted Fanny again. The next day when her sister had still not come, Claire sent a note round to Skinner Street to ask for her. In her diary Mary wrote, 'but she does not come'.

Perhaps the note did not arrive quickly or was kept from her, or perhaps Godwin did not see the need for disobedience to his instructions just because his daughter had lost a child. Whatever the case, Fanny came five days later, walking all the way through the pouring rain and arriving 'wet through'. She dried herself and stayed to comfort Mary; then she dined with them, leaving at past nine in the evening. The sisters seemed close at last.

Fanny valued being needed and Mary valued the compassion. But on her return to Skinner Street Fanny experienced the ice in Godwin, for, despite Mary's tragedy, the death of her first baby, he continued refusing to speak to her and Shelley; he kept up his resolution even when he saw the pair in the street. Notwithstanding his accepted reliance on Shelley's money, he now declared the young man 'wicked'.[15] Perhaps he knew something more about their tangled relationships; perhaps Claire had dropped hints when she had been with them in Skinner Street, or perhaps Charles had done so.

The death of her baby two weeks after its birth affected Mary more than the others seemed to realise. One night she dreamed they had rubbed the small corpse so that it became alive again, and she admitted, 'I think about the little thing all day'. In her misery she desperately wanted Shelley to herself and the insensitively cheerful Claire out of the way. Indeed, she felt comfortable only when Claire was in bed – she sometimes stayed there all day – or out of sight. For a while she managed to persuade Shelley to drop his notion of the commune but he would not agree to send Claire away. 'I fear it is hopeless,' Mary recorded, 'not the least hope', the prospect 'more dismall than ever'. It was 'indeed hard to bear'. [16]

Fanny was now a comfortable presence. She did not intrude on Mary's life as Claire persistently did and the blood relationship seemed stronger. Both Mary and Shelley appreciated Fanny's coming with news, sometimes bringing letters that had arrived at Skinner Street. She also delivered the clothes and books her sister needed. Up early, she could easily spirit them out of the house without being noticed. Indeed, Fanny became Mary's main connection with the lost world of family and Scottish friends. As a regular visitor she often remained for dinner and heard Mary's accounts of Shelley – and probably her complaints about their stepsister. Shelley too made her feel wanted. He listened eagerly to her tales of 'the politics of Skinner Street & its allies'. It pleased Fanny that sometimes he would find a coach for her or walk her home part of the way. It was the first time she had had him to herself since the early days in Skinner Street. Perhaps Godwin had relented a little or Fanny had become more cunning.

❧

Since Sir Bysshe's death Shelley had entered into serious negotiations with his father over the inheritance, always refusing to settle for a life interest in part of the immense property in return for prolonging the entail on the rest – in many ways a good deal, but one that would prevent him raising immediate money on the estate for himself and Godwin. In May he and the new Sir Timothy came to an agreement whereby Shelley would acquire an annual £1,000 income – out of which he would allow Harriet £200 – £2,900 to settle unpaid bills and loans, by no means all of them, and a lump sum of £4,500 on top. Desperate for immediate cash, he told his father that one debt was the £1,200 promised to Godwin. On receiving this however, he handed over only £1,000 keeping back £200; the outstanding sum would arrive later in November, he promised Godwin, after a further settlement with Sir Timothy.

At the end of May the money had been paid to Godwin and Claire, though noting that 'Riches seem to fly from Genius', happily wrote to Fanny that she was 'quite delighted' to learn that 'Papa had at last got a

£1,000'.[17] Their papa was less so: Godwin had counted on the full amount. He was facing a legal battle for precisely the missing sum: settling one lot of debts with the £1,000 would provoke arrest by the other unpaid creditors. Significantly there was no longer any real pretence that the bookselling business would be saved by this injection of capital, just that Godwin should be kept out of prison. He thanked Shelley for the money 'in a style of freezing coldness'.[18]

Shelley would not waste the extra money he had gained from the settlement on paying debts; instead he would find new lodgings for them all, perhaps big enough for a larger commune. In the meantime he wanted to avoid creditors and it was as well to be out of London. So towards the end of April he took Mary for a couple of nights away alone to the Windmill Inn, Salt Hill, in modern Slough. Imagining herself a dormouse, she revelled in the 'green fields & acorns', thoroughly enjoying herself. They asked Claire to look out for the new lodgings while they were away, but, irritated by this trip *à deux*, she refused; so Mary asked Hogg to search instead.

It was possibly during this outing that Mary, happy to be parted from Claire, became pregnant again. Presumably she and Shelley did not try even her father's faulty contraceptive system: Godwin seems to have believed that he and Mary Wollstonecraft could avoid pregnancy by following the popular but discredited *Aristotle's Masterpiece*, which taught that frequent sex reduced the likelihood of conception – it was widely noted that whores were seldom pregnant – and that it occurred most easily during the few days after menstruation. Their daughter Mary had been the result of this faulty system.[19] Shelley probably knew more than Godwin, who was twice caught out when pregnancy ought to have been avoided. In 1819 Shelley wrote a note on contraception which might have referred to a vaginal sponge, a common method known to enlightened doctors in the early nineteenth century, and there are periods of literary busyness when perhaps he and Mary decided she should not get pregnant and so used this method. And yet Shelley impregnated Harriet at least once after the point where he considered his marriage dead, which surely he cannot have intended. On the whole it seems that he took little trouble and liked fathering children well enough; he imagined them growing up with his own views. But he was not much interested in the actual process of child-rearing – he was unconcerned with his and Harriet's children after an abortive effort to claim them.

On their return from Salt Hill, Shelley and Mary moved into 26 March-mont Buildings, off Brunswick Square. Claire came with them. Mary was freed from her presence only when, with the money Godwin considered his and which Shelley's creditors were demanding, Shelley paid for Claire to go on an extended visit to Lynmouth. Since her only outing in all these months was a few days away with her stepmother, Fanny must have been desperately in need of a break herself. But Shelley, so keen to lavish his money on visits for the other Godwins, failed to consider her needs.

Insult was added to injury when she found that Claire had left for Lynmouth the day before her own twenty-first birthday without any warning or farewell. She was deeply hurt. Claire explained that she and Shelley had kept Fanny in the dark because of her loyalty to the Godwins. Shelley had not forgotten her part in luring Claire away with bogus stories.

CHAPTER 21

CLAIRE

WHY DID CLAIRE go to Lynmouth in May 1815? And why should the Godwins not be told ahead of time? Why had Fanny not to know?

The answer to the first question is possibly that an irritable Mary could not take Claire's presence any longer and insisted on a period of separation. Having tried home once more, Claire was not prepared to return to Skinner Street, and the Godwins' respectable friends were not content to take her in. There were no welcoming Baxters on offer for this compromised teen-aged girl.

The answer to why no one in Skinner Street was allowed to know is less clear. Later Mrs Godwin pretended she had friends and relatives in Lynmouth and that her daughter had gone to these, but clearly the trip was undertaken without her knowledge.

Before Mary and Shelley took Claire with them on their elopement, Mary had perhaps followed her stepmother in seeing Claire as more or less a child. '[S]he is only sixteen,' wrote Mrs Godwin, 'and as childlike in her manners and tastes as if she were only twelve – no young man would feel much interest in her I think at present.'[1] Even when Claire went off with Shelley and Mary, Mrs Godwin continued to insist that Shelley saw Claire as a little sister. In Calais, where she pretended he had been pursued by Marshall, Shelley had been 'not in the least in love with [Claire]; but she is a nice little girl, and her mother is such a vulgar, commonplace woman, without an idea of philosophy, I do not think she is a proper person to form the mind of a young girl'.[2] The description of herself here sounds genuine and suggests some of the rest may be so too. Yet before the journey was over Mary would be irritated at the flirtation between Shelley and the 'nice little girl'.

That Claire was in love with Shelley in the erotically charged atmosphere of London after their return seems evident; that he was sleeping with both sisters is less clear. Many friends and onlookers assumed that he was; infatuated with his own sister-in-law, the radical journalist Leigh Hunt was told to follow Shelley's example and bed her. Ever since the triangular elopement of 1814 explicit rumours had been circulating about Shelley and Claire. Even Shelley's close friend Peacock mocked him for his 'two wives'. When Godwin suddenly called Shelley 'wicked', did he too suspect or know something, stung perhaps by what Claire had let slip while in Skinner Street?

Shelley encouraged Claire in a role that distinguished her from Mary. While he had yearned for the intellectual equal whom he now found in his knowledgeable lover, he also relished the mentor role which he had played with Harriet. Here the 'unformed' Claire was of more use; she was an eager pupil, a new Harriet but more moody, volatile and exciting. When taught by Shelley she even found a pleasure in learning the Greek characters and four tenses of the verb 'to strike'. Shelley had written of 'the irresi[s]tible wildness & sublimity' of Mary;[3] 'wildness' he could find in even greater abundance in Claire.

Much later, Shelley wrote of Claire as 'Constantia', a soaring comet (and the name of Charles Brockden Brown's heroine whom he had once so admired): 'O Comet beautiful and fierce, / Who drew the heart of this frail Universe/ Towards thine own'. He described a 'power' in Constantia/Claire which 'from thy touch like fire doth leap'.[4] Mary evoked ideas of sublimity; like Harriet before her, she rarely suggested anything quite so erotic as that fiery power.

The first time Shelley and Claire were indisputably alone together for a night was shortly after the death of Sir Bysshe at the beginning of 1815. Eager to know the contents of his grandfather's will, Shelley decided to visit Field Place. Leaving Mary alone just days before she gave birth, he went off with Claire to a village close to his old home, then continued on by himself, only to be refused entry at the door. Shelley and Claire stayed at least one night together in an inn, and possibly now at last, if not before, they became sexually intimate in the way Claire seemed long to have wanted. Shelley described himself as 'an harp responsive to every wind'.

Times alone were too few, and Claire became increasingly jealous of Mary through the early months of 1815. In turn Mary anxiously watched the growing emotional attachment of her lover and stepsister. Each young woman looked in the other for new signs or hints of intimacy.

Mary tended to become especially reserved at times of crisis and dramatic scandal. She and Claire were inveterate journal writers and record keepers but Mary's journal between 13 May 1815 and 21 July 1816 is missing. The loss may suggest that something more than her usual irritation at the flirtations and fugues of Shelley and Claire was occurring. She was pregnant again and must have noted that Shelley tended to look abroad at such times.

Mary's moody attitudes hint that she, like Claire, was jealous. She was desperate for her stepsister to go away and for a long period. This time Shelley agreed. Peacock offered to marry her for convenience but this was hardly a Wollstonecraftian act. Lynmouth was the answer, the place where Shelley had spent one of his most peaceful times with Harriet – Claire could stay in the same house with the kindly landlady. The £200 Shelley had kept back from Godwin could be used to finance her visit. She set out for Lynmouth on 13 May. When she finally heard of the trip, Mrs Godwin would gloss the cause: 'Mary was so jealous, Claire would not stay with her.'[5]

She was said to be in poor health. Perhaps it was her old liver complaint, but there were suspicions that Claire was hiding a more delicate predicament. If the trip was to cover up a pregnancy, the stratagem worked. At least Fanny was kept in the dark – or if she had suspicions she repressed them when she wrote to Claire. There is no mention of a baby from this time, so, if one existed, presumably it was miscarried, stillborn, aborted or secretly disposed of. Claire later showed herself devoted to a child but not determined to hold on to it.

In Devon, whatever her physical status, Claire calmed down; she wrote to Fanny in late May, 'After so much discontent, such violent scenes, such a turmoil of passion & hatred you will hardly believe how enraptured I am with this dear little quiet Spot.'[6] With Fanny she tried for a tone of weary sophistication, considering herself matured by the upheavals of the last months. Remote Lynmouth had a beach on the Bristol Channel and hills rose steeply behind it. The scene was not quite pastoral – too many scolding wives and drunken husbands – but the cottage had jasmine and honeysuckle over the window and a garden full of roses. It was a shame the two gentlemanly families were absent, Claire wrote.

Fanny doubted her stepsister could ever exist alone. Much later Claire admitted her loneliness in Lynmouth and portrayed the episode more dramatically: 'a mere child I was driven from all I loved into a solitary spot, without a friend to soothe my affliction, without even an acquaintance with whom to exchange a word, day after day I sat companionless upon that unfrequented sea-shore, mentally exclaiming, a life of sixteen years is already too much for me to bear.'[7]

The truth was somewhere between the two posturings. Claire was better pleased to be 'at Liberty' than if she had stayed with approved friends in London or with her parents in Skinner Street but she had to work hard to make herself and others believe that she was 'as happy when I go to bed as when I rise'. It is unlikely that she boasted to Mary, as she did to Fanny, about her enjoyment of the 'serene & uninterrupted rest I have long wished for': her conclusion that majestic mountains give 'a sober temperature of mind more truly delightful & satisfying than the gayest ebullitions of Mirth' would certainly have raised a smile in the stepsister so often irritated by her unseasonable spirits. Happy to be without Claire, Mary recorded, 'Clary goes', drew a line, then wrote, 'I begin a new journal with our regeneration.'[8]

In one way or another they had, over the winter, all been ailing. To invigorate themselves Shelley and Mary decided to follow Claire and take a holiday by the sea as well. When Shelley chose Torquay Mary must have glanced anxiously at the map and been relieved to discover that the resort was eighty-two miles from Lynmouth. They again took *Fleetwood* to read: the story of a man whose life was destroyed by jealousy.

By late June 1815 they were wandering around the West Country, talking of their next long-term move. Fleetwood's Wales had twice attracted Shelley: first Elan Valley, then Tremadoc. His experiences had been mixed but the scenery always beguiled him. Mary liked the idea – 'oh its much better [I] believe not to be able to see the light of the sun for mountains than for houses', she had written the year before; they would move to Wales and settle there. Like Harriet (and Mary Wollstonecraft before them) Mary often indulged a vision of ideal family life in a quiet rural place.

But the following week the plan changed. Now they must live in Windsor, to be near Peacock, who had moved out of London to Marlow, a small town on the Thames in Buckinghamshire. Shelley was constantly altering plans, lodgings and places to live, doing so without consulting anyone and without hesitating. But there is something more than his inordinate restlessness behind this particular change of purpose. There is also something obscure about the movements of all of them, including Claire, over these weeks.

On 1 July Shelley left Torquay bound for Marlow, where he would inspect a house for himself and Mary. A month later Mary appears to be staying alone in Clifton near Bristol. From there she wrote to Shelley at their old lodgings in Marchmont Street, Bloomsbury. He had, it seems, not found a house after all and Mary was weary of being without him; she was lonely and desperate to join him somewhere. She had a surge of fear that she had been abandoned.

What terrified her was that she had written several letters to Claire in Lynmouth and received no reply. The circumstance suggested that her stepsister was no longer in Devon. Could she have gone back to London to meet Shelley? Could Shelley and Claire be there alone together?

It was not an unreasonable fear. However Claire boasted in letters to Fanny of her inner resources and love of solitude, she longed for Shelley's company and she wrote to him often from Lynmouth. It was nearly a year since, as little more than adventurous children, they had all eloped to Switzerland; they now seemed centuries older. Whatever she had then been, Claire was, her stepsister knew, no longer a child.

Fear made Mary as abject as her mother had been when she felt Imlay withdrawing. 'I cannot bear to remain so long without you,' she wrote to her lover, 'pray pray do not stay away from me'. Then she asked directly: 'Pray is Clary with you?' [9]

Unlike Imlay, Shelley responded positively to the appeal, sorry that he had reduced Mary to such abjection. He took a comfortable house in Bishopsgate near Windsor Forest and Marlow with rural views and a staff of servants. Her comment on a later move catches her reaction: 'A house with a lawn a river or lake – noble trees & divine mountains that should be our little mousehole to retire to – But never mind this – give me a garden & *absentia Clariae.*'[10]

In early August he and Mary were settled in Bishopsgate together and Claire was once more in Lynmouth. If she had indeed been alone with Shelley in London and had made a bid for his exclusive or paramount love, she had failed. She was not invited to the Bishopsgate house any more than Fanny or Harriet; Mary had '*absentia Clariae*' at last. Peacock was present but the commune of women was for the moment in abeyance.

While no invitation went to Fanny, and she did not yet presume to visit without it, Charles Clairmont did come to stay. Thoroughly sick of Skinner Street and its crises, he much approved their calm life of reading and boating. Shelley had even abandoned the vegetarianism which had been so taxing to his pregnant women; he ate mutton chops and drank beer. It seemed idyllic.

Yet Shelley was not content. He remained unmoored. He did not want an exclusive relationship with Mary and never quite settled into even intellectual domesticity: there would always be a gap between himself and those he loved, between the real and the ideal – the 'anti-type' of 'all that is best and most beautiful in the world'.[11] And he continued to hanker after the sexual freedom that had been so inspiring in James Lawrence's exotic romance of free love, a freedom that would take the individual to a higher plane of experience than mere sex with an individual woman. He had translated Godwin's earlier hatred of enforced monogamy into something altogether more yearning and transcendental. He might have said of love as he did of political change: 'I am one of those whom nothing will fully satisfy.'[12]

He was writing a new long poem, *Alastor,* in which he depicted an explicit but strangely unfocused and self-centred, almost ruthless sexuality; it warred here with an equally seductive death. Harriet had accused Shelley of losing his political edge, his care for others, his care for her, his care for anyone but himself; his father shrewdly remarked of this new poem that his son showed in it he 'wants to find out one person on earth the Prototype of himself'. Much later Mary herself commented that *Alastor*, in contrast to *Queen Mab* with its sympathy and hope, 'contains an individual interest only'.[13] Despite its richness and possibilities, Harriet could have been forgiven if she had found in it an allegory of herself as the worthy and modest Arab maiden who brings food and watches over the hero, and of Mary as the passionate veiled maid into whose 'panting bosom' and 'dissolving arms' he folds his frame. Or perhaps Mary might wonder if he could possibly mean herself and Claire.

᠁

In October, paid for by Shelley, Claire visited Ireland with her brother Charles. He was turning his back on the bookshop and investigating prospects of joining a distillery firm. But without the necessary capital nothing came of the idea and both Charles and Claire were again in London by the end of the year. She was still living off Shelley, who in March sent her £41. With the odd night in Skinner Street she was now alone in London, part of the time in their old lodgings in Arabella Row where Mary's baby had died. There were intermittent visits from Shelley but most of the time she was by herself in the city. It was an exhilarating existence for a young girl of seventeen.

Shelley had, she knew, encouraged a relationship between Mary and Hogg; probably he had had one with her. Why could she not now love where she wished? Why could she not become a fully fledged 'Nairess', as in Lawrence's romance, choosing her man rather than waiting to be chosen? Claire had always wanted to behave with éclat; now was her chance. There were other fascinating, scandalous men besides Shelley in the world and one was, unlike him, famous as a poet. Probably Claire mentioned the idea to Shelley; he would surely have approved and encouraged it.

Lord Byron was the most celebrated writer of the day, dominating the literary marketplace, lionised in all the salons of London. He had irrupted sensationally on to the literary scene in 1811 with his exotic epic *Childe Harold*. Even the daughters of the intellectual Godwin household read his poetry and responded to his popular image. During their quick courtship, Shelley and Mary pored over his early love verses, and when the three of them were together in lodgings they read his *Lara,* an oriental tale of a dark moody hero whom all of London associated with its aristocratic author. Byron had become a romantic idol and it would have been strange if the young girls in Skinner Street had not day-dreamed a little about him. The Byronic hero would appear obsessively in Mary's later fiction, as Claire noted. Even Fanny would beg tales of the romantic lord and find excitement and solace in *Lara*.

In January 1815 after a career of bisexuality which included a very noisy affair with the married Lady Caroline Lamb, who sent him locks of her pubic hair, Byron had married the cousin of Lady Caroline's husband, Annabella Milbanke, and moved into a grand house in Piccadilly. Before the year was out Lady Byron, scandalised by her husband's revelations and violent, manic behaviour, close she thought to insanity, slipped out of the marital home with her newborn baby and rejoined her parents. She would never live with him again and Byron had seen the last of his daughter. By January 1816 a separation had been agreed and the whole of London knew that Lady Byron accused her husband of attempting to bugger her and of incest with his half-sister Augusta. Byron was shocked at his wife's departure, which he seems not to have expected: 'she – or rather – the Separation – has broken my heart – I feel as if an Elephant has trodden on it … I breathe lead.' The separation had as extreme social as emotional results: it 'has literally made me as much an object of proscription – as any political plot could have done – & exactly the same as if I had been condemned for some capital offence', Byron wrote.[14]

With most of fashionable London ignoring him, he was planning to leave England as soon as possible. In no mood for further scandals, he was perhaps more open to new acquaintances. In any case it was difficult to resist a persistent, bubbly, attractive girl like Claire. Comically echoing Shelley's first letter to Godwin – 'You will be surprised at hearing from a stranger' – Claire approached him as an 'utter stranger', one who stood 'on the edge of a precipice'. She, a woman of 'unstained' reputation without guardian or husband, was throwing herself on his mercy and confessing her love 'with a beating heart'. It was of the utmost 'importance' that he see her. Byron replied warily, 'Ld.B. is not aware of any "importance" which can be attached by any person to an interview with him – & more particularly by one with whom it does not appear that he has the honour of being acquainted.'[15]

Several more letters from Claire gave her romantic life story as a sort of wild child thrown on the world, equivalent to the heroine of 'The Ideot', a story she had begun during the elopement two years before, a Godwinian girl educated in 'mountains & deserts', knowing only her own impulses and committing 'every violence against received opinion', but amiable, noble and sweet as well. She probably sent the story to Byron as part of her self-presentation. Her letters were signed with a signature and seal provided by Shelley that suggested a gentry status.

Later in life Claire portrayed herself in vulnerable terms, as a young and poor 'romantic girl'.[16] At the time she appeared brazen and pushy, but Byron was not displeased with the effect she made when he granted her an interview in late March 1816 in Drury Lane. Claire was entranced at the attention from a man whose amorous verses and sultry oriental tales enthralled all London.

For the moment he was impressed. Claire, just eighteen, had a fine singing voice. It would inspire Shelley to ecstatic sexual poetry: 'The blood is listening in my frame'. Now Byron addressed to her one of his most charming lyrics:

> There be none of Beauty's daughters
>> With a magic like thee;
> And like music on the waters
>> Is thy sweet voice to me: ...
> ... the spirit bows before thee,
> To listen and adore thee;
> With a full but soft emotion,
> Like the swell of Summer's ocean.[17]

It was enough to turn a wiser and older head than Claire's. Soon she had her way with him. For Byron it was a casual affair, one of many, but there was some piquancy in it: he enjoyed trying to shock her by showing her letters in cipher from his half-sister Augusta, hinting at the erotic nature of the relationship.

In practice Claire was as unconventional as Byron; in theory probably more so. With literature as midwife, especially the writings of Mary Wollstonecraft, she was being reborn as a youthful freethinker who was prepared, like her heroine, to flout convention and follow desire. By her mid teens Claire had become both erotically and emotionally experimental. Mary Wollstonecraft had more than once suggested a *ménage à trois*. Claire had already tried this route. In her last novel, *Maria*, Wollstonecraft advised women to gain experience 'while experience is worth having, and acquire sufficient fortitude to pursue your own happiness'.[18] Claire was ready.

She appealed to Byron for what they had in common; yet they were at different stages: he was paying for his nonconformity while she was just beginning to savour hers. To him she was a rather wayward, 'odd-headed girl', and he had little sense of her potential as an adult. To her Byron was an exciting development, a super Shelley all of her own. Her fascination for this celebrity of the day hid from her his ultimately sexist views of women.

Her forwardness was not unexpected in a girl who had lived around Shelley and Mary for the last year and a half and told her parents of her 'total contempt for the laws and institutions of society'. It might suggest once more that the relationship with Shelley had at one stage become sexual and that she now regarded herself as a woman who could seduce rather than wait for seduction. Or, since she claimed she would give Byron something he did not expect, she might have been referring to her virginity – the surprise could hardly be a child since it was too soon for that, nor would Byron much have welcomed it. Whatever the facts, so began what she later called her ten minutes of '*happy passion*'.[19] She would be pregnant almost at once.

For all her pushiness, Claire had an inkling that Byron might not want her for long or for herself alone. She bombarded him with importunate letters: 'I do not expect you to love me; I am not worthy of your love, I feel you are superior.'[20] Like Mary fearing that she appealed to Shelley primarily through her parentage, Claire came to suspect that for Byron her charm was her connection with Shelley and the Godwins, a group nearly as notorious as himself. Byron claimed he admired *Queen Mab*, which Shelley had sent him, and he was enthusiastic about Godwin's novels – once, hearing that Godwin was in 'dire need', he had offered to donate to him £600 from his publisher's payments – though a later publishing dispute allowed the Tory John Murray to ensure that no funds reached the old radical. Claire knew Byron would be intrigued by the daughter of Godwin and Mary Wollstonecraft. It was a trophy she could bring him.

For all his fascination, Byron was cautious. Other people's unconventionality did not much appeal to him, and he tended to see Shelley's high-minded sexual freedom in terms of his own louche libertinism. But he allowed Claire to propose a meeting between himself and Mary. For it Claire was anxious to control his behaviour: Mary was ignorant of the sexual affair and Byron must not judge her by her stepsister. Mary had a scandalous reputation but she was a proper lady in manner.

Mary was intrigued and a meeting was arranged, stage-managed by Claire, who was almost offering Mary to Byron, rather in the way Shelley had offered Hogg to Harriet and Mary. After the encounter she told each of the good effect made on the other. She also used that of Byron on Mary to pry out his destination abroad – Geneva in Switzerland – information he might have been loth to confide to the ardent Claire. Although she told him that the Shelley ménage was waiting to hear further news about Sir Bysshe's estate before travelling to the Continent, Byron cannot have imagined they would so suddenly be influenced by his own movements.

While busy seducing Byron, Claire continued to crave Shelley's admiration as much as ever: when Byron called her 'a little fiend', she teasingly asked Shelley whether she was not rather of a 'gentle disposition'. Writing to Byron the next morning she flirtatiously repeated Shelley's flattering response and suggestively referred to him as the 'man whom I have loved & for whom I have suffered much'.[21] Shelley and Byron enjoyed terrorising their women companions with their devilish ways and imaginings. Claire exploited their similarity.

CHAPTER 22

HARRIET

ALTHOUGH SHELLEY PROBABLY accepted and encouraged Claire's pursuit of Byron, it meant that during these months he was missing her wholehearted attention. On 24 January 1816 in Bishopsgate Mary had given birth to her second child, a boy whom they named William in honour of Godwin (soon he was affectionately known as Willmouse). He was less puny than her first infant and she hoped his star would be more fortunate. It was thus a moment similar to the time when Harriet had been in Bracknell with her new baby, Ianthe, taking less notice than usual of her husband. Although keen on women breastfeeding, Shelley was impatient with infants and too much mother-love; later Mary fancied 'your affection will encrease when [Willmouse] has a nursery to himself and only comes to you just dressed and in good humour'.[1]

With his lover out of town and involved with the new baby, and Claire preoccupied with Byron, Shelley was often alone in London, pursuing a lawsuit with his father while trying to borrow more money for Godwin. Unusually, then, he was without constant female companionship.

Throughout this time Harriet was still living in her father's house. She was, however, a married woman and not always chaperoned. Perhaps now, despairing of her husband's return, she met and was attracted to another man. There were two barracks with numerous army officers quite close to Chapel Street. If she took a lover he may have been the Colonel Maxwell whom Godwin named to his Scottish friend William Baxter. Many years later Claire, presumably taking her facts from her mother, mentioned 'a Captain in the Indian or Wellington army' who had become Harriet's lover; he was sent abroad and, according to Claire, Harriet assumed he had abandoned her as Shelley had done.[2] This would be horrifying, for somewhere during the spring or early summer of 1816 Harriet had become pregnant.

But there remain arguments against the Captain Maxwell scenario. In June 1816 Harriet was writing from her father's house, where her sister was with her. She offered aid to Mr Newton whose wife, Cornelia, was fatally ill: if Harriet could be of any help to her and her children she would 'fly to give comfort to the distressed'.[3] Some time in the summer she also visited Mrs Boinville at Bracknell to console her during her sister's illness. There she gossiped bitterly about Mary and Shelley, gossip with which Mrs Godwin was regaled when she visited in September and which in part caused her to turn ruthlessly on Fanny. These images of Harriet do not fit well with a woman in the midst of an affair or concerned with the retention or loss of a new lover.

There can be an alternative explanation. Since baby Charles Bysshe as the heir had been demanded in court to make legal various financial transactions – he never actually came – Shelley had had to deal with Harriet; he therefore called round at Chapel Street. She was still in love with him, still receptive to his charm. Her father was largely supporting her and his grandchildren, and he would wish a reconciliation between husband and wife for everyone's sake, including his own. He would want to give the young couple every opportunity to be alone and to learn to love each other again. Claire later declared that, after many quarrels, Shelley and Harriet 'embraced'.

It is not impossible, then, that, during a visit in the spring of 1816, while Mary was preoccupied in Bishopsgate and Claire was gadding around with Byron, Shelley once more found sympathetic companionship with the loving Harriet, still legally his wife, still very young and beautiful, and that he made her pregnant for a third and last time.[4]

Crabb Robinson, who knew of Harriet's new pregnancy and later interested himself in a custody case concerning Shelley's children which the lawyer Basil Montagu was pursuing for Shelley, remarked: 'It is singular that it was not suggested to Basil Montagu by Shelley that he was not the father of his wife's child. Mrs. Godwin had stated this to me as a fact. Basil

Montagu thinks it improbable.'[5] The 'child' here might be Charles Bysshe, the heir, since Mrs Godwin had been suggesting that Harriet was unfaithful to Shelley *before* he abandoned her, but it is an odd expression for a living, named boy and in a case concerning his custody. If Charles Bysshe was not Shelley's he would not be the Shelley heir: surely if Shelley was suing for custody of a boy Crabb Robinson had heard Mrs Godwin say was not his biologically, he would have made more of it in this passage – his diaries do go into considerable detail.

So, although the words bear various interpretations and may be diary shorthand for longer conversations, they may also be construed to mean that Shelley did not declare to his lawyer that Harriet had not been made pregnant by him. This was curious if he had any doubts, since, although the unborn child was not an issue in the case, Shelley needed to denigrate Harriet – and consequently his opponents the Westbrooks – as thoroughly as he could. A child conceived out of wedlock – even if their marriage existed only on paper and Shelley had deserted her – could still be used to impugn his wife's morals.

CHAPTER 23

FANNY

IN HIS IMAGINATION Shelley constantly saw the hoped-for revolutions in society and psychology as volcanic eruptions. In reality volcanoes could be disastrous. In April 1815 Mount Tambora erupted on the island of Sumbawa in present Indonesia, killing 92,000 people. It resulted in a huge cloud of dust which by the spring of 1816 had settled into the stratosphere over Europe. Sunlight was diverted back into space and the lands beneath the cloud became dark, dank and melancholy. The cause of the dark spring and summer was unknown until the twentieth century, but the effects were noted all over Europe.

Travelling down from Scotland in late April, Godwin was caught in deep snow. In Hampshire Jane Austen contemplated the damp cottage walls and swollen pond and wrote in what would be her last completed novel about her heroine Anne Elliot's autumnal depression and loss of bloom. All over the country rain fell and the spring became the coldest in recorded history. The year of Mary Wollstonecraft's death had seen unusual storms and turbulence, and both Fanny and Mary had been raised on stories of that memorable year. This was worse.

Fanny was feeling the full weight of her mother's legacy. All the young women in the Godwin household shared the excitement of her ideas; they accepted the value of female as well as male intellectual effort, but all of them knew or were learning the difference between male and female narratives, the coincidence of free love and pregnancy for women, the male ability to skip out of family and country when matters became too complicated. With her troubled life and demanding theories, Mary Wollstonecraft's was sometimes a difficult inheritance. For Fanny she was in addition a woman who had twice thought to kill herself and abandon her child.

Godwin wrote, 'The human intellect is a sort of barometer, directed in its variations by the atmosphere which surrounds it.'[1] With the departure in 1814 of Shelley, Mary and Claire, Fanny was left only with Godwin as an emotional and intellectual anchor. Mary Hays, an admirer from twenty years earlier, remarked of him, 'I respected his reason, but I doubted whether I could inspire him with sympathy, or make him fully comprehend my feelings.' His daughter Mary told a friend that Godwin's 'feelings or passions ... were very faint. He professed to be guided by reason in all things. Pathetic and sentimental passages in books he skipped as nonsense.'[2] With her tendency to be moved by life and literature, Fanny must have irked him with her feeling heart and overflowing sympathy.

And Godwin was more self-absorbed than ever. Crabb Robinson remarked, 'He made me feel my inferiority unpleasantly'; on one occasion he described his friend 'in high spirits, but hardly in good spirits. He laughs long and loud without occasion, and mingles with this causeless hilarity great irritability. He is vehement and intolerant.'[3] Coleridge reported a conversation to Southey, '"Yes–Sir! just so! – of Mr Southey – just what I said –["] and so on more Godwiniano – in language so ridiculously and exclusively appropriate to himself, that it would have made you merry – it was even as if he was looking into a sort of moral Looking-Glass, without knowing what it was, & seeing his own very very Godwinship, had by a merry conceit christened it in your name, not without some annexment of me & Wordsworth'. More cattily he continued, 'I was disgusted at Heart with the grossness & vulgar Insanocaecity of this dim-headed Prig of a Philosophicide.'[4] Godwin abused Wordsworth, Coleridge and Southey for selling out to the government, but he was no doubt irritable with others for less serious offences. Fanny was always on hand.

With mingled anxiety and eagerness she had played her role as go-between. She had been warmed by her close relation with Shelley and Mary, and occasionally Claire, but she had also known their criticism, their mockery of her poor spirit and their lack of concern about her life and future. When Mary and Shelley seemed so comfortably settled in Bishopsgate she felt even more excluded – her temporary intimacy with them had lapsed with their need for her.

When Willmouse was born, Shelley wrote at once to Skinner Street to give the news, making the bitter point that at least Fanny and her stepmother would be glad to hear that Mary was safe. After the first birth, while Claire and Shelley rambled round town, Fanny had rushed to her sister's side and, when the baby died, she had struggled to visit Mary through the pouring rain. But this time her presence seemed uncalled for and she did not see her little nephew for a month. Then, still without an invitation, she took matters into her own hands and simply travelled out to Bishopsgate.

She arrived late in the evening just as Shelley and Mary were settling down to sleep. She knocked at the door and told them she had come to see how they were; she stayed talking until half past three, leaving the room only so that Shelley and Mary could finally get some sleep. Since this was the time when decisions had to be made about her own future and relationship with the aunts in Dublin, she might have wanted to consult them as well as see the new baby. Or perhaps she thought they might ask her to stay with them there and then, especially since Claire was absent. It was a fair distance from London to Bishopsgate for a young woman to travel alone, and it was not cheap. But Mary had not got rid of one sister only to have another thrust on her.

Fanny had pressing reason for wanting to escape Skinner Street, for matters had deteriorated still further between the two households and she was, as ever, caught in the cross-fire. In February 1816, entangled again in a dispute with his father and creditors and constantly importuned by Godwin for the £200 he thought he was owed from the previous payout, Shelley had echoed the fictional character Fleetwood by declaring, 'I shall certainly not delay to depart from the haunts of men.'[5] Godwin was appalled – Hogan, his most pressing creditor, was hassling him for £300, and his friend Josiah Wedgwood, less patient than his dead brother Tom, was demanding his long-owed £500. So Godwin tried to be conciliatory. He lamented the estrangement. While he would never condone what Shelley had done, he might just forgive, he said.

The effort lacked tact. Shelley was sick of the hypocrisy, of Godwin's harshness and cruelty, of the contempt they had to put up with. Godwin confused him, Mary and Claire, with 'prostitutes and seducers'. 'Do not talk of *forgiveness*', he snapped, 'my blood boils in my veins'. Shelley asked the question long avoided between them: why was the older man so right-eous? How could he for the sake of getting money continue corresponding with a man he declared he hated – and in so haughty a manner? Several of Godwin's friends, Crabb Robinson for example, were similarly bemused.

The quarrel spiralled upwards in high literary style, concluding with Godwin's declaration that 'torture cannot wring from me an approbation of the act that separated us'.[6] When on 24 March Shelley called three times at Skinner Street he was refused admittance. It cannot have been comfortable in a home where Fanny alone tried to defend Mary and her lover.

With the distance between the two households she could no longer take messages as before, and Charles was not around to negotiate either. He had grown sick of his nagging mother – thirteen-year-old William called her an 'untamed outlaw' – and disgusted with the 'unworthy occupations' of the bookshop; so, after the failure of the distillery scheme he had, with financial help from Shelley, decamped to France, from where he refused to write to any of them.[7] It was a great blow to the Godwins and their creditors – and to Fanny, left more isolated than ever. Even Marshall hardly came to the house now, for he too was deep in debt. As a result the main role of negotiator fell on Tom Turner.

Godwin had supported Turner in his law studies, so he was an obvious alternative to Charles and Fanny. But, since Shelley had two years earlier attempted to seduce his beautiful wife Cornelia, his involvement was bound to inflame the situation. Turner had not forgotten; he did not like Shelley and always thought him stagey and histrionic. He now began to insinuate that the failure to supply instant money was choice rather than inability – 'If he is really inclined to get the money there is no doubt of his power to do so,' he wrote to Godwin.[8] Initially Shelley suspected Turner only of having 'entirely misapprehended the whole case'; five months later he accused him of acting with 'duplicity', eventually concluding that he had 'some malignant passions' which he sought to gratify.[9]

Though not able to travel and negotiate, Fanny was still the main social link between them all, deputed to write to Mary and Shelley from Godwin about his needs. As a result she felt acutely that she was in the middle of the rift being widened by Tom Turner. Whatever her own views, she was again implicated in the quarrel on the Godwins' side. In the furious letters her stepfather made her write he left no room for a postscript from his scribe, nowhere for Fanny to express her sense that there should be no sides or even that she felt on the wrong one.

Since Mary and Shelley had gone off without her in 1814 she had rarely been entirely happy but, now deprived of them once more, she felt even less valued. Godwin seemed to have stopped talking much to her and their communal excursions, dinners and trips to the theatre had become less frequent. She brooded alone over a missing letter from Aunt Everina, wondering whether Godwin had received and replied to it. If so, what had he said? What could they all be plotting? At the back of her mind was always the sense of her diminished future, the life of schoolteaching in Ireland which, as matters continued to deteriorate in Skinner Street, Mrs Godwin must often have told her to prepare for.

In the spring Everina had come to visit the Godwins, most likely to discuss Fanny's future and, as usual, the Primrose Street property. The rents had now collapsed altogether. If, despite their straitened circumstances, her aunts still wished to have her, either they were in no hurry or Fanny was reluctant to join them, since she did not return to Ireland with Everina as might be expected. Instead they parted out of sorts with each other. Again it was sad that aunt Eliza Bishop's failing health prevented her from taking the lead in dealings with her niece. For someone in low spirits the bracing and abrasive Everina was not the best tonic. The delay must have aggravated Mrs Godwin: Fanny was, after all, nearly twenty-two. Like the brother contemplating his sister in Jane Austen's *The Watsons*, Mrs Godwin probably made it clear to her stepdaughter that she was now a weight upon the family.

Back in Dublin Everina had written a long letter to Skinner Street. This is the one that had gone astray. Waiting for it, Fanny felt the oppressive silence. She wondered in her usual way whether she was to blame. Had Everina been offended, perhaps by her reluctance? Given her stepmother's obvious desire to be rid of her in these dismal months when she was without either of her own children, Fanny was anxious to show she had not alienated her only close relatives.

Finally, a note came from Everina and Fanny was relieved. The silence had been due to the loss of the letter and to her aunt's 'anxieties and sufferings'. Even when she had been Fanny's age, Everina had liberally complained of her health and spirits, as Mary Wollstonecraft had remarked while grumbling back. Fanny must have noticed how much she had in common in temperament and situation with her Wollstonecraft family.

She replied at once, but, ignorant of the contents of the lost letter, she wrote uncertainly. She imagined her aunt had written about her again going to Ireland but was anxious neither to seem to assume this nor to let Everina assume she would accept. She could promise only to 'answer [the letter] in the most deliberate and frank manner' when another copy was sent. Her main purpose now was to show 'how much affected, I am by the return of your confidence, and affection, which I trust my conduct and character will secure to me through life, even under the greatest misfortunes'. Whatever they had felt earlier, her aunts had evidently overcome any worries they may have had about the outrageous doings of her sisters: Fanny was untouched by Mary's and Claire's scandals. Eliza was ailing and Everina was worried about her and their work – presumably the illness further depleted their income. Eliza had had rheumatic pains when young and they had probably continued. Fanny wished she could be of use but it was, she said, 'impossible'.[10]

The word is difficult to interpret. Was she simply too far away and so could do nothing? Or was it 'impossible' for her to leave the Godwins? Curiously she made no offer of specific help to Everina, perhaps feeling it presumptuous. Or, despite being grateful to her aunts, perhaps she feared being sent to them from everything she held dear. It sounds as though she valued Everina and Eliza's continued affection but was also pretty desperate not to have to go to them. She was even thinking of moving to France instead – maybe with Shelley and Mary when they travelled abroad, as they declared they intended to do. Her head ran on possibilities and she suggested that 'a trip to the Continent' would benefit her sickly Aunt Eliza. The suggestion, when received, must have reminded Eliza of her many years of longing for Mary Wollstonecraft to rescue her and transport her to a welcoming France.

The day before Fanny wrote back to her aunts, Godwin set out for Edinburgh to negotiate with his publisher about his new novel, *Mandeville,* which he intended soon to finish. In December 1815 he had asked Constable, to whom Charles had been apprenticed, for a £500 advance to give him sufficient peace of mind for this project. He was confident of his abilities: comparing himself with the most famous novelist of the day, Walter Scott, he wrote, 'my talent for novel-writing is not inferior to that of any known author now living'.[11] Not persuaded, the experienced publisher declined, and offered the sum in exchange for half of Godwin's royalties; the money would come only when Godwin handed over two volumes in January 1817. They agreed terms and signed the contract in Edinburgh.

Godwin was pleased: 'All is well,' he wrote home to Skinner Street. As in Ireland sixteen years earlier, his welcome in Scotland had been 'flattering', with many people desiring to see 'the monster'.[12] He had his portrait painted and met the famous Edinburgh literati, Dugald Stewart and Francis Jeffrey; he dined with the novelist Henry Mackenzie, stayed a night with Walter Scott at his home in Abbotsford and on his way back visited a quarrelsome Wordsworth at Rydal Mount. Now, returning to London after a month, he was feeling like an important man again, 'on fire' to get on with his work. He hoped that Shelley would organise a settlement for him to take his mind off money.

His hopes were soon dashed. He entered his house in Skinner Street to discover that, the day before, Shelley, Mary, Claire and Willmouse had all run off again. Shelley had always planned a continental trip in the future but Claire had, it seems, persuaded him to go at once to Geneva. So a week after Byron left England, Shelley, Mary and Claire were en route, wrongly expecting him to be in Geneva before they arrived. From Dover Shelley wrote to Skinner Street, 'I leave England – I know not, perhaps forever.' Godwin had, he said, first inspired his understanding: 'It is unfortunate for me that the part of your character which is least excellent should have been met by my convictions of what was right to do.' More to the point, he stated, 'I shall receive nothing from my father except in the way of charity. Post Obit concerns are very doubtful.'[13] To Godwin's horror it sounded like a valedictory letter. Yet Shelley promised the Godwins £300 in the course of the summer.

Gossip started immediately. Once again the baronet's heir had gone off with two young ladies – and to a fashionable continental resort where the wicked Lord Byron was known to be heading. The papers expected considerable copy. Rumours were everywhere. It was even said that Byron was having an affair with a Mrs Shelley. Godwin preyed mercilessly on Shelley, to be sure, but it sometimes seemed that Shelley studied to make Godwin an object of mockery.

He was furious. Why had they not waited for him to return? In fact, tired of his high-minded frostiness and belligerent demands, Shelley had chosen the day for departure precisely to avoid Godwin. When rebuked for his secrecy, he responded, 'we are not on those intimate terms as to permit that I should have minutely explained to you the motives which determined my departure … I can easily imagine that you were disquieted by it.'[14]

CHAPTER 24

FANNY

THIS SECOND REMOVAL again turned Fanny's world upside down. Shelley and Mary had gone off once more without consulting or telling her – or taking her with them. And again they had favoured Claire. They had, too, removed Willmouse, whom she had come to love: 'I sometimes consider him as my child & look forward to the time of my old age & his manhood,' she would later write.[1] Fanny and Harriet were left behind, each living in a house with disapproving parents. Obsessed with the same couple, they could make no common cause. Each brooded alone.

For Fanny, Shelley's and Mary's departure came at the worst possible moment, for she and her sister had just quarrelled. Mary had snapped at her, declaring her 'sordid or vulgar' for worrying about Godwin's money and for not siding with them against him. Fanny was stung by the accusation. She had come to accept her sister's schizophrenic attitude to Godwin, but she thought it strange that she was being blamed for loyalty to *Mary's* father. In an emotional letter to her sister, despite a lifetime of calling Godwin 'Papa', she pointedly referred to him as 'your father'.

The abrupt exit had prevented any reconciliation and Mrs Godwin could build on this while Shelley and Mary were away. She taunted Fanny with her unappreciated loyalty and love. Perhaps taking a hint from comments made by Claire when she had visited Skinner Street, she now told her stepdaughter that she was a figure of fun to Shelley and Mary, that they constantly made her their laughing stock, the butt of satiric remarks. Combined with Mary's accusations of sordidness and vulgarity, such revelations of contempt were hard to bear.

And always she continued to grieve for the poor and downtrodden she saw around her and worry over what could be wrong with the country. Years later Mary would admit that she herself was often accused of 'lukewarmness' in reforming causes; she was not, like Godwin, her mother and Shelley, passionate about bettering the world. She wanted people to improve but she saw this happening naturally. In 1838 she would admit, 'I have never written a word in disfavour of liberalism but neither have I openly supported it.' Fanny was different, closer in this respect to Mary Wollstonecraft, who felt deeply the social woes of her country. Fanny always experienced others' miseries on her pulse and was desperately sad when she thought things could not quickly change.

Yet she could also stand back and analyse what was happening. Part of the trouble was meteorological in this dark year, for by now the volcanic effect from Tambora had reached England with a vengeance. A Norwich creditor called in his debt from Godwin 'owing to the distress of the country'. It was late in the summer and yet the harvest was still green in the fields: 'I fear the sun will not come this year to ripen it,' mused Fanny. Indeed, they were heading for the worst crop failure of the century. The *Cambrian* newspaper reported that the apple and pear trees in Herefordshire had suffered 'severely from blights' and would yield only a sparse crop.[2] There were few strawberries, that fruit that best expressed an English summer, and Harriet in Chapel Street lamented she could not send summer fruit to her sick friend Mrs Newton because of the cold spring. In Skinner Street the Godwins lit fires in their rooms each day.

Political troubles complemented the dreary weather. After the elation of victory at Waterloo in 1815 the national mood had soured. No longer could hatred of France bolster patriotism; people began to look more closely at the class-ridden society they had defended. Fanny was restless, curious to know the whys and wherefores of people's sufferings. Why with military victory had the poor sunk further into poverty?

A Corn Bill had been passed regulating imports to keep prices high and prevent a sudden collapse in the incomes of landowners; its effect on the lower ranks was harsh and vicious, especially as wartime enclosures had pushed many from their small pieces of land and taken their rights to common pasturage. The huge national debt, run up over twenty-two years of war, could only be paid off in peace with a thriving economy, of which there was little sign. Crabb Robinson, who often called on the Godwins, remarked that 'England is destined, having survived the shock of War, to sink under her financial embarrassments. I am persuaded that England must *decline*.'[3] The shortfall was made up by heavy taxes.

Fanny tried to talk of the popular miseries with Godwin, to hear him explain the cause of the distresses she saw all around her. But she noticed he did not much heed them. His visions were more abstract, more principled, more about the moral than the social economy. Although so antagonistic, he seemed close to the *mode* of the government, which thought it could avoid working-class agitation by controlling moral thought and building churches. Shelley too, though troubled by social injustice, tended to see it in general hyperbolic terms: the groans of the wretched unheeded amidst the infamous revelry of the rich. Sometimes he satisfied himself with the unpleasing traces of misery: in the Lake District he had noted that industry contaminated a 'peaceful vale and deformed the loveliness of Nature with human taint'; dead children were found floating in the river, killed by their working mothers.[4] Often he had helped the industrious poor but he tended to recoil from the fecklessly destitute; Fanny felt for the suffering, whether worthy or unworthy.

She pieced together what she could about causes and remedies from her own observations, from newspapers and opinions of acquaintances such as David Booth, the friend Mary had met as a young girl in Scotland three years before. Booth told her that peace had brought the end of the country's manufacturing dominance; now the Continent was free to rival Britain's industries, to make its own goods and pay lower wages. So, as Fanny put it, 'millions of our fellow countrymen [are] left to starve'. A few months later the truth of this was brought home to Booth when he witnessed food riots in Dundee. Meanwhile the British navy no longer needed canvas, and his parents-in-law, the Baxters, were reduced to poverty when their business collapsed; their employees were laid off.

Even hope for the future was suspended. The glut of English manufactured goods would not be used up for seven years. It was a long time – a third of Fanny's life. In Staffordshire and Shropshire, Ironbridge and the

Potteries, those centres of the early Industrial Revolution, there were, Fanny heard, 26,000 unemployed men. Meanwhile the Bilston colliers were dragging huge wagons of coal from the Midlands all the way down to St Albans and Oxford. They were heading towards London and Carlton House in the touching, futile hope that the Prince Regent, living there in his usual extravagance, would listen to them and make things right. Disliking such direct approaches, the government sent magistrates to St Albans to keep the colliers out of London.

Fanny was also helped towards understanding by Robert Owen, with whom she agreed and disagreed. In the summer of 1816 he came to dine at Skinner Street and talked lengthily with her about the state of the nation. She thought about his words. She was Godwinian enough to realise that a change of government ministers would never be enough; a change of system was wanted. But she did sometimes wonder if, instead of waiting for Godwin's individual transformations of mind, the country might do better listening to Robert Owen's more paternalistic socialist views, based as they were on a thorough understanding of the evils of industrialism.

Following his journey to inspect conditions in factories, where he had seen children under ten abused and crippled by working fourteen hours a day in hot, polluted conditions, Owen had been pressing Parliament to regulate industry and ensure better conditions for labourers. He had his strong utopian side as well: he imagined a time when all men would be equal and no one would have to work more than two or three hours a day. It sounded attractive.

Yet, thinking over the ideas, Fanny came to the conclusion that they were too 'romantic'. They demanded action from the top: they took power from those needing help and depended too thoroughly on the rich agreeing to give up their riches. To achieve success, reformers had to do business with the rulers (something Godwin deplored). Also, although she confessed herself 'sick at heart' when she contemplated the misery of her countrymen, the utopian notion of equality that Owen held troubled her. She could not at once put her finger on what was wrong.

Probably they also discussed education – Fanny remembered her visit with Aaron Burr to Lancaster's school in 1812, an experiment Owen had supported though uneasy at some of the methods. He insisted that he himself had improved on the approach in his own New Lanark schools.

Learning from the Swiss educational reformer Pestalozzi, he believed that no child should ever be punished; only affection for the teacher could make pupils dutiful – they should be spoken to 'with a pleasant voice and in a kind manner'. Such ideas would have struck a nerve with sensitive Fanny, who had known rather different treatment for much of her life, and they fitted well with what Mary Wollstonecraft had proposed. Other aspects of the curriculum might have surprised her – and certainly displeased Godwin: children were not to be 'annoyed with books', Owen ruled, but instructed by familiar conversation and entertained by singing and dancing lessons.[5]

Owen admitted to difficulties in finding suitable teachers to follow his methods in his schools; perhaps Fanny was desperate (and idealistic) enough fleetingly to hope for a position in a village school in Scotland rather than one in Dublin with one disagreeable aunt.

CHAPTER 25

MARY

AS THEY LEFT England, Claire wrote gaily to Byron that he was about
to receive 'the whole tribe of the Otaheite philosophers'. The remark had a
whiff of incest, for the Otaheite philosopher – Diderot's imaginary Tahitian
sage – allowed untrammelled sex. Having heard his hints about Augusta,
Claire assumed the allusion – probably to his own words – would please
Byron.

When they were in Geneva he could have Mary as well as herself, she
told him, making again that triangular relationship which had excited and
pained her with Shelley; 'you will I dare say fall in love' with Mary for 'she
is very handsome & very amiable & you will no doubt be blest in your
attachment ...' Claire's imagination leapt onwards: she would redouble her
attention to please Mary, for she 'would not stand low in the affections of
the person so beyond blest as to be beloved by you'. She herself would be
happy simply to be Byron's asexual friend or attendant: 'I have no passions; I
had ten times rather be your male friend than your mistress.'[1] In fact, though
Byron enjoyed seducing both men and women, he did not hanker for a
commune of free love, especially one with so operatic a participant.

The Shelley trio left England in high spirits, and in better style than
two years previously. Now they were travelling in Shelley's coach – still
unpaid for – instead of on foot and donkey. But, while they moved more
easily, the weather proved equally uncomfortable. The day in 1814 when

they left London had been one of the hottest the girls had experienced in their sixteen years; the spring and summer of 1816 were the wettest in living memory.

On the journey Claire looked forward to meeting Byron again and Mary was hoping to have Shelley more to herself now she saw Claire absorbed elsewhere. Again they were all reading Mary Wollstonecraft and writing journals, letters and accounts while the baby wailed, an interruption Godwin had once confessed ruined his concentration.

Despite their last quarrel Mary wrote lengthily and in detail to Fanny, copying out much of what she wrote; she had a shrewd eye to the publication she would make of these and her accounts of her previous trip. Together they would form a travelogue catching impressions of the war-torn countryside and people; there was little about their own interactions.

This time the French, morose in 1814 before Napoleon's final adventure and defeat, were downright hostile. They resented the nationals from a country that had subdued them and reimposed the detested Bourbon monarchy. As Shelley remarked to Peacock, 'The discontent & sullenness of their minds perpetually betrays itself.'[2]

Withstanding the hazards and the cold of the Alps, they arrived in Geneva before Byron. Claiming to be husband, wife and sister, they took cheap rooms within the expensive lakeside Hôtel d'Angleterre in Sécheron, on the northern bank of Lake Geneva a mile or so from the town.

A fortnight later Byron rolled up in his stately coach modelled on that of his hero Napoleon. He was so tired that he declared his age a hundred in the hotel register. Claire harassed him at once. As a result he was reluctant to meet Mary and Shelley, thinking that any association might tie him tighter to his importunate lover. But then one day, as she saw Byron coming in from a boat off the lake, Claire led Shelley and Mary to the quayside; the meeting which she hoped would ensure her hold on the famous poet had to take place.

To Lord Byron's doctor, John Polidori, urged by the publisher Murray to keep an account of his employer's life this summer, Shelley appeared rather different from the charismatic figure he had cut with the Godwin girls in Skinner Street: 'bashful, shy, consumptive', Polidori wrote. His complicated home life was summarised as 'separated from his wife; keeps the two daughters of Godwin, who practise his theories; one L.B.'s'.[3]

For a short while Claire thought her scheme had worked since Byron accepted her attention. As he later wrote to Augusta, it was hard to refuse a girl who had scrambled 800 miles for the pleasure of having intercourse with him, especially when he had slim opportunities elsewhere. But soon it was apparent Claire had miscalculated: after an initial awkwardness Byron was a great deal more interested in Shelley than in her, bored by her demanding humility.

Both poets were physically striking: Shelley had the advantage of height and fine if not handsome features compared with the shorter stockier Byron with his thick sensual lips. But Byron's voice was mellifluous and soft where Shelley's was a high tremor – the voice of a child, Claire called it. They had rank in common, though the lord overtopped a baronet's heir. Yet Byron had a less socially secure beginning: for all his grumbling about his father's tyranny, Shelley had known only privilege and significance; Byron had spent his early untitled, fatherless childhood in Aberdeen with a suffocating mother. Both were close to large fortunes; yet both were in hock to moneylenders.

Soon the pair of poets were going off together to talk, leaving both young women behind. As he had for Hogg and Godwin, Shelley reinvented his life for Byron and Polidori, who recorded it with his own inflection: 'Gone through much misery, thinking he was dying; married a girl for the mere sake of letting her have the jointure that would accrue to her; recovered; found he could not agree; separated; paid Godwin's debts, and seduced his daughter; then wondered that he would not see him. The sister left the father to go with the other. Got a child. All clever.'[4]

Mary loved Switzerland, which recalled Scotland to her. She wrote ecstatically to Fanny, describing the lake as blue as the heavens sparkling with golden beams. Momentarily the weather grew mild; there were birds, flowers, a pale moon, grasshoppers, and the sight of Willmouse playing outside and growing in strength; Mary and Shelley began a routine of writing and studying Latin and Italian, followed by walks in the hotel gardens. When Shelley was not with Byron she had him more to herself than for some time.

The sunny weather soon failed and the prevailing gloom of rain and clouds returned, punctuated by violent electric storms. In the beginning of June Shelley and Byron took lodgings a few miles outside Geneva on the opposite bank from the Hôtel d'Angleterre, with views of the Jura. The Shelley house, Maison Chapuis, now destroyed, was close to the lake at the small village of Montalègre near Cologny, a secluded 'bird's nest among leaves'. Byron moved in a few hundred yards away, to the Villa Diodati, a mansion with terraced gardens and viewing balcony on three sides, directly up from Shelley's house.

The proximity – and the resulting intercourse – was convenient for the owner of the Hôtel d'Angleterre, who made the Villa Diodati one of the attractions of his establishment; he provided telescopes so that guests could spy on the wicked doings of the poets and their shared harem, then shudder enjoyably. Imagination rioted and Byron's bedsheets and tablecloths hung out to dry became the wicked nightwear of the scandalous Godwin girls. One English expatriate recorded, 'Our late great Arrival is Lord Byron, with the Actress and another family of very suspicious appearance. How many he has at his disposal out of the whole set I know not ...' Byron was also said to be ravishing the city virgins at night.[5] As he remarked, 'Heaven knows why – but I seem destined to set people by the ears.'

They lived in relative social isolation from the rest of British and Swiss society. 'I never gave "the English" an opportunity of "avoiding" me,' Byron wrote, 'but I trust, that if ever I do, they will seize it.' With Polidori he did, however, visit the celebrated Swiss-French author, Madame de Staël, in her nearby mansion of Coppet. His effect there became legendary: 'It is true – that Mrs. Hervey (She writes novels) fainted at my entrance into Coppet,' Byron recalled, '& then came back again; – on her fainting – the Duchesse de Broglie exclaimed: "This is *too much* – at Sixty five years of age!"'[6]

To such grand if unconventional ladies – Jane Austen apparently refused to meet Madame de Staël when she was in London – Mary and Claire must have seemed a couple of bedraggled teenaged girls in the entourage of a rakish young man. Godwin had dined with Staël a couple of years before but made rather a poor impression. There is no record of his daughters visiting Coppet.

By now Claire was not only on occasion warming Byron's bed but also acting as his scribe. At night he would compose the third Canto of *Childe Harold,* then send the sheets with corrections to Claire in the late morning when he rose; she would copy them out in fair hand. Byron visited Shelley after breakfast and later Mary, Shelley and Claire would walk up to Diodati after Byron had dined alone about five; when it rained, as it often did, they all stayed at Diodati.

It was a comfortable routine, but Byron soon tired of Claire's part in it.

He made his attitude clear. Claire responded with begging letters, offering to come to him at any hour for any purpose.

❦

Few episodes are more written about than the night of 16 June which prompted the writing of *Frankenstein*. Before it there were many conversations with Shelley, Byron and Polidori about the nature of man and the exciting new science which suggested that life was a matter of the body alone and needed no divine spark. If there was no soul, then the body was at man's disposal. Why could not man create life? That women appeared to create it in a natural way was dull compared with the notion of life made through intellectual endeavour.

The ideas excited Mary, as did the theme of men wrecking family life with their utopian ideals. For beneath the new theories lay the layers of her own experience, of her dead mother, of her difficult father and his fictions, *Fleetwood* and *St Leon*. From all of these she had derived a sense of the awesome power of environment. What happens if, though man is born good, he is treated badly, especially within the family that should nurture him? What misery and evil must ensue?

The amazingly wintry weather added to the intellectual and emotional ferment. Lightning flashed from the mountains, electricity at its most violent. So nature assisted them in creating a mood. They decided to stay up through the night reading a French translation of German Gothic tales, one concerning the reanimation of a corpse's head. Then they themselves should write their own tales. So it began – or so it was later said.[7]

Years on, in 1831, when the summer of 1816 and the genesis of *Frankenstein* had become legendary and most of the actors were dead, Mary described her trouble with thinking up her own ghost story. She then provided a description of a dream she had had, proper genesis of a great Gothic work. She had a vision of a creature who stood at the bedside of his creator with 'yellow, watery, but speculative eyes'.[8] The creator/father flees from his creation/child in horror. So, a virtual orphan, the Creature will become an outcast with no escape except suicide.

Shelley too had startling visions – perhaps in response to Mary or perhaps he provided the model she copied in her 1831 account. Two evenings after the night of Gothic tales, according to Polidori's diary, they all assembled again at Diodati, recapitulating in a way the frantic nights Shelley had shared with Claire in London. At midnight, much impressed by Coleridge's fantastic poems, Byron repeated the lines from 'Christabel' about the false friend's withered witchlike breast. Shelley looked at Mary and thought of a woman with eyes instead of nipples (this part of the female body troubled him, for he also declared that the demonic Eliza Westbrook had exposed her breasts to him, displaying 'two glaring eyes in place of nipples').[9] He ran shrieking from the room. Water was thrown on his face, then Polidori administered ether. Byron was surprised: 'I can't tell what seized him,' he remarked, 'for he don't want courage'.[10]

Just twenty-one, Polidori was also caught up in the glamour of the poets; sensitive and prickly, he alternately vied for Byron's attention and competed with him. He had joined the entourage in some excitement but was soon hurt by his employer's habit of mocking him and making him the butt of jokes. Polidori would be dismissed at the end of the summer, return to England and publish his own vampire tale. It was based a little on a fragment written by Byron after the famous night of ghosts, but far more on Byron himself as a predatory destroyer of other people's lives. The story expressed Polidori's sense of the society in Diodati, a sense of what it was like to live in the light of other people's genius and of their social and psychological power. His tale ends with the hero's sister glutting 'the thirst of a VAMPYRE'. During the summer of 1816 Byron thought Polidori was falling in love with Mary. They had this in common, that where Polidori definitively made Byron into a vampire, Mary transmuted Shelley's morbid and disturbing effect into similarly iconic characters: Frankenstein and his Creature.

To Byron's irritation, a publisher printed Polidori's story as 'The Vampyre: a Tale by Lord Byron'. As such the work had huge success, but Polidori had sold the copyright and received little for it. Two years later, after gambling away what money he had, he killed himself with prussic acid.

❧

In late June 1816 Shelley and Byron left Polidori, Mary and Claire behind and went off together for a brief tour of the lake. They visited places resonating with the passion of Rousseau's *La Nouvelle Héloïse*. At one point the boat nearly sank and Byron pleased Shelley by noting it was the spot where the heroine Julie and her lover Saint-Preux capsized and where they were tempted to plunge into the lake together. Shelley was fascinated by such moments of *Liebestod*.

Since Claire was pregnant, during the trip the two men probably discussed her condition, about which Mary still seems not to have known. When they returned, perhaps still affected by their near shipwreck – this 'prospect of death' produced 'a mixture of sensations', he noted in a letter to Peacock – Shelley made a will leaving £6,000 to Claire and a similar amount to whomever she named, presumably meant for the baby she was carrying; it made the huge sum of £12,000 in all.[11]

In *Political Justice* Godwin had written that when society became perfect it would probably not be known who was the father of any child. But in an imperfect era Byron puzzled over the matter. He noticed that by the time Shelley, Mary and Claire left Geneva, Shelley had not been having sex with Claire, and this he thought might suggest the child was his – indeed he once imagined, like Shelley with Ianthe, it could become his 'comfort' in old age. Yet he asked a doubting friend, 'Is the brat *mine*?' He had reason for doubting: he tended to use contraception – 'Don't forget the Cundums', he urged his friend John Cam Hobhouse on 27 April 1816, when expecting Hobhouse to join him in Geneva.[12] (At the same time, 'Cundums' or no, he did manage to get gonorrhoea more than once and he did father another illegitimate child.)

There were certainly doubts in Claire's case. Byron noted that Shelley, despite not sleeping with Claire in Geneva, was quite prepared to help her through the birth. Later Shelley's concern for the baby, in due course named Allegra, and his readiness in 1818 on her behalf even to sacrifice the health of his and Mary's new child Clara, suggested that he might have thought the baby his, although he must also have felt responsible for a girl he had origi-nally enticed from her mother and home and who, since Byron was showing so little interest, could well, without his protection, wind up on the streets. Allegra's death at the age of five led to an outpouring of grief from Claire which turned primarily to blame of Byron. But there is also a strange remark within a caricature she made of Shelley: 'He looking very sweet & smiling. A little Jesus Christ playing about the room He says. Then grasping a small knife & looking mild I will quietly murder that little child.'[13] We may here be in the region of abstractions and the small knife be the satire with which Claire imagined Shelley destroying the 'child' of orthodox religion. Or perhaps she had a momentary sense of his fatal carelessness with a real one.

Whatever they all believed, the idea that Shelley was sleeping with both sisters and had fathered a baby with Claire persisted after they all returned to England. Visiting the Shelley ménage, David Booth wrote to his wife, 'They have a little child, "Miss Auburn," of which your father could not procure the history. Is she not [Claire's]? She and Mary live with Shelley alternately when he is in London, and in these cases Mr. Godwin tells me that they have never been able to persuade Clare to sleep a single night under her mother's roof. She has, says Mr. Godwin (with great simplicity) an unconquerable fear of ghosts and will not sleep in a room alone. She therefore goes to Shelley's lodgings every night.'[14] Perhaps neither Byron nor Shelley – nor Claire – knew who the father was.

Mary and Shelley planned a tour of the Alps. Byron refused to accompany them but they took Claire, rather subdued by her lover's constant rebuffs. Byron was reading a *roman à clef* about the ending of a relationship between Madame de Staël and Benjamin Constant. Thinking perhaps of the affair with Claire, he remarked, 'it is a work which leaves an unpleasant impression – but very consistent with the consequences of not being in love'.[15]

Towards the end of July, leaving Willmouse with his Swiss nurse, Shelley, Mary and Claire set out. The tour began in Chamonix, a straggling resort town full of English tourists seeking the sublime sights of Switzerland closed to most of them through the twenty-two years of war. At the Hôtel de Londres Shelley wrote their separate names as unmarried people in the visitors' book, then in Greek declared himself an atheist and democrat on his way to hell, a joke or a riposte to fear. From Chamonix they saw pinnacles of ice shining though the pines, then the clouded summit of Mont Blanc. 'I never knew I never imagined what mountains were before,' Shelley told Peacock. 'The immensity of these aerial summits excited, when they suddenly burst upon the sight, a sentiment of extatic wonder, not unallied to madness.'[16] Next day they went on mules up the precipitous mountain slopes towards the peaks. Through the rain they looked along six miles of the *mer de glace* with its icy waves.

Noting their destructive and growing power, Shelley saw the Swiss glaciers and mountains as vivid images of encroaching desolation, symbol of Necessity. Mont Blanc became for him a vast animal with frozen blood.

In the poem it inspired him to write, he speculated that 'silence and solitude' might be 'vacancy' – or that the vacancy could resonate only with the human mind's imaginings. Mary stored up the image of the ice waste to people it with the egoistic Frankenstein and the monster he created and forced to become evil through his freezing indifference.

Back in Geneva on the evening of 27 July they were reunited with Willmouse and collected their letters. One was from Charles Clairmont, whiling away time in France and now asking for money from Shelley to support himself. Another concerning arrangements with Sir Timothy demanded Shelley return at once; another told them that the furniture of their Bishopsgate house had been sold, probably to pay debts. Soon they would receive letters from Fanny and Godwin, of course detailing Skinner Street troubles. Godwin had returned from Edinburgh to new debts, had tried Constable for an immediate advance and been allotted £200, again on condition that two volumes of the new novel were submitted by January. Since the money went to pay debts on previous publishing ventures he had 'as yet gained nothing on his novel'. He was frightened of 'the terrors of the law' closing in on him and desperate for 'the relief so long expected' from Shelley: 'If I am disappointed in this, if my affairs in the meantime go to a wreck that can no longer be resisted, then the novel will never be finished.' Fanny was aware of the hyperbole of her stepfather, but his affairs did now have a most 'serious and threatening aspect', she told them.[17]

Shelley had dispatched £10 to Godwin before he went on his tour; now he sent another £10 to Charles.[18] Then he and Mary went into Geneva and bought a gold Swiss watch for Fanny back in London. It was an appropriate gift: in times of sudden poverty Shelley would easily part with his own gold watch; Fanny, in thrall to others, was more in need of keeping time.

On 2 August, leaving a rather puzzled Mary behind, Claire and Shelley went up alone to the Villa Diodati. Presumably they intended to talk about Claire's pregnancy. The conversation was not altogether satisfactory: Byron was prepared to accept the child as his on the two conditions that he himself had nothing to do with the mother and that the mother pretend to be the child's aunt. He suggested the baby be brought up by his half-sister Augusta among her large brood of children rather than in the unconventional Shelley ménage – he noticed that they had not yet managed to raise an infant successfully; this way reputations would be preserved. To persuade Augusta to take the child he declared it 'a new baby B'.[19]

Byron is 'a slave to the vilest and most vulgar prejudices', Shelley told Peacock.[20] He, Shelley, would take care of Claire through her pregnancy. Indeed he seemed sometimes at this stage keen to raise her child using his own libertarian principles – though Mary cannot much have relished the notion. He was, however, always concerned that Byron should acknowledge and support it, however slavish might be his ideas. The scandal of fathering a child with Claire was far greater for Shelley than for Byron.

While they had been away, the notoriety of the group had increased and more and more visitors were arriving in Geneva expecting to enjoy Byron, Shelley and the Godwin girls as one of the sights. It was said that the poets and their entourage had 'found a pact to outrage all that is regarded as most sacred in human society … atheism, incest, and many other things'.[21] The furore upset Mary, who did not visit Diodati again though Byron still came down to the Shelley house. Claire continued copying manuscripts.

On 29 August Mary, Shelley, Claire with Willmouse and the Swiss nurse set off for England. By now Mary knew Claire was pregnant and cannot have been quite sure by whom. Whatever she knew of Byron, she did not care the less for him. She had been happy in the attention of two poets, admiring and loving both. Claire simply provoked her former lover's scorn by declaring that she loved and would love only him for the rest of her life.

'I never loved nor pretended to love her, but a man is a man, and if a girl of eighteen comes prancing to you at all hours there is but one way.' About to travel to Venice and enter the most promiscuous period of his life, Byron was in no mood for monogamous sentimentality. To Augusta he summed up the affair: 'a foolish girl – in spite of all I could say or do – would come after me – or rather went before me – for I found her here – and I have had all the plague possible to persuade her to go back again – but at last she went. – Now – dearest – I do most truly tell thee – that I could not help this – that I did all I could to prevent it – & have at last put an end to it. – I am not in love – nor have any love left for any, – but I could not exactly play the Stoic'. His next mistress, a Venetian baker's wife, would be accomplished but unintellectual; above all she would not 'plague' him – 'which is a wonder'.[22]

Many years later, Claire remarked that Byron was an example of the contemptible result of 'Intellectual Greatness' divorced from 'moral Greatness'.[23] The Skinner Street training would always show.

CHAPTER 26

FANNY

FANNY HAD LEARNT from Godwin's *Memoirs* that she had been named after Fanny Blood, her mother's dear friend. As a young adult Mary Wollstonecraft had for some years intended spending the rest of her life with Fanny Blood, whose dying after childbirth she witnessed with anguish in Portugal.

She had also been close to Fanny's brother George Blood, especially when she was a governess in Ireland hating her aristocratic employer. George had pleased her by calling her the 'Princess'. He had some reason, since for several years she had been the benefactor of his feckless parents at considerable emotional and financial cost to herself.

Once she became a writer and mixed with London intellectuals, Mary Wollstonecraft outgrew George Blood, and the pair lost touch. Around 1790 George had wanted to marry Everina, but, either because she thought him beneath her or because she simply did not like him enough and preferred her own company, she had refused. She had left her sister Mary to write the letter rejecting him.

After Mary Wollstonecraft's death, George Blood had done better in Ireland than any of the sisters might have expected: he married, had eight children and became an accountant to a mining company. In May 1816 he was visiting London and he took the opportunity to come to Skinner Street to dine; for the first time he saw the girl named after his dead sister.

Familiar from childhood with Godwin's flamboyant and intellectual friends, Fanny was a little surprised to see in her mother's old companion a kindly, rather uncultivated person: 'George Blood is not a man of superior intellect but has great wealth of feeling and great goodness of heart.' He was still much in awe of Mary Wollstonecraft and spoke enthusiastically about what she had meant for him and for the world. Indeed he continued to venerate her 'as a superior being'.

He told Fanny stories of when he and her mother had been young together making their way in an unwelcoming world, and of her love for his sister Fanny, whose talent in drawing, painting and illustrating books – perhaps he brought one to show her namesake – foreshadowed Fanny's own skill. The letters Mary Wollstonecraft had written to him then had been intimate, expressive and also overwhelmingly melancholy and self-pitying. If Fanny saw them now she would have met not only the luminous shining mother she so revered but also a young woman who, like herself and at much the same age, could succumb to periods of gloom.

Despite being rather quicker than her mother to spy George Blood's intellectual limitations, the meeting with a man so familiar with and admiring of Mary Wollstonecraft impressed Fanny and gave 'balm' to her heart. 'Every thing he has told me of my mother has encreased my love and admiration of her memory,' she reported. When George Blood 'ventured to hope that her daughters were not unworthy of her,' Fanny snatched at his words. She was used to being told by Mrs Godwin of her failing in obedience and by Mary and Claire of her timidity and feeble spirit. The frequent criticisms had disheartened rather angered her – to such an extent that she had stopped feeling herself the equal of her sister, or indeed the daughter of an exceptional mother. But George Blood's visit inspirited her: 'I have determined never to live to be a disgrace to *such a mother,*' she now declared – with hindsight a rather ambiguous resolve. It was not enough to overcome the melancholy sense of unworthiness that had settled on her in the last months, and she added, 'I have found that if I will endeavour to overcome my faults I shall find being's to love and esteem me.'[1] It was an odd phrase explained by the context – for she wrote these words to Shelley and Mary: it was their 'love and esteem' she craved despite what Mrs Godwin told her of their contempt.

❦

The nonchalant unconventionality of the households in Geneva appalled the Godwins when they heard the gossip brought back by visitors to Switzerland. Their financial predicament was worse than ever for, with Shelley noisily and notoriously absent, Godwin was again hounded by creditors. With nothing more available from Constable, he had only the young man's promise of £300 during the summer to borrow against and, in desperation, he turned again to the moneylender William Kingdon, who had lent him £75 when he married.[2] He also tried to negotiate with a solicitor acting for tenants of Sir Timothy, to whom Shelley had promised long leases in the future (so getting round the ban on issuing post-obits). Something might come of this, Godwin believed, but they had to plan 'for the possible contingency of your father's surviving your life & your son's'. Needing documents which Shelley held, he rifled through his London lodgings but found nothing: 'This is the first fruits of your unfortunate absence,' he told Shelley.[3]

The novel he was proposing cannot have helped the mood in the house. However wonderful it appeared to Fanny – and himself – it was also a book of immense gloom. *Mandeville* had the usual Godwinian theme of a man cursed by his response to another's overbearing personality: of the hero he wrote, 'He loved his sadness, for it had become a part of himself … In reality he rather vegetated than lived; and he had persisted so long in this passive mode of existence, that there was not nerve and spring enough left in him, to enable him to sustain any other.'[4] People who serve Mandeville catch his gloom. No wonder Peacock would later mock the book for its morose misanthrope.

Despite its theme, Godwin was happier writing his novel than not. Things were worse when he stopped. The debt to Kingdon had to be paid by the end of June. The expiry date went by with no sign of the £300 from Shelley. As a result he could concentrate on nothing, not even writing. Wretchedly, Fanny looked on, lamenting she could be of so little use. Despite his anger, presumably Godwin passed on Shelley's good wishes at the end of a business letter: 'Remember me kindly to Fanny both for her own & for her sister's sake.'[5]

The letters she received from Mary were wonderfully descriptive, but Fanny, although finding them precious, must sometimes have noticed their lack of involvement with herself and felt she was holding public documents. It was good that Mary felt as 'happy as a new-fledged bird' and had 'escaped from the gloom of winter and of London'.[6] Fanny however was still there, left in the gloom with no icy pinnacle to pierce it. 'England … has been dreadfully dreary & rainy,' she wrote at the end of May.[7]

Mary's letters were expensive. Fanny had not a sou of her own, as she put it, expressing a rare resentment at her dependent state. Shelley could enjoy the drama of poverty, say he could live on £50 a year, and make toy boats out of paper money, while he ran up debts for furnishings and fabrics he had no intention of paying, simply because he could obtain credit. He knew nothing of the disempowering lack of money Fanny experienced. Recipients of letters had to pay postage and she was forced to ask Mary to write small, so there would be no need of a second sheet which would make her letter more expensive. Every penny Fanny used came from the Godwins.

The letters Fanny wrote back to Mary and Shelley in the summer of 1816 form the clearest window on her mind during this crucial time. They show swings in mood depending on her health and the treatment she received, but they also show excitement and immense enthusiasm. They could be despondent in parts but they were never despairing.

At first she admitted that, under the shock of their going, she had sunk into 'torpor'. But then she explained that this was in part because she, usually so well, had caught a heavy cold. She shivered in the damp, chilly summer. The weather was often as dismal in Geneva as in London, and under its influence Byron wrote his poem 'Darkness', describing an imagined time when the sun did not return at all and 'the icy earth/ Swung blind and blackening in the moonless air'.[8] Yet Fanny wistfully imagined that for Mary and Claire the cold weather could become 'an adventure to look back upon with pleasure'. The letters they wrote from Switzerland bore her out for they described the drama of violent storms which excited the spirits. But in England everyone's spirits simply sank with the glum weather. She was not unusual.

When she made her confession of 'torpor', Fanny was writing to Mary and Shelley on the end of one of Godwin's icy letters of reproach and demand. He had given her some space to append her own words – more economical with paper than sending a separate letter. But, wary of Mary's scorn of her submissiveness, she insisted that, although she was writing with the permission of 'Papa', Godwin was not reading her words. She herself sealed the letter. And Godwin was scrupulous for, although he so often used Fanny to plead for money, here she was left to write what she wished. The result was a bizarre juxtaposition of Godwin's frigidity and, despite her violent cold and dark mood, Fanny's affection.

First she pushed money matters aside: 'I do not chuse to interfere further than I am obliged,' she admitted. Her subject was herself. Her attitude to them all was hardening: she was desperate to make herself understood and appreciated.

After an effort to be entertaining by recounting George Blood's visit, she alluded to the recent quarrel with Mary. Reliving the moment, she found the formality of letters Godwin had taught them all as children breaking down. She almost sobbed: 'believe my dear friend's that my attachment to you has grown out of your individual worth, and talents, & perhaps also because I found the world deserted you I loved you the more'. She continued in her now bitterly humble manner, revealing how demolished she had been by her sister's harsh words: 'What ever faults I may have I am not *sordid* or vulgar. I love you for *your selves alone.*' Given her intense affection for Godwin it must have been hard for her to write this, for she knew that Godwin 'loved' Shelley for what he could get from him – not long afterwards he would openly admit his dislike.

Godwin had preached that self-pity was unworthy and before she concluded her letter she tried to pull herself together, to resume her old service role. She told them to kiss little William 'again & again' for her and apologised for Godwin's cold note, glossing it as a cover for 'great kindness & interest'. She was so used to patching up quarrels and smoothing the surface of other people's lives that such comments came involuntarily.

It was hard for Mary among the poets and mountains to understand the extraordinarily isolated and vulnerable position of her half-sister and the pain of rejection she was feeling – to appreciate what Fanny called 'the dreadful state of mind I generally labour under & which I in vain endeavour to get rid of'. Certainly this scrawled letter, appended to Godwin's, was miserable and in a later one she apologised for writing 'in some degree in an ill humour'.[9] But, apart from her violent cold, her only explanation was that she was harassed on all sides.

13. The Villa Diodati on Lake Geneva, rented by Lord Byron in summer 1816; there he was visited by Claire, Shelley and Mary, who conceived the idea for *Frankenstein* while at the Villa.

14. William (Willmouse), beloved son of Mary and Shelley; he died at the age of three.

15. Percy Bysshe Shelley: one of the major Romantic poets, charismatic heir to a baronetcy and large fortune; according to Mrs Godwin, he was loved by Fanny, Mary and Claire.

16. Lord Byron: popular and notorious Romantic poet, friend of Shelley and Mary and, briefly, lover of Claire Clairmont, who bore his child Allegra.

17. Address on one of Fanny's pleading letters to Mary and Shelley, written during the dark summer of 1816.

CAMBRIAN POST-COACH,
AT REDUCED FARES,
From the MACKWORTH-ARMS INN, SWANSEA,
TO THE
BELL-INN, GLOUCESTER, and BUSH INN,

18. An advertisement from October 1816 for the Cambrian Coach, the public vehicle in which Fanny made her last journey from Bristol to Swansea.

19. The Coroner's Bill for Inquests, Quarter Sessions Roll for 1816: 'Oct 10 Body at Mᶜworth arms'; the body, unnamed and unclaimed, was Fanny Wollstonecraft's.

20. The Mackworth Arms in Wind Street, Swansea, where Fanny killed herself.

21. Shelley's three fragments of poetry inspired by Fanny's suicide; 'Thy little footsteps on the sands …', 'Her voice did quiver as we parted …' and 'That for those who are lone & weary …'

22. Shelley's drawings of steps, possibly leading to a grave and a flower pot. The wording reads: 'I drew this flower pot in October 1816 and now it is 1817'.

23. Marble memorial to Mary and Percy Bysshe Shelley in Christchurch Priory Church, Dorset, England, suggesting the idealisation of Shelley after his death.

24. William Godwin in 1832, the year of his son's death and four years before his own at the age of eighty.

Despite its expression of love, Mary was not impressed. She told Fanny to stop being so dismal, to quit writing so much about her misery.

෯

Fanny complied. By the time she wrote again at the end of July, just as Shelley, Mary and Claire were returning from the Alpine excursion, her cold was better and she had cheered up. She told them all of the visits of Robert Owen. Now, musing further on what he had said, she found she was back with her favourite theme: the subject of (male) genius and what was owed to it. His notion of equality did not take it into account.

'I would not like to live to see the extinction of all genius, talent, and elevated generous feeling in great Britain,' she wrote. She was prepared to give up Robert Owen's seductive vision of a world where all people would be properly fed and achieve plain simple manners to nurture her idea of a '*poet* a painter and a philosopher'. Her life had in a way been founded on the service of genius, perhaps her mother's, certainly Godwin's and Shelley's. If the concept was meaningless, what had been her purpose? Even now she was distressing herself by writing letters in the belief that Godwin needed and deserved money because he was composing his 'very best' novel. She was an idealist, like Shelley.

His poetry was having a profound effect on her. She thought it could become curative, a sort of therapy, and, like the art of Godwin, was worthy of intense devotion. With Shelley, she believed that poetry was 'an interpenetration of a diviner nature through our own ... It compels us to feel that which we perceive, and to imagine that which we know. It creates anew the universe.'[10] Writing before Shelley penned these words but no doubt having heard him make such visionary claims in conversation, Fanny was both stating her inner convictions and making a plea for Shelley's attention when she declared that, for her, poetry was a sort of benefaction of the human race: 'It is impossible to tell the good that *poets* do their fellow-creatures – (at least those that can feel), ' she wrote. '[W]hilst I read I am a poet – I am inspired with good feeling's, feeling that create perhaps a more permanent good in me, than all the every day preachments in the world.' Only poetry made ordinary everyday life bearable and gave hope for oneself and the future of mankind. By poetry she did *not* mean the old-fashioned sort full of dying swans and sighing Delias but the new Romantic verse of Wordsworth and Coleridge, Shelley and Byron.

In the letter and elsewhere Fanny caught the visionary transcendental aspect of Shelley's art – that which made him so impatient with earthly impediments. It called directly to her. So she was saddened to hear from Mary that he was not writing much. He *must* write, must continue his 'divine' mission. Godwin and Shelley were twin poles of her imaginative universe, but it was Shelley's world she desired now to inhabit.

They had asked for books, especially Coleridge's poems – the acute effect of 'Christabel' on Shelley had made them want the real text. She was eager to comply but had not been able to get hold of it or 'Kubla Khan'. As for other books, she admitted she had no money to lay out for them. She was 'a dependant being in every sense of the word'.

To encourage them all to write at length and in detail she gave some literary gossip. Coleridge was making efforts to obtain opium despite living with a doctor who was supposed to control his habit. The politician and playwright Sheridan was dead – Godwin and his son had gone to the funeral, but Fanny had not. She did not care for his cynical writing or his drunkenness. Romantic in her admiration for the Poet, Fanny, like Claire, also cleaved to older eighteenth-century notions of art's involvement with moral worth, on which Godwin had nurtured them all.

In this long letter to Mary and Shelley the plea for inclusion was forthright: 'I had rather live all my life with the Genevese …' Fanny wrote. 'I should like to visit *Venice & Naples*'. She had had little contact with her aunt Eliza Bishop, and could not have known how closely her longing to share her sister Mary's life recalled her aunt's desire to be made part of the earlier Mary Wollstonecraft's glamorous Parisian existence. When she begged news about the more vibrant world they inhabited, Fanny imagined Mary and Shelley enjoying themselves *en famille*, dipping little William into the lake. Here she echoed her own mother's letters to Imlay in which she too painted imaginary pictures of a cosy domestic life beyond her grasp. With her letters her sister Mary had invited 'the ethereal part' of Fanny to travel through the 'magic of words'; Fanny was looking for a more mundane invitation.

She was fascinated by Byron and she asked for descriptions of his face, voice and habits, indeed any gossip and anecdotes they could give. She visualised life on the banks of Lake Geneva with Byron coming into their house in a careless, friendly, dropping-in manner. Were the scandalous rumours true? She hoped he was not really a *detestable being* since, though she loved the poet, she wanted also to respect the man. What had Byron been writing? Was he sending the poems to England? Tell him, she wrote, 'that you have a friend, who has few pleasure's, and is very impatient to read the poems written at Geneva'. She had seen the first cantos of *Childe Harold* much earlier but had recently been reading his *Turkish Tales*, with their brooding obsessive heroes who looked only to death to cure them of guilt or misery. She had allowed these poems to 'cheer' several gloomy hours.

Yet, however much she managed to forget herself in poetry, the summer of 1816 was a painful and lonely time for Fanny. Only she of all the older children had failed to escape from Skinner Street. Mary and Claire were in Geneva and Charles had not been heard from for a year. He did not write because he was ashamed to admit his pleasure-seeking way of life abroad, but to Fanny his silence meant he had forgotten her too. And Mrs Godwin dripped away at her.

During his visit to London, George Blood had spoken about her coming to live in Ireland (he was a friend of her aunts) and, with still no invitation from Shelley and Mary, there seemed no exit except this. Despite Eliza Bishop's concern over Claire's contamination of Fanny, the sisters had re-established reasonable relations with the Godwins. Now in early August they visited London again and Fanny's future was their subject. As Francis Place had hinted, it was time Godwin put his grown girls to work and Fanny too knew the moment had come. She told Mary, 'my future fate will be decided' with this visit; she would know 'what my unhappy life is to be spent in &c &c'.

She dreaded rejection or embrace. And now she may have shown some reluctance to be with her aunts and accept the drudgery of schoolteaching, for it is curious that in their extended stay she saw so little of them. She was not reclusive; she liked art and had recently been with Godwin to an exhibition of Italian cartoons and pictures at the British Institution in Pall Mall – though rather typically Godwin directed her gaze from what he considered the lesser Raphael cartoon, 'The Miraculous Draught of Fishes', to the one depicting Paul preaching at Athens: 'papa who was with me made me turn immediately to the south'.[11] She concurred with his judgement – St Paul became for her another man of genius who could with his powerful words act on the minds of his listeners. Fanny intended to go again to the Institution before the exhibition closed – perhaps this time she would be alone and freer. Later in the summer she made a special trip to the Dulwich art gallery south of the river to see pictures by Murillo, Guido and Titian. So her lack of visits to her aunts is strange. Perhaps she was trying to avoid committing herself.

CHAPTER 27

MARY

BY THE TIME Shelley and Mary returned to England in early September they had abandoned the frankness advocated in *Political Justice*. Secrecy was imperative – everyone, including the Godwins, would suspect Claire's child to be Shelley's. Entirely in the dark, Fanny waited for them to arrive in London, expecting to see as much of them as she had when they were last there and she had run their errands.

But they did not come. Instead, they travelled through Fanny's birthplace of Le Havre direct to Portsmouth, a sea voyage of twenty-six hours. Then Mary and the pregnant Claire, now passing as Mrs Clairmont, went straight to Bath. The story for friends in London was that Claire was poorly and that Bath had been recommended for a cure.

The two women took pleasant lodgings at 5 Abbey Churchyard near the Pump Room. Yet Mary disliked the town; she judged it dull and fashionable. The choice had been entirely due to Shelley's concern for Claire, not herself. In literature Bath was a place where ladies in delicate distress went to hide until they could decently re-enter society.

Mary had hoped that, as Shelley had promised, they could have settled down without Claire. Now she begged her lover to go with her alone to a mountain place to live – the dream of Wales again. He promised they should in the future – but for the moment he was too entangled for such a move. Instead he expected Mary to care for her stepsister through her pregnancy while he made flying visits to London. As with Harriet, he had high expectations of his women.

Discontented herself, Mary made no effort to soften Fanny's renewed sense of exclusion; she gave no excuses for their absence from town. She had been happy with Shelley in Geneva, where Claire had been absorbed in Byron. But now they were back in England her stepsister annoyed her as much as ever, and there seemed no immediate chance that Shelley would send her away. Still, Mary hoped for better things – he had, he said, now determined to settle somewhere in the mountains one day soon.

Then, with his usual abrupt change of mind, he decided they should move to be near Peacock in Marlow. He went straight there from London, and, three days later on 15 September, invited Mary to join him at Peacock's place. They could look together for a house. She should leave Willmouse and his nurse with Claire, he announced, a duty Claire did not much relish – unlike Fanny she did not dote on the boy.

Mary enjoyed her visit to Marlow, although, loyal to Harriet, Peacock did not entirely warm to her. While there she did not take the opportunity to go on to London to meet Fanny, although the distance was not much more than her sister had travelled when they lived out in Bishopsgate. Fanny continued to wait in Skinner Street. She had not seen Mary since before her sister had so suddenly left for Geneva after their quarrel.

CHAPTER 28

FANNY

WHEN HARRIET HAD written to her straying husband in 1814 she had worried about his health. More recently, when Mary left Bath for Marlow, Claire had told her to make sure that Shelley wore a greatcoat and did not walk too much. Fanny too claimed a stake in Shelley by being concerned with his bodily wellbeing. When she met him on one of his secret visits to London – he was still being pursued by creditors – she told him he did not look well: he should be careful of himself. He did at times appear sickly, but the continual absorption of all the women suggests they used concern for his health to assert proprietorship or beg his attention.

He had come to town to complete financial agreements with his father and deliver to the publisher John Murray the later cantos of *Childe Harold*, Byron's manuscript which Claire had copied out. He stayed at his old lodgings in Marchmont Street where he had 'No companions but the ghosts of old remembrances, all of whom contrive to make some reproach to which there is no reply'.[1] He also came to sign a new will.

Clearly Fanny did not impress her needs on him, for he remembered just about everyone except herself and Godwin. Apart from the huge legacy to Claire, he settled the residue of his estate on Mary, left £6,000 in trust for Harriet and £5,000 each to their children Ianthe and Charles; Byron and Hogg were to have £2,000 each and Peacock a ready £500 and £2,000 for the purchase of an annuity.

He was also arranging a mortgage on his inheritance to obtain in due course a further £3,500, a sum tied up with a financial agreement with Sir Timothy. By paying Shelley's (considerable) new debts his father hoped to free the estate from further claims; the debts should be paid directly and Shelley should not have control of the money; nonetheless Shelley hoped he would have sufficient funds to pay Godwin the promised £300.

Fanny knew nothing of her absence from the will, or of Shelley's complex relationship to his inheritance, but he may have mentioned his hopes for easier money when he met her on the evening of 10 September, the anniversary of Mary Wollstonecraft's death, or again on the 24th. She was glad to see him on both occasions and asserted herself to entertain, in the process making yet another appeal to him and her sister. Mary had sent her a letter describing their domestic life in Bath with Willmouse. It sounded beguiling.

In both meetings Fanny brought news from Skinner Street – Godwin's acute anxiety over the Kingdon loan, of course, but she also spoke excitedly about his progress with *Mandeville*. Without belief in her stepfather's art it was hard for her to accept her part in his incessant begging. She gossiped about the *roman à clef* Lady Caroline Lamb had written concerning her affair with Lord Byron, and in the second meeting she grumbled a bit about her unfriendly stepmother. Mrs Godwin had visited the Boinville family in Bracknell and come back in a foul mood, having learnt what people were saying about them all.

Then Fanny got in her plea, indirect but quite clear. She had heard they were all living a studious and contented life in Bath, with 'calm philosophical habits', so very different from the anxious, snappy household in Skinner Street. She would relish such an existence, she said. She loved to hear that Willmouse was in good spirits.

Shelley was often unaware of the effect he had on people and how enticing he could be when actually intending something far more muted – this had happened with Hogg and Elizabeth Hitchener. Possibly then, without being explicit, he sowed in Fanny's mind the idea that she just might be welcome to them. But, if Shelley had ample proof of Fanny's emotional dependence on himself and her sister, he also knew of her loyalty to Godwin; he dared not tell her of their real situation in Bath. So again no clear invitation came, and Fanny was left wondering why she, so useful to them when they were in need, was ignored when they arrived at more prosperous times.

For she assumed they *were* prosperous. Buoyed up with the excitement of the large sums of money he was hoping for, Shelley probably forgot that he was still a debtor on the run, visiting London secretly to avoid creditors and supporting an incorrigibly indebted Godwin. So he sent out financial messages that Fanny read more positively than he meant and she had more hope than usual. She had forgotten his habits of hyperbole.

Back home Shelley wrote to Byron inviting him to join them. He painted a cosy domestic picture of himself, Mary reading by the fire, the cat and kitten under the sofa and Willmouse asleep – probably the kind of description he had just given verbally to Fanny. But Byron was in Venice in the midst of new loves – he knew what an invitation from Shelley entailed and he had no wish ever to see Claire Clairmont again.

On the day Shelley visited London and met Fanny, Everina Wollstonecraft and Eliza Bishop left for Dublin. Just before they went Godwin paid a call on them. Fanny did not accompany him, although by this time it was decided that she would visit them for a long holiday fairly soon. After that a decision on her future would be made. Whatever doubts there had been on both sides, and whatever was later asserted (Mary Hutton declared that Everina, whom she detested, had rejected Fanny), there seems no particular slight, and their departure does not appear to have upset Fanny; it is unclear exactly who was on probation in the projected arrangement.

After Shelley and her aunts had left, Fanny sat down to write to Mary. She told her sister how 'pained' she was for the financial setbacks Everina and Eliza had suffered, especially since the loss worried them so much. But again her primary concern was not Ireland or any new life she might have there but Mary and Shelley, and she used her letter to follow up her hints given to Shelley in their recent meeting, and to make clear again her longing to be rescued.

To be more persuasive she tried to display herself as an attractive intellectual companion as well as the useful helper and carer she had been for so long. She heard Claire had a piano; Fanny would look out for music to send her. Shelley had spoken about his new poem 'Mont Blanc', written in Switzerland. Its 'extatic wonder' affected Fanny. Perhaps Shelley had recited it when they met; she begged him to make her a copy of the poem, as well as of his letter to Peacock describing his thoughts on the mountain: 'you cannot think what a treasure they would be to me,' she added.

Her visit to the Dulwich art gallery had made her think about painting and poetry. Paintings were not nature; they appeared a poor second and did not satisfy her. Poems were different. The subject of the Poet was still engrossing her. 'It is only poets that are eternal benefactors of their fellow creatures,' she wrote, 'the real ones never fail of giving us the highest degree of pleasure we are capable of – they are in my oppinion nature & art united – & as such never failing.'[2] Such thoughts were both exciting and exalting. It was wonderful both to read sublime poetry and to be intimate with the geniuses who wrote it, even if they were physically at a distance. Fanny's quotidian life might be dismal but the imaginative life fed by poetic visions could be rich indeed.

⸙

But then, a few days later, everything changed. The depression that had fallen on her when Shelley, Mary and Claire dashed off to Switzerland earlier in the summer, returned magnified and poetry was not enough to lift it. There were three main causes.

First and most significantly, there was no response to her appeal for inclusion, no answering enthusiasm. It was a severe blow. She had never before so openly expressed her desires to them both. By 3 October when she wrote to Mary and Shelley again, Fanny had taken the rejection thoroughly to heart.

Second, there was a further and worse financial catastrophe in Skinner Street. Despite the large settlement he was negotiating with his father primarily aimed at settling past debts, Shelley found he had only £248 in ready money. Throughout the fraught summer of 1816 Godwin had been counting on the promised £300 in his tortuous dealings with creditors. Only this money stood between him and bankruptcy, he constantly declared. Now, on 2 October, Shelley told Godwin that the money could not be found. All he could send – and that was generous in the circumstances – was £200, keeping £48 back for himself. He had need of it. Claire was soon to move into separate lodgings at 12 New Bond Street to become, in Byron's words, 'a Mamma incog.'.[3] Shelley would be paying for two establishments.

The blow was severe and Fanny was at home to witness it. She watched Godwin's face darken as he read Shelley's letter; it was like 'a thunderclap'.

She was aghast, for Shelley had not prepared her for this. Indeed he had been buoyant; consequently she had raised Godwin's hopes. Why had he deceived her? Surely he could see that she would feel responsible – and be blamed – for any misunderstanding.

She was used to Mrs Godwin's reproaches but now Godwin, seeing prison looming before him, joined in. She struggled to defend Shelley and Mary, and herself. 'My heart is warm in your cause – and I am *anxious most anxious* that papa should feel for you as I do both for your own, and his sake,' she wrote. She was especially upset that the added anxiety was interrupting Godwin's novel. His mind should be 'free and disengaged' for writing, she told Shelley and Mary in her letter. No doubt her stepfather looked over her shoulder as she wrote these words but, since she so passionately believed in his work, she also expressed her own views. It was Shelley's and Mary's duty to do everything in their power to help a man of his talents – after all, she may have reflected, she herself was doing just that. Fanny's passionate underlinings here – Godwin must have support 'for *his own* and the *world's* sake' – indicate that she was also projecting on to him some of her own barely repressed desires.

And there was more: the cheque Shelley sent for the smaller amount was made out directly to Godwin rather than to a third person – the usual ruse her stepfather required to hide his scandalous dependence on Shelley. Godwin was incensed and sent it back, demanding by return of post a duplicate with a more obscure recipient. His letter was cold and hectoring: he would not accept 'a cheque drawn by you and containing my name', he told Shelley.[4]

There was a third reason for her plunge downwards. In her chats with Shelley she had been unusually honest about her feelings for her stepmother. Mrs Godwin disliked Shelley and Mary equally and was saying the usual harsh things about them around town. Now she learnt that they themselves were entertaining their friends with tales in which she became the equivalent of the cruel patrician in Godwin's finest novel, *Caleb Williams*, who hounds his worthy servant almost to death with his lies. The stories must, she thought, originate in Fanny's gossip with Shelley – perhaps it was only now that she knew of the meetings. As before, when Mary and Shelley had first left for the Continent, she could vent her fury only on her stepdaughter.

All the years of irritation at the girl inherited from a more universally favoured wife surfaced. Fanny had been nothing but a nuisance since her birth – her existence had made her mother emotionally dependent on the adventurer Gilbert Imlay, while more recently Mrs Godwin had ruined her health bringing up and feeding this orphan. There were, after all, so many nearer claims on their purse. Probably in her anger she brought up the demand of the Wollstonecraft sisters that her own daughter Claire be banished because this young woman, with no blood connection, was in the house.

Six months earlier Godwin had assumed Fanny's affection for his wife, for he had written from York, 'Remember what I said to you of my desire that you should write to me, particularly of what you observe of the state of Mamma's health & spirits, & the things of which she would not willingly write. Do not alarm me unnecessarily; but do not keep me in the dark ... I hope she will not know of my having written this ...'[5] But now Fanny, usually so careful, admitted openly, 'Mamma and I are not great friend's'; Mrs Godwin had lashed out at her 'in a passion' and was neither 'just' nor 'amiable'.

It was Fanny's turn to be angry, not with Mrs Godwin, whom she had never loved, but with Shelley, whom she did. Her freedom with him, which she thought appreciated, had not only failed to appeal but had backfired. Shelley had betrayed her confidence.

She was used to his melodramatic stories – she had heard them even before he appeared in Skinner Street, when he made the commonplace Timothy into an operatic tyrant. As Hogg remarked, 'He was altogether incapable of rendering an account of any transaction whatsoever, according to the strict and precise truth, and the bare naked realities of actual life.'[6] But surely he could see how unwise it was to blame Mrs Godwin for 'hounding' him and Mary if the information could be laid at Fanny's door. He and Mary cannot have thought of her insecure position in Skinner Street and the needs which they themselves were not proposing to fulfil:

> I either related my story very ill to Shelley or he paying little regard to what I might say – chose to embellish a story out of his own imagination for your amusement – which you to[o] have coloured to your own mind; and made what was *purely accidental;* & which only occured *once* a story after the manner of Caleb Williams – [viz] – of 'Mamma, persuing you like a hound after Foxes.'

Even the unpleasant Mrs Godwin, Fanny declared, had some virtues: and, she added half-heartedly, she would 'never do either of you a deliberate and deadly injury'.[7] Since Mary and Shelley were old scandal, the 'deadly' gossip may well have concerned Shelley and Claire. If harmful tales were being spread, continued Fanny, then it was probably by Harriet. Or more likely they came from their own servants; Mary and Shelley were always leaving their letters around for everyone to see.

Fanny wrote abruptly and frankly, and she felt uneasy with her unusual tone. She had at times accused herself of torpor, ill humour and melancholy; now she was adding resentment, an emotion she had hardly allowed herself in her short life. It was a cross letter, but still not a despairing one.

When she received it Mary labelled it 'stupid', she was irritated by Fanny's scolding.[8] It was ridiculous to talk of 'virtues' and their stepmother in the same breath.

☙

Shelley did not immediately answer Godwin's letter demanding the change of name on the cheque and, in the interval, perhaps the older man thought that at last with his peremptory tone he had gone too far. It would have been natural for him and his wife to become even more querulous than usual, to find fault with anyone who would accept it.

In fact Shelley was not *especially* offended, used as he was to Godwin's impertinence. He did as requested. On 7 October he sent a new cheque without Godwin's name on it.

But before the new cheque arrived Fanny acted. She would accept no more blame or abuse, and she would no longer be anyone's instrument. She would take her future into her own hands, as the others had all done. She would leave the Godwins and Skinner Street for ever.

PART IV

CHAPTER 29

FANNY

WHERE WAS SHE going?

Later the Godwins wished people to believe she was on her way to Dublin to join her aunts. It seems unlikely. If the Wollstonecraft aunts had rejected her in any way, why go to them? If not, and Godwin's later letter makes no such claim – indeed he says her going was still being discussed – why not take sufficient money for the journey; surely Shelley and even Godwin would have helped her for such a purpose. She or Godwin would certainly have written ahead to Everina and Eliza to announce her coming and her non-arrival would have produced a flurry of letters. Besides, the quickest and cheapest way to Dublin from London was through Holyhead, not Bath.

Godwin also later claimed that he expected she was going to her death. He knew the crescendo of abuse she had recently suffered, mainly from his wife, and he might have supposed an extreme reaction. But, again, this is unlikely. She left no note for him as his daughter Mary had done when she crept out of his house two years before, and the letter she next wrote had nothing ominous about it.

So, since she certainly went to Bath, everything seems to point to her going to Shelley and Mary.

She had been melancholy while they were away in Switzerland and had eagerly awaited their return. She had received long letters and the gift of a fine gold watch; she had expected their attention when back in England.

Throughout the summer of 1816 she had written excitedly about what Shelley's poetry meant to her and of her longing to lead his and Mary's philosophical life and to visit distant places. She was surprised not to meet her sister when she returned, but Shelley had sought her out in London on each visit and she had made her pleas to him. Now a month had passed since their return with no clear invitation.

The last time she had seen Shelley they had talked intimately and her recent cross letter could not erase the fact. She had scolded him in the past – when he had first abandoned the Godwins without notice – and he had accepted it with good grace. She cannot have expected this rebuke to have unduly offended him, especially since he and Mary must have known she wrote in part at Mrs Godwin's prompting. Mary was her sister and she had intermittently got on with Claire in a sisterly sort of way. Surely none of them would be unwelcoming if she actually arrived in Bath. She would let them know she was coming.

If she wrote her letter to Mary and Shelley before she quitted Skinner Street, she could have posted it before she boarded the coach: the daily mail to Bath left from the Swan with Two Necks, Lad-Lane, at 7.30 in the evening and arrived at the Lamb Inn in Bath the following morning at 9.30. But probably she waited till she reached Bath, then sent the letter by hand – it was later claimed it was dated 8 October.[1] Mary recorded receiving the letter the same day; its contents were perhaps annoying but could not have been unduly worrying, for she and Shelley went about their business in the ordinary manner, Mary having a drawing lesson and reading Clarendon's histories of the English revolution, the pair of them walking out together.

Before she left the house Fanny dressed herself nicely for her journey. She put on stockings marked 'G', then her mother's stays marked 'MW'. Claire Clairmont had thrown off stays as part of her emancipated stance, possibly after she read Shelley's description in *Queen Mab* of Morality 'dressed up in stiff stays' glimpsing her own 'disgusting image'. But they enhanced the figure and Fanny chose to wear them, as Mary Wollstonecraft had done.

Over the stays she put a blue striped skirt with white bodice. On top of this she wore a brown pelisse lined with white silk and trimmed with lighter brown fur; she had a hat to match. In her pocket she placed the new gold Swiss watch that Mary and Shelley had sent her. Then she took a little bag which contained her red silk handkerchief, her brown-berry necklace and a small leather clasped purse in which she placed her small amount of money. She was dressed to make a pleasant impression.

Bath was 106 miles from London. She probably took the coach that left at about one in the afternoon of Monday 7 October. If so, she made the familiar walk to the Saracen's Head Inn at Snow Hill near Skinner Street. This coach was not the fast mail and the journey took nineteen hours; she would arrive in Bath at the Greyhound Inn around eight o'clock in the morning of Tuesday 8th; Shelley and Mary would receive her letter soon after this. She would have the whole day ahead for seeing them.

Presumably this letter (now lost) requested a meeting with them all. But it was of course out of the question. Now six months pregnant, Claire must not be glimpsed. Also, Mary, who had parted irritably from Fanny before she left for Geneva and had recently been cross with her scolding, may not have wanted to deal with another sister or to share Shelley further. Fanny could not be invited to their lodgings. Probably it was decided that Shelley should go to meet her alone at the coaching inn where she was waiting. He would have to put her off somehow.

So Fanny, nicely dressed and eager, met a different man from the one she had prattled to so unguardedly a few weeks before in London. Shelley had long believed himself persecuted for his politics, but with the rumours circulating in the country he now felt – or was persuaded by Mary to feel – the social anxieties that had dogged Godwin for so many years. He had become involved in a battle with Harriet for the custody of his heir Charles, so he had to be concerned with his reputation. This was now intimately tied up with Claire's as well as Mary's. Fanny was devoted to Godwin, he knew, and he assumed she would tell him and his wife the true state of things if she saw her bulging stepsister. To save Claire's reputation Fanny had to be rejected.

❧

No prose record of a last meeting exists but Shelley put his intense and complicated feelings into poetic fragments. These form the only account of what may have happened.

In them Fanny appealed to Shelley but did not directly convey her love for him – in which he later came to believe, as Claire always did. Unable to recognise acute, unpackaged suffering, he could see no urgency in this needy affection. He withheld himself, ignored her appeal and left Fanny to go off alone.

Feeling and deflecting blame, Shelley originally opened his fragment of poetry with the lines:

> Friend had I known thy secret grief
>> Should we have parted so.

But he changed his mind and wrote instead:

> Her voice did quiver as we parted,
>> Yet knew I not that heart was broken
> From which it came – and I departed –
>> Heeding not the words then spoken.
> Misery – oh misery
> This world is all too wide to thee!

His verses petered out into the odd lines: 'Some secret woes had been mine own – ...'. He had first written 'griefs' but 'woes' seemed closer to what Fanny had probably felt. Then came at last the understanding of her predicament: 'that for those who are lone and weary/ The road of life is long and dreary'. The fragments end with the words: 'Some hopes were buried in my heart/ Whose spectres haunted me with sadness.'[2]

❧

To Fanny nothing now remained except death. She wanted to go where she would be unobserved by those she had cared for but who had not cared enough for her.

❧

Claire had noted Fanny's sensitivity. Mary Wollstonecraft found the same quality in herself and lamented its double-edged nature, for it opened a person to suffering as well as to art and nature. When still bolstered by a Christian hope of an afterlife that made sense of the miseries of this one, Wollstonecraft had written in a letter,

> [R]efinement genius – and those charming talents which my soul instinctively loves, produce misery in this world – abundantly more pain than pleasure. Why then do they at all unfold themselves *here*? If useless, would not the Searcher of hearts, the tender Father, have shut them up 'till they could bloom in a more favorable climate; where no keen blasts could blight the opening flower. Besides sensibility renders the path of duty more intricate – and the warfare *much* more severe – Surely *peculiar* wretchedness has something to balance it![3]

Fanny had been left with no such hope and faith, nothing to balance '*peculiar* wretchedness'. Writing in her life of Mary Shelley, F. A. Marshall summed up this aspect of Fanny's predicament with partial truth:

> Full of warmth and affection and ideal aspirations; sympathetically responsive to every poem, every work of art appealing to imagination, she was condemned by her temperament and the surroundings of her life to idealise nothing, and to look at all objects as they presented themselves to her, in the light of the very commonest day.[4]

Although Fanny had a temperament to be hurt, she was not, I think, 'condemned' by it. Instead, circumstances were against her. She was poor, dependent, and made to feel a burden despite carrying so many burdens for others. And without even Charles Clairmont in Skinner Street she had been bereft of any person to take the weight of the Godwins' fretful anxieties. She depended solely on the sympathy and hopes vested in Shelley and Mary; 'I am afraid her affections were with them,' wrote Godwin. Now these had failed. As idealistic as Shelley, she needed gentle treatment; she could no longer register disappointment for, after two years of minimal satisfaction, she had suffered finally a repulse of the sort that could not be forgiven.

From the moment she read her mother's works and her stepfather's *Memoirs* of Mary Wollstonecraft she knew of her own suicidal legacy. She also knew of Patrickson's death two years earlier, and had been brought up on Godwin's rationalist views. Suicide was not for her, as it was for a pious Christian, a diabolical temptation to be overcome. If, according to *Political Justice*, the 'assassin cannot help the murder he commits any more than the dagger', then the suicide lacked moral responsibility for her act.

There was, too, Shelley's poetry with its otherworldly desire, its yearning for ineffability and a kind of transparency: 'Death is the veil which those who live call life:/ They sleep, and it is lifted'. He speculated that 'death is slumber,/ And that its shapes the busy thoughts outnumber/ Of those who wake and live'.[5] Mary related to the Godwinian enlightened side of Shelley and Claire to the macabre, strange and Gothic. Both found their brains 'whizzed with giddiness, about idealism', however.[6] Fanny was ready to give ultimate significance to this aspect of Shelley's poetry; there she encountered the unmistakable yearning for death as the gateway out of physical or material life, the mingled desire for and fear of the life of a wraith.

Fanny's death would not be radiant like that of the Poet in *Alastor* – the whole poem resembled a magnificent suicide note – but its existence and power over her imagination could help ease her into the notion of death as a choice over life when she too had had enough of 'chains and mossy walls'.

Perhaps amidst mountains it was possible to imagine oneself what one contemplated, but in a world without colour or majesty, in dirty streets under a leaden sky, only other people's visions could raise her out of dinginess. Mountains and snows might be stained but they had a moment of purity. In the gloom of her mind and her environment no such moments were forthcoming – that is unless she could make contact with the source of visions, the Poet. Perhaps on this last meeting Shelley could have persuaded her of his truth: 'we might be all/ We dream of, happy, high, majestical'.[7] But he did not try.

◦৯

Fanny wanted the Godwins, Shelley and Mary to know what she was doing and why, but to lack the power to stop her. She must write to them all and then go from the place stamped on her letter so she could not be intercepted. She needed a room in a town where she would not easily be found.

The next stop on the main coaching route from Bath was Bristol, only fourteen miles down the road. It was easy to find a coach, for they went very frequently and took only two hours. When she arrived in Bristol Fanny probably spent the night at the Bush Tavern in Corn Street, one of the inns from where transport set off to South Wales.

She now needed the means to kill herself. After she was rescued from her suicide attempt in 1795, almost exactly twenty-one years before her daughter followed her example, Mary Wollstonecraft had described the horror she had felt at the process of drowning. The year before she had tried drugs or poison, probably laudanum, and been saved through Imlay's swift action. When she came to imagine suicide in her fiction in *Maria* she gave her heroine a dose of laudanum. Fanny aimed at a peaceful but definite death in the way her mother had tried and prescribed and for which the poetry of Shelley seemed so often to long. She would need a potent drug and a place where she would not be disturbed.

Laudanum was widely available and widely used as an analgesic, though it was not easy to commit suicide with it, as Napoleon found when, defeated, he tried to kill himself. But when taken in sufficient quantities it slowly caused coma, and it was remarked that women frequently chose the option because it did not disfigure the body. Fanny would have known the quantity required. She was aware of addicts among her acquaintances who lived on an average daily dose of an ounce or two – though Coleridge, whose opium habit she had mentioned to amuse Shelley, consumed up to five ounces of the drug a day, so that his pupils were perpetually wide and his skin pale and leaden. She probably also knew the poem 'The Maniac', which her mother's old friend, the beautiful but crippled 'Perdita' Robinson, had dictated in a frenzied delirium after swallowing eighty drops of laudanum to dull the pain of her rheumatism.

At some point, then, Fanny used part of the little money she had left to buy laudanum; there was a chemist and druggist shop, Hassall & Williams, in the same street as the Bush Tavern in Bristol. The most popular formula was 'Sydenham's Laudanum', devised in the mid seventeenth century: strained opium mixed with cinnamon, cloves, saffron and canary wine. An ounce cost 8d.

Very early next morning, 9 October, she wrote to Shelley and to Godwin, declaring to both: 'I depart immediately to the spot from which I hope never to remove.' She told the Godwins in particular that she was 'disgusted with life' – implying that they had made her so. To Shelley she wrote that she would be dead by the time he received her letter but that she would like him to bury her.[8] She knew he felt the pathos of the unmarked grave. He often imagined his own dead body and the earth that would house it. When hounded by creditors he saw himself 'starved to death' in a damp cell; when hurt by poor reviews, he pictured his own unknown tomb. The Poet's body in *Alastor* is signalled only by a transitory mound of leaves.

Unlike so many of her previous letters, those Fanny wrote from Bristol, which survive only in snippets in other people's accounts, were from herself alone. No one was looking over her shoulder or dictating what she wrote. No Godwin guided her pen and Mrs Godwin could not exaggerate and muddy her message. She had lost Mary and Shelley when she failed in her many pleas to join them; she was now in a way losing the Godwins, to whom she had given her loyalty for too long. She brooded over what she had never quite complained of before: the blame that had come to her most of her short adult life. She had once tried to ingratiate herself with her letters but now she had become forthright. It was no wonder that her correspondents destroyed these.

Before retiring to bed in Bristol Fanny purchased her place on the early-morning Cambrian coach to Swansea, which left at 6 a.m. on Wednesdays. It was a town she may have gone through when she visited Wales two years before, and the London coach went there after Bristol. The journey took sixteen hours.

It was not easy to cross the River Severn below Gloucester since there were no bridges after that point but there was a three-mile ferry crossing lower down the river at the New Passage. It was a difficult, windy uncomfortable place and travellers found themselves 'slipping and sliding, falling and floundering, in the slimy mud' as they crossed the beach to reach the open boats.[9] Harsh weather often made the journey much longer than was advertised. Paterson's *Roads* of 1822 records that the ferry-crossing fee for a four-wheel carriage was 12s; this made the fare expensive, and after paying for her ticket Fanny had 8s 6d left. She would have been an inside passenger since she had no need to save her money by travelling cheaply outside.

Her friend Aaron Burr left records of the many accidents and inconveniences accompanying public coach travel which he encountered in England: the desperate scramble to book a seat, coaches departing without passengers who had paid for their passage upfront, coachmen stopping every few miles for a drink or a wench. But the hundred-mile coach ride between Bristol and Swansea this time passed without incident, and Fanny behaved sedately; hers was a dry, stony grief. She was used to controlling herself, and other passengers noticed nothing odd in her demeanour. She told them that she intended to go on from Swansea to Ireland.

She was, of course, proposing no such thing, for she had already written her letters of intent. Shelley often imagined death near water and Swansea fitted this notion, but death in a staging place, simply en route to somewhere else, fits more with Fanny's sense of her own rootless existence, the rootlessness not of Shelley's constant journeyings but of not belonging where she was: 'I could lie down like a tired child, / And weep away the life of care … Till Death like Sleep might steal on me'.[10]

The Cambrian coach arrived at the Swansea coaching inn, the Mackworth Arms in Wind Street, on Wednesday 9 October at 10 o'clock at night. Fanny asked for an upper room to herself. She looked like a 'most respectable' lady and the innkeeper William Jones assumed she could pay; a room was assigned to her. The Mackworth Arms fronted a handsome, well-paved street, the principal thoroughfare of Swansea. Both in position and facilities it was considered a good house, especially useful for those doing business in the town since it was close to the exchange for corn, fish and vegetables as well as to St Mary's Street, where the butchers' market was held. The inn was a bustling place, with ceaseless coming and going on its lower floors. No one would pay much attention to a young woman who wanted to be left alone.

When she arrived Fanny drank tea in the parlour. Then, before she went upstairs, she told the maid she was very tired and would put out her candle herself. She would need no service or attention. She may already have written her suicide note when she was at Bristol at the point when she sent her letters to Shelley and Mary and to the Godwins, or, more likely, she wrote it now. She could expect it to be printed in the newspaper, for it was quite usual for suicide notes – a form made popular in the eighteenth century – to be published in the press after they had been read out at the inquest. She would have seen many during her life; they often disposed of their writers' property, but Fanny was careless of this, the gold watch probably being her most valuable possession.

While making clear her views in her note, Fanny avoided her mother's threatening posture towards Imlay: 'in the midst of business and sensual pleasure, I shall appear before you'. Fanny had given up hope of influencing anyone, even in death:

> I have long determined that the best thing I could do was to put an end to the existence of a being whose birth was unfortunate, and whose life has only been a series of pain to those persons who have hurt their health in endeavouring to promote her welfare. Perhaps to hear of my death will give you pain, but you will soon have the blessing of forgetting that such a creature ever existed as

The reference to an unfortunate birth echoed Mary Wollstonecraft, who had written her lessons for infants primarily 'for my unfortunate girl'. Unlike her mother in her angry suicide note, Fanny mainly quoted life rather than literature – she had had enough of her family's dramatising – and the substance has the sound of Mary Jane Godwin, who claimed she had lost 'youth and beauty before the natural time' in her struggle with Godwin's children. Fanny's old playmate Henry Reveley was judging at second and third hand when he recorded, 'after Mr Godwin's second marriage with the widow Clermont the neglect and ill-treatment of her stepmother drove Fanny to despair'.[11]

But others too were implicated in the tragedy. If the first part of the note addressed those in Skinner Street, the second less clearly did so. Fanny would not imagine the Godwins feeling much 'pain'. This she would ascribe to her sister perhaps, more likely to Shelley, the only one she had recently seen. He must feel some grief, but not perhaps for very long. Pity was strong in him but, as with Godwin, self-pity was stronger. The utopian dreams had always centred on self.

Having written her note now or earlier, she took the laudanum and lay on the bed without undressing. In *Alastor* Shelley imagined a final earthly vision: 'the great moon, which o'er the western line/ Of the wide world her mighty horn suspended'.[12] It was autumn, so quite dark; Fanny's last view was the little inn room, perhaps by muted candlelight before she snuffed the candle out herself.

❧

When her body was discovered in the morning it was modestly clothed.

Beyond her brown-berry necklace her possessions told a pathetic story – the small amount of money for a person leaving home; the now useless watch which had not been proof of special care from the givers; the stays that marked how her body and life had been bound by her mother's; the stockings from a family that had not quite nurtured her. She had probably signed her words as Fanny Godwin, perhaps as F. G. – perhaps even as her birth name Imlay – so assumed there would be no questioning who she was. Since the newspaper followed her note with five asterisks the reporter might have learnt it had been 'Fanny', her usual signature at the end of letters. Since she had identified herself, she would not have expected her body to be rifled. If she had written to Shelley to ask that he bury her, she would have assumed it in better hands than those of servants and coroners.

The coach from Swansea to Milford Haven for the crossing to southern Ireland set off next day, Thursday 10 October. Those who had heard Fanny was planning to travel must have been surprised when she did not appear. The innkeeper and servants grew worried. They knocked on the door of her room, received no answer, then forced entry. Fanny was found dead, with the remains of a bottle of laudanum on the table beside the suicide note.

The offices of the local newspaper, the *Cambrian,* were located in Wind Street near the Mackworth Arms. Costing 7d, this popular weekly paper featured local and national news – of drowned men near Swansea and frame-breakers in Nottingham – as well as advertisements for patent medicines, properties to be let or sold, meetings of religious groups such as the Christian Knowledge Society, and competing coach routes. It was published at Messrs. Murray and Rees every Saturday morning. News received even late on a Thursday night for printing throughout Friday could be included in the paper.[13]

The reporter needed to step only a few yards down the street to speak to the innkeeper and, very likely, attend the inquest. By the time the newspaper conveyed its contents, there was no name on the note. It had been 'torn off and burnt'. Perhaps the reporter would see the body, but the facts concerning it were probably obtained from the inn people or from the early stages of the inquest, which was always held soon after a corpse was found. The week following the death, the *Cambrian* recorded the 11 October verdict on Fanny as 'Found dead', the issue of 12 October having gone to press before the inquest concluded.

CHAPTER 30

SHELLEY *and* GODWIN

SHELLEY AND MARY received the first letter from Fanny on 8 October. This was the day she probably met Shelley in Bath. The next day, in the evening of the 9th, arrived the 'very alarming' letter. This she had posted together with her note to Skinner Street before she boarded the Cambrian coach for Swansea: the mail for London left Bristol at four in the afternoon, unloaded the Bath post two hours later and continued its speedy journey, arriving in London at 8 o'clock the next morning.

The second letter was therefore with Shelley long before Fanny checked into the Mackworth Arms late at night on the 9th. He was shocked by its despairing and perhaps reproachful contents; he 'jumped up thrust his hand in [his] hair', exclaiming, 'I must be off'.[1] Leaving Mary and Claire in Bath, he set out for Bristol, from where the letter had come. The pursuit to death was so constant a motif in Shelley's poetry (as in Godwin's and Mary's novels) that, once again, life seemed encroaching on literature.

Only a week previously he had been to Bristol on some business, so he probably had contacts he could interrogate about movements of coaches and passengers. He would quickly know that Fanny was not in the town – in any case her letter had told them that she did not intend to stay but make her deathplace somewhere distant. He left messages with people asking for information as soon as any trace of her was discovered.

He was back in Bath by two in the morning of the 10th, just before or after Fanny took her overdose. Mary and Claire had waited for him, fearing the worst. Perhaps now, imagining the deed done, Mary prevailed on him to be cautious – there was another scandal in the making and one that would bring the most unwelcome attention on all of them. Fearful for Claire's reputation, he saw the point.

If the matter were to be hushed up he would need funds. He would also need them if he were to arrange a burial. It was probably for these reasons that Shelley wrote to his bankers asking for money to be sent by return of post.

Soon he was back in Bristol, where he found 'more certain trace' of where Fanny had gone; he now knew she had headed for Swansea.

From here on, matters are difficult to untangle. If he knew Fanny was in Wales, why did he not go straight there?

It is just possible that he did, so arriving even before the reporters and authorities were apprised of the death. He would then have seen both body and note. But it is unlikely, for, according to Mary's journal, he was back with her by 11 o'clock that evening.

Part of the night Shelley slept in Bath; then he set out early on the 11th. He travelled by post horses straight from his lodgings to Swansea. Not constrained by coach times or by lumbering vehicles, he made the crossing by the nearest ferry and travelled in far quicker time than Fanny's public coach. Knowing the coaching inns, when he arrived he would not have needed to scour Swansea for Fanny's whereabouts but could enter the Mackworth Arms straightaway. There he would learn at once that a respectable young woman who had got off the Bristol coach had killed herself and that an inquest was being held. Years later Shelley told Henry Reveley that he tracked Fanny down with 'post horses … but when he came up with her at the Inn she was already a corpse'.[2] He would have been at the inn before the *Cambrian* finished printing its story on its third page later that day.

❧

The inquest on Fanny was held by the coroner John Charles Collins, who, as was required, immediately summoned twenty-four men – at least twelve jurors were wanted. They had to view the body to see if there were any marks of violence; since there were none, no surgeon need be present. Perhaps the corpse was still at the inn, for it had been found only twenty-four hours earlier – or, since the innkeeper would have wanted it out of his establishment as soon as possible, it might have been taken to the gaol or workhouse close by, housed in the intact part of the old castle.

Witnesses were called: those who found the body at the inn and people who had travelled with Fanny; they made their statements, were questioned, then signed a record of what they had said. When the jurors and coroner were satisfied that murder could be ruled out, the question remained whether they were looking at suicide, insanity or accidental death.

The macabre penalties for suicide were still sometimes enforced, especially in Wales – though class mattered everywhere: rich suicides managed somehow to get into Westminster Abbey, it was noted. In Swansea shortly after Fanny's death a jury over which Mr Collins presided pronounced a former sailor of nearly eighty, Jeffrey Vallet, 'Felo de se'. They could not do otherwise, for 'So determined was this hoary wretch on his own destruction, that he actually greased the rope by which he suspended himself to a hook in the ceiling, and when discovered his feet were resting on the floor.' His body was buried at the crossroads at dawn.

Sometimes an affecting story emerged from an inquest, like that of a young weaver who loved a farmer's daughter. He discovered her heart was another's; they quarrelled and he begged her to accept a silk handkerchief in memory of him. She refused. When later she went to milk the cows, she found her lover hanging on a willow tree, suspended by the handkerchief she had rejected.

Except in such clear-cut cases, often juries wanted to avoid the penalties of suicide and brought in verdicts of 'insanity', as they did for a couple in mid Wales who poisoned themselves with arsenic earlier in the year. In Fanny's case, despite the suicide note and laudanum, they were even kinder. She was labelled neither a suicide nor insane, simply 'dead'.

The coroner then granted a warrant for the body to be buried. At the end of the proceedings the documents were sent to the sessions which would be held the following week in Swansea.

So, some time during this day, Friday 11th, while he was in Swansea, Shelley had to make a decision whether to identify Fanny's body and give it a decent burial, or whether to refuse involvement and let Mary Wollstonecraft's daughter be buried alone without mourners, so saving the remnants of respectability to which the Godwins – and he – now clung.

Clearly he reached his decision, for the body was not claimed. Commenting a few months later, Mary's Scottish friend David Booth remarked that 'Shelley is certainly insane, he does everything he can to become notorious'. But it was not the case now: it was one of the few times when he was of the same mind as the Godwins. He was ignoring the rousing words he had written in Ireland: 'It is a very latitudinarian system of morality that permits its professor to employ bad means for any end whatever.'[3] Perhaps, rather, he was remembering the novel that had inspired him in early manhood, Charles Brockden Brown's *Ormond*: there the rejected Helena writes a suicide note to the hero, then kills herself with laudanum; he leaves the funeral arrangements to those who can suspend their grief: '*I* cannot attend to them,' he declares.

Despite the jurors' oath to give 'a true verdict' and not 'spare any through fear, favour, or affection' there are many examples of inquests being influenced for all these reasons – and through bribery. Although Shelley made intermittent efforts to shake off the gentleman with what Claire called his 'lackadaisical' air, to many who met him he appeared a person of consequence and he usually impressed people with his status and credit. He could not remove the stays marked 'MW' and the Swiss gold watch but these by themselves would not be enough to alert others, including the newspaper reporter, to Fanny's identity. Since Fanny's name was once on the note it is likely that Shelley now removed it – presumably money changed hands between him and the coroner and subsequently the reporter. The newspaper gave the curious detail that the name was torn off and burnt. This would be easy enough – anyone could get a candle, but Shelley, fascinated with fire, also carried a tinder box whose flame he loved to hold till it burnt his fingers.

He stayed the night of 11 October in Swansea to see the newspaper report on Saturday 12th. Then he returned to Bath with the 'worst account'. He did not see the funeral and it is unlikely that he paid for anything 'respectable', since such an action would have required at least a fictitious name; the *Cambrian*, which related the inquest verdict the following week, would surely have mentioned the fact.

The Godwins too had received Fanny's suicidal letter of intent from Bristol. It arrived in Skinner Street in the morning of the 10th, the day after the similar one arrived for Shelley and Mary closer by in Bath. Godwin left for Bristol on the coach, perhaps the evening mail from Lad-Lane – he had reached only Salt Hill in Slough by tea time. If he travelled by the mail coach through Bath, he would have arrived at eleven the following morning at the Bush Inn, where he recorded dining later in the day; perhaps he tried to glean information at the same time. He may now have heard that Fanny had boarded the Cambrian coach two days earlier – and that another man had also been in search of her, following the trail to Swansea.

This would explain Godwin's next move. He returned to Bath, perhaps expecting more news there, most certainly hoping he could prevent Shelley from taking an incautious step and allowing the probable scandal to become public knowledge.

On arrival in Bath he wrote to Mary, Shelley and Claire, presumably ordering discretion (the recipients were certainly discreet since the letter has not survived) – then he took a walk to the Circus and the Crescent to calm his nerves. Afterwards he went to bed at York House close to Mary and Shelley's lodgings at Abbey Churchyard.

In the morning, instead of calling on them he boarded the coach back to London, eager to be away, perhaps fearing that Shelley would get in touch after receiving his letter of instruction. He breakfasted at Calne in Wiltshire, dined at Reading and arrived back in London in time to sleep in his own bed. Carefully he noted down his route in his diary, together with the names of his fellow passengers.

The next morning he received certain news of Fanny's death in a letter from Shelley. It expressed sympathy for what the Godwins must be suffering. While he would not identify the body, Shelley wrote that he would return to Swansea, probably to give Fanny a proper burial. The notion provoked a response from Godwin by return of post: 'Go not to Swansea, disturb not the silent dead,' he commanded.

Having only Fanny's letter from Bristol, Godwin appears not to have known that Fanny had stopped in Bath. He therefore believed that the blame for her death fell squarely on himself and his wife, especially if Shelley recounted the suicide note which suggested a connection with Mary Jane. Always morbidly anxious about what others thought, he was frantic to stop

Shelley doing more and implicating them: 'My advice & earnest prayer is, that you would avoid any thing that leads to publicity,' he wrote to Shelley. He did not want his sympathy – 'I do not see ... that sympathy can be of any service to me.'

> Do nothing to destroy the obscurity she so much desired, that now rests upon the event. It was, as I said, her last wish. It was the motive that led her from London to Bristol & from Bristol to Swansea.
>
> ... Think what is the situation of my wife & myself, now deprived of all our children but the youngest [their son William]; & do not expose us to those idle questions, which to a mind in anguish is one of the severest of all trials[.]
>
> We are at this moment in doubt whether during the first shock we shall not say she is gone to Ireland to her aunts, a thing that had been in contemplation. Do not take from us the power to exercise our own discretion. You shall hear again to-morrow.
>
> What I have most of all in horror is the public papers; & I thank you for your caution as it might act on this.
>
> We have so conducted ourselves that not one person in our house has the smallest apprehension of the truth. Our feelings are less tumultuous than deep.[4]

Shelley agreed to what Godwin asked. There would be no further visit to Swansea, no identification of the body, and no public arrangement for burial. The Swiss gold watch fell from notice. Shelley might have suggested it be used to pay for a funeral but there is no record of such a transaction. Most likely Fanny's coffin and interment were at the parish's expense.

☙

The Swansea quarter sessions for Michaelmas opened on 15 October, five days after Fanny's death. They were partly held in the Mackworth Arms. According to the Minute Book, the bill (£16. 15s. 6d.) for the coroner John Charles Collins was approved a couple of floors away from the room in which Fanny had died. Bodies found dead, through suicide or misadventure, were named when possible. In the Quarter Sessions Rolls for 1816, fourteen dead bodies are listed as being charged, most of them drowned. Fanny's body must have been among the anonymous ones, for an entry on the sheet is dated 10 October and states 'Body at Mc worth arms'. The coroner's expenses for Fanny's body were £1. 0s. 9d. This may have been his fee for the inquest or included the price for a cheap pauper burial. In larger cities bodies were buried together in 'dense-pack'd corruption', twelve or so to a grave, and later in the century Swansea too put ten or more bodies in pauper graves in its municipal cemetery.[5]

Pauper burials struck fear into onlookers; even the very poor tried to avoid the degradation by investing their pennies in burial societies. When Charles Lamb described a parish funeral, he visualised a coffin of naked planks coarsely put together, no pall to hide it, carried by drunken men. It gave the impression that the dead had been a person of bad life, someone unworthy of Christian ceremony. Meeting one of these 'meagre processions', he felt 'out of humor and melancholy all the day after. They have a harsh and ominous aspect.'[6]

Just before she died Mary Wollstonecraft described the pathos of such a burial:

> I have … been shocked beyond expression when I met a pauper's funeral. A coffin carried on the shoulders of three or four ill-looking wretches … hastening to conceal the corpse, and quarrelling about the prey on their way. I know it is of little consequence how we are consigned to the earth; but I am led by this brutal insensibility, to what even the animal creation appears forcibly to feel, to advert to the wretched, deserted manner in which they died.[7]

The quarrelling was connected with the gruesome fact that bodies of paupers and suicides, uncared for by friends and relatives and quickly buried, were much prized for freshness by 'resurrection men' who stole and sold them to anatomy schools.

> Rattle his bones over the stones,
> He's only a pauper who nobody owns.

CHAPTER 31

GODWIN

CLAIRE WROTE TO Byron that she was distressed by the manner of Fanny's death: 'I passed the first fourteen years of my life with her, and though I cannot say I had so great an affection for her as might be expected, yet she is the first person of my acquaintance who has died and her death so horrible too ...' At times Fanny had cared for and mothered Claire, but the younger girl had never filled Fanny's life as Mary, Shelley and Godwin had done.

Possibly Claire remained unaware of her part in the final rejection. She did not publicly discuss Fanny until she was an old woman, when she claimed that Shelley and Mary had not told her of the death for several months to spare her feelings: the letter to Byron disproves the claim but perhaps the changed story indicates a residual sense that she had been unhappily involved. And her later reflection on herself, now like Fanny perceived on the margins of the great Shelleyan love story, might serve for her stepsister: 'can I forget the bitter experience that I learned ... that a woman without rank, without riches, without male relatives to protect her, is looked upon by men as a thing only fit to have her feelings and her rights trampled on'. [1]

Following his principles, although he had cared deeply for Fanny in the past, Godwin did not publicly mourn her. Even with Mary Wollstonecraft he had been quick to resume his life and he would later rebuke Mary for grieving for the loss of her children – sorrow, he said, left a person a 'prey to apathy and languor of no use to any earthly creature'. A week after Fanny's death he was back writing *Mandeville,* the dreary novel for whose comple- tion she had been so anxious. In his journal he simply recorded 'Swansea'.

As his letter to Shelley declared, his horror was for the scandal that would be caused should the suicide be known. The man who had published his wife's love letters to another man in 1798 had by 1809 the 'strongest antip- athy' to the posthumous printing of a friend's diary. He was now prepared to go to extremes to avoid public intrusion into his private life, and he took active steps to explain Fanny's disappearance by anything other than the truth. She was, he claimed, on an extended vacation.

Even Charles Clairmont, away on the Continent, was fed this story – belatedly. Claire wrote to him in December 1816 but failed to mention the suicide of their stepsister. In August 1817 Charles was asking after Fanny. He wondered if she could help him get money from the Godwins. He inquired whether Shelley was seeing her often: the inquiry came ten months beyond her death. A full year after it, Mary prodded Shelley: 'Have you written to … (what I dread to ask) C.C.?' (Later Claire invented a rather different sequence of events: she said her brother was so upset by Fanny's death that he became ill and depressed – he had to go to France to recover.)[2]

No letter went to Everina Wollstonecraft and Eliza Bishop until nearly six weeks after Fanny died and after the first rumours had faded; then both Godwin and Mary wrote. Everina replied at once to Mary but not to Godwin, although they resumed contact later on. Nearly twenty years later her niece, Edward Wollstonecraft's daughter, Elizabeth, now living in Australia, corresponded with Aunt Everina about her cousin Fanny. Eliza- beth wanted to know as much as possible about the death but knew the subject was still very painful to Everina.

To the more suspicious or those who expressed surprise at the length of her absence, Godwin admitted that Fanny had died in Wales, but of a cold. To the Baxters he wrote in the spring of 1817 mixing truth and lies: 'From the fatal day of Mary's elopement, Fanny's mind had been unset- tled, her duty kept her with us: but I am afraid her affections were with them … Last Autumn she went to a friend in Wales – and there was a plan settled about her going from thence to spend a short time with her Aunts in Dublin, but she was seized with a cold in Wales, which speedily turned to an inflammatory fever which carried her off.'[3] Godwin liked the specific term inflammatory fever and used it often in his correspondence concerning his stepdaughter.

Others were led to believe she had died in Ireland. Some heard or suspected the truth and Charles Lamb told Crabb Robinson of 'Fanny Godwin's or rather Wollstonecraft's death' by her own hand. Two years later Mary Hays informed him that Fanny, now called Imlay, had never been to Ireland but had hanged herself in England. It was, commented Crabb Robinson, a former devotee of *Political Justice*, one of the many catastrophes that could be blamed on Godwin's early writings. Fanny had 'adopted Godwin's opinion … She was pitied and respected.' In his journal he wrote 'Poor Godwin! How sadly visited he has been in his own family for the errors in speculation which his early works may have disseminated!'[4]

The Godwins collaborated in their stories. When she could, Mrs Godwin took the line her husband had put about, that Fanny 'had been living some time with her mother's relations'. When he had to admit the suicide Godwin followed his wife's idea, that Fanny had killed herself because she loved Shelley and Shelley had always loved Mary and not her.[5] (Significantly he never used rejection by the aunts to deflect blame from himself and his wife.) Claire too assumed that Fanny loved Shelley. She may have heard the same from Shelley himself as well as from her mother. It is unlikely that any of them could have known for sure. Fanny had had no confidant.

CHAPTER 32

HARRIET

HARRIET SHELLEY HAD had little contact with Fanny and the two young women had never conversed intimately. The initial coolness had intensified as Fanny adhered more tightly to the people she loved: any common cause would have destabilised the emotional basis of her precarious life. But rumours of the suicide undoubtedly reached Harriet and reinforced the progressive opinion she and Fanny had taken from Godwin and Shelley, that no sin attached to suicide and no afterlife made it threatening.

By the time Fanny travelled to Swansea to die Harriet was heavily pregnant. If she had been impregnated by Shelley, she had to understand her further abandonment by him, for he had not been to see her before leaving for Geneva and had not sought her on his return. What she never knew, however, was that in November he was trying through Hookham to find her whereabouts. It is not clear why – perhaps he feared the consequences of his earlier action and suspected she might be near her time.[1]

He failed in his attempt, for by then Harriet's life had become obscure. The only definite facts are that in early September she had left her parents' house. She had probably gone with their agreement since she moved out with the help of her father's friend, a plumber named William Alder. She rented a whole floor in nearby Elizabeth Street, just off Hans Place, where Mary's first child had been born; there she passed as 'Mrs Smith' for, whoever was the father of the child she was carrying, she would be disgraced if her situation were made public: the whole of London had heard that her husband was living with the two Godwin girls. Mr Westbrook had wanted a reconciliation with Shelley – hence his presence at the second marriage ceremony – but, when Harriet failed to achieve this, and revealed herself as pregnant as well whether by Shelley or by another man, he may have grown censorious and wanted her out of his house: there is, however, no evidence that she was summarily expelled and she always remained in close touch with her sister. She would not be in need: she had money from her family and her allowance from Shelley, and her lodgings were both spacious and respectable.

According to her new landlady and the maid, Harriet lived reclusively; she appeared gloomy and unwell, and spent a lot of time simply staying in bed. Mr Alder said she had 'labored under lowness of Spirits' for several months.[2] In her misery one day she wrote to Mrs Boinville asking her to come to her at once; if she did not, Harriet would kill herself. According to Boinville family tradition the letter was delayed in the post.

On 9 November, after eating a hasty dinner at four o'clock in her lodgings, Harriet left the house in Elizabeth Street. The landlady never saw her again. Neither did William Alder. The Westbrooks learnt of their daughter's disappearance and grew anxious; after a week had passed, they asked Alder to have the local ponds dragged. But nothing was found.

On 10 December a body was discovered in the Serpentine River, a common refuge for Londoners 'sick of life's miseries'. It was taken to the Fox and Bull Tavern, reception place of the Royal Humane Society which looked out for suicides. According to the *Sun* for 11 December, the body was that of a 'respectable female' with a 'valuable ring on her finger' – the detail indicated there had been no robbery, hence probably no murder; the body was 'far advanced in pregnancy'. William Alder identified the corpse. A shocked Hookham, who had recently been trying to find Harriet, heard the news and informed Shelley.

Accounts differ as to what had happened. On the one hand the person who discovered the body floating on the surface thought it had lain in the water some days, not weeks; the corpse appears to have been recognizable as Harriet, where a month-old one, even well preserved, would probably not have been, and the ring was not used for identification as one might have expected had the body been much decomposed. These aspects point to an account stemming from Claire (through Mrs Godwin) which has Harriet, very much alive after 9 November: on that date she simply moved into a mews lodgings to await the birth of her child – although why she should need to do so is unclear. In this account Harriet did not kill herself until about 7 December, so that her body would not have been long in the water when it was discovered.

On the other hand Godwin always believed Harriet died on 9 November, the day on which, after weeks of misery, she disappeared from her Elizabeth Street home; the inquest seems to have assumed the same and, if she were not missing, why would Eliza, still living with her parents and always in touch with her beloved sister, allow Alder to drag the nearby ponds in mid November? A corpse on land would certainly have decomposed during a month, but in cold water it could more easily have been preserved, possibly weighed down with stones which would have prevented it floating to the surface when bloating began (1816 was, after all, an exceptionally cold year). Then at some point it might have become dislodged and risen.

Whether fooled once more by Shelley or despairing at the plight into which she had fallen by following his unconventional principles, Harriet had certainly killed herself. And the body now discovered was undoubtedly hers. She was given a lengthy but partial inquest, in which people who knew her identity remained discreet; probably it was Mr Westbrook who ensured that a full account did not find its way into the newspaper.

Like Fanny, Harriet received the kindly jury verdict, 'found dead'. Since the daughter of the landlord at the inn where she was taken knew her, she had been 'tenderly' laid out and 'with care', and, according to Peacock, her body was carried to her father's house before receiving a proper funeral. She was buried as 'Harriet Smith'.[3]

As with Fanny, so with Harriet: Shelley and the Godwins quickly wove stories round the event and the life leading up to it. The Skinner Street family made her into an adventuress who had trapped a rich young gentleman into marriage. Shelley's version of her ending deflected blame from himself: Harriet had been 'driven from her father's house, & descended the steps of prostitution until she lived with a groom … There can be no question that the beastly viper her sister, unable to gain profit from her connection with me – has secured to herself the fortune of the old man – who is now dying – by the murder of this poor creature.' To Mary, and later Byron, he declared again that Harriet was more or less murdered by Eliza Westbrook for the sake of their father's money. Yet, despite this vilification, when he wrote to Eliza demanding his children, Ianthe and Charles Bysshe, he accepted that Mary *alone* would appear as 'the cause of your sister's ruin' – no other was noted. He made no mention in the letters, either to Eliza or to others, of his wife's pregnancy by another man.

While vilifying Harriet and the sister who had so long supported her and his children, he insisted on his own righteousness: 'Everything tends to prove, however, that beyond the mere shock of so hideous a catastrophe having fallen on a human being once so nearly connected with me, there would, in any case have been little to regret ... every one does *me* full justice; – bears testimony to the uprightness & liberality of my conduct to her.' Although he claimed he was much affected by the 'dark dreadful death' of Harriet, he believed that Fanny's had given him 'far severer anguish'.[4]

In the years after his own death the unblemished saintliness of Shelley became the family purpose. As Mark Twain remarked of an early biography by a family friend, Edward Dowden: 'Percy Bysshe Shelley has done something which in the case of other men is called a grave crime; it must be shown that in his case it is not that, because he does not think as other men do about these things.'[5] Mary wrote, 'I vindicated the memory of my Shelley and spoke of him as he was – an angel among his fellow mortals – lifted far above this world – a celestial spirit given and taken away, for we were none of us worthy of him,' a picture far from Hazlitt's red-faced, shrill-voiced man with 'a fire in his eye, a fever in his blood, a maggot in his brain, a hectic flutter in his speech, which mark out the philosophic fanatic'.[6]

Harriet's sad story failed to fit the passive saintly image, and Shelley's first wife was portrayed spending her last months in poverty moving from man to man, until she ended little better than a prostitute – a crowded descent in which Shelley, whether or not the father of her child, may have believed. Peacock however always maintained it was his 'most decided conviction that her conduct as a wife was as pure, as true, as absolutely faultless, as that of any who for such conduct are held most in honour'. Probably, as usual, the truth was somewhere in between.

Like Fanny, Harriet left a suicide note – or *possibly* she left one, for the handwriting is not totally convincing. Unlike Fanny's note, placed by the bedside, Harriet's note is not mentioned by her landlady or the maid at the lodgings, was not available at the inquest, and the Westbrooks did not use it in the later custody case; it turned up for sale in 1895. Yet it sounds genuine and sadly echoes Fanny's authentic note. Mentioning no lover, it addresses '[m]y dearest & much belo[ve]d Sister' Eliza: 'do not regret the loss of one who could never be anything but a source of vexation & misery to you all … Too wretched to exert myself lowered in the opinion of everyone why should I drag on a miserable existence embittered by past recollections & not one ray of hope to rest on for the future'. It also addressed 'dear' Shelley, declaring a continuing love: 'I never could refuse you.' It was signed, for no one tore off this signature, 'Harriet S—'[7]

✧

Unlike Fanny's suicide, Harriet's was proclaimed by Godwin, for it promised to give his daughter a 'good match'. Fanny's death had the effect of bringing him and Shelley together and effecting a reconciliation as no other event since 1814 had done; Harriet's death continued the process.

Godwin summoned Mary to Skinner Street, where her lover was now welcomed. Shelley remained unenthusiastic about marriage but, according to Mrs Godwin, Mary pressured him into it — 'if you do not marry me, I will do as Harriet did'. Shelley turned pale and agreed. (Another of Mrs Godwin's versions gives a more central role to herself — *she* threatened Shelley with Mary's suicide if he did not comply.) Two weeks after learning of Harriet's drowning and after dining at Skinner Street for the first time on the previous evening, Mary and Shelley were married at St Mildred's Church, Bread Street, in the City.

The proud Godwins were in attendance: Mary would one day be Lady Shelley, 'a future ornament of the baronetage', wrote Godwin. To the Baxters and Booths he succinctly described events: 'My first information you will be very glad to hear. Mrs Shelley died in November last and on the 30th December Shelley led my daughter to the altar.' It was not a formulation that much appealed to these Scottish Puritans — they also disliked seeing Godwin flatter Shelley 'by terming him the son of a baronet'.[8] To his brother he was more expansive:

[Mary's] husband is the eldest son of Sir Timothy Shelley of Field Place in the county of Sussex, baronet. So that, according to the vulgar ideas of the world, she is well married; & I have great hopes the young man will make her a good husband. You will wonder, I dare say, how a girl with not a penny of fortune, should meet with so good a match. But such are the ups and downs of this world. For my part I care but little comparatively about wealth, so that it should be her destiny in life to be respectable, virtuous & contented.[9]

Mrs Godwin was just as eager to impart 'the agreeable intelligence', and she wrote to Godwin's publisher: 'I have now the pleasure to announce that Mr. Godwin's daughter, Mary, has entered the marriage state with Mr. Percy Bysshe Shelley, eldest son of Sir Timothy Shelley, Baronet, of Field Place, Horsham, Sussex.'[10]

CHAPTER 33

MARY *and* SHELLEY

THE EFFECT OF Fanny's death on Mary is hard to gauge. Later she would write of her horror of people 'dragging private names and private life before the world' in these 'publishing, inquisitive, scandal-mongering days', and she applauded reserve and a 'common silence'.[1] When she published Shelley's lines beginning 'Her voice did quiver as we parted' she did so without explanation and she omitted much of what tied the poem and surrounding comments to Fanny's death. On the day she learnt of the suicide she recorded simply 'a miserable day' in her journal.[2] She bought mourning clothes or, more probably, cloth, then spent some of the day sewing. A few months later, after Harriet's death she remarked, 'Poor dear Fanny if she had lived until this moment she would have been saved for my house would then have been a proper assylum for her' – she knew that Fanny always wished to be with them.

On the anniversary of her baby girl's death Mary had a dream 'of the dead being alive'; possibly Fanny joined her dead niece to haunt her.[3] Yet she kept the haunting private: when she published her first work, the *Six Weeks' Tour,* she avoided mentioning her sister as the recipient of the letters she printed. Years later, when she attempted to write her father's life, she did not emulate his frankness over Mary Wollstonecraft but simply noted his first marriage without any reference at all to his wife's daughter. Edward Trelawny, a friend to whom she communicated many incidents from her

early years, was allowed to assume that only she was the child of Mary Wollstonecraft and the others in Skinner Street all the children of Mrs Godwin.

Yet there must have been pain. In *Manfred,* in part calling on the trau-
matic disruption of his tie with his half sister Augusta, Byron has imagina-
tively caught what might have been the sisters' relationship at the end:

> Though thou seest me not pass by,
> Thou shalt feel me with thine eye
> As a thing that, though unseen
> Must be near thee, and hath been.

Close to the anniversary of Fanny's suicide, when Claire's daughter had
been born, Mary wrote to Shelley that she saw in the little girl's eyes something that reminded her not so much of the Fanny she had known as of
their mother's description in *Letters from Sweden* of her as a small child with
intelligent eyes and great vivacity. Possibly she and Shelley had again been
relating the dead Fanny to this always haunting − overwhelming − book.
'But this is a melancholy subject', she ended.[4] It was, after all, for the sake of
Claire and this child that Fanny had been repulsed.

The secrecy of diaries and biographies could not be sustained in fiction.
The book Mary was writing as Fanny passed through Bath on her way to
die was *Frankenstein*.

In the story young Victor Frankenstein grew up in a loving family. In
Skinner Street only Fanny among the girls had supported the notion of
the nuclear family and the 'amiableness of domestic affections', as the 1818
preface to *Frankenstein* described the atmosphere of a happy home. Having
read the wrong books and assumed the wrong ambitions − to be admired by
the whole human race − Frankenstein tears himself from his loving family
to follow his utopian dreams and study alone, until he fashions from the
ugly dead a man as ugly as the dead and flees in horror. His flight condemns
his creature, who, following Godwinian precepts, is benevolent although
susceptible to life's blows. Maddened by constant rejection, he understands
that his uncaring creator may be hurt through those he loves. So he kills

Victor's little brother, William, the resonant name of Mary's father, brother and son. Victor too is a resonant name, for Shelley used it when as a boy he published poetry with his sister Elizabeth.

Chapter 5 of *Frankenstein*, written in Bath immediately after Fanny killed herself, begins the new story of Justine.

This is another tale of cruel parenting. Both Caroline, Frankenstein's mother, and the orphan Elizabeth, his intended wife, are unselfishly feminine; both die young. So does the loving Justine, but she is even more unfortunate, in life as in death. She has a volatile Catholic mother who 'could not endure her' and makes her feel to blame for everything, even her siblings' misfortunes – much as Fanny had been blamed. At twelve, near Fanny's age at the time of Godwin's explanatory discussion with her, Justine enters the Frankenstein family as part daughter, part servant, a kind, frank-hearted, grateful little girl, especially liked by Victor but never regarded like Elizabeth as a potential wife – a matter perhaps of class, appearance and temperament. Her adoption into the Frankenstein family will be her downfall.

Justine loves the baby William and adores Victor's mother, who, when she falls ill, is attended by Justine. Yet, when she dies, Justine's huge grief is little noticed by Victor and Elizabeth. Her early vivacity and joy disappear.

When the Creature kills little William he plants on Justine the beloved mother's miniature that had before hung round William's neck. So she is blamed for the murder. She is tried and executed. Many are sorry for her, knowing that the sentence is unjust, but no one acts to save her. Elizabeth gains the court's approbation by expressing concern and a momentary guilt: 'I wish,' she cries 'that I were to die with you.'

In this new character of Justine, scapegoat of the Creature and in a way his alter ego, one might see some reference to Fanny. Both real and fictional women kill themselves – for Justine's apathy and ultimate passivity amount to this – out of lowliness of spirit and to escape the world's injustice. Knowing she is innocent, Justine nonetheless confesses her guilt; like Fanny she has too often been blamed. It is as if she cannot bear the notion of her own innocent pain any more, as if she wants to quit a life in which, for all her care and good intent, she could be blamed for wearing a mother's picture and for causing harm to other children, a life stemming from a birth that was 'unfortunate'. Nothing, the novel seems to say, can take the place of the lost family. Stepmothers are not mothers and Justine can be no more secure in the Frankenstein circle than the Creature. But, where he murders, then kills himself, she as a woman kills only herself.

◌

On the day of his marriage to Mary, Shelley wrote to Claire: 'I will not tell you how dreadfully melancholy Skinner Street appears with all its associations. The most horrid thought is how people can be merry there!'[5] The abuse, the mockery, the indifference of which they had all been guilty, preyed on his mind – but there were friends, dinners, a little unaccustomed and welcome fame to distract him. And in due course he too could be merry.

Yet Fanny's death affected him deeply in moments. He told Byron so. Having seen her in London and almost certainly Bath, he had been the last of her generation to know her alive; perhaps only now accepting her passion for him, he saw himself rejecting her with a poetic theatricality. He had refused an appeal as urgent as any made by those he had rescued.

If in reality Fanny's death made few ripples – Shelley continued reading *Don Quixote* and obsessed about his own health: he began to record in grams exactly what he ate – in the imaginative realm where he lived much of the time he could accept her death as significant. He had done no wrong in neither saving nor burying her, for she had chosen her release and her earthly remains were unimportant. She had embraced a death whose mystery he himself always longed to penetrate. There need be no guilt or sorrow. But Fanny had not gone to die in a spirit of ecstatic enquiry, rather of resentment and despair. He could feel anguish for the real person he had known, the one who had lived in the world and been neglected by it. If her death and his implication in it did not quite make him a 'changed man', as Claire reported, he did perhaps intend for a while to act 'more cautiously to women'.[6]

On the reverse side of the paper on which he wrote the lines, 'Her voice did quiver as we parted' – words he did not show to Mary – Shelley repeatedly sketched steps going down. Perhaps they led to a tomb – what he had failed to give Fanny? He also drew drooping flowers: one flower was being devoured in its pot by a fleshy mouth-like leafbulb – a plant killed where it grew.

Among the doodles is the line, 'Breaking thine indissoluble sleep'; below that is the word 'miserable'; and written beneath that is the sentence: 'It is not my fault – it is not to be attributed to me'. Maybe he had erased his guilt; perhaps he was using the manoeuvre Peacock had noted: Shelley's 'imagination often presented past events to him as they might have been, not as they were'; or perhaps he feared that he *was* to blame, that if the Poet was, as Fanny had so recently written, 'never failing', the man had been.

Goethe's *Faust*, Part I, ends with Faust's vision of the woman he seduced and abandoned awaiting execution for killing her child. When Shelley translated the lines concerning the doomed woman he made two subtle changes:

> Her eyes are like the eyes of a fresh corpse
> Which no beloved hand has closed, alas!

Goethe's original phrase, 'someone dead', has become in Shelley's version a 'fresh corpse' and the 'loving hand' is now the 'beloved hand'. It is hard to imagine that he failed to think of Fanny when he modified these lines.

Some months – possibly a year – seem to have passed after he doodled and sketched on the manuscript where he had written 'Her voice did quiver as we parted'; then he returned. He now inscribed his flowerpot, 'I drew this flower pot in October 1816 and now it is 1817'. Over the other drawings he wrote 'These cannot be forgotten – years May flow'. And, above the earlier words 'It is not my fault – it is not to be attributed to me', he now added 'When said I so?' In moments he must have felt a sort of shame, for the earlier words if for nothing else.

He had been reading again from *Letters from Sweden,* the book which best expressed the hope of Fanny's early life and which had charmed both him and Godwin. There Mary Wollstonecraft described how, separated from her lively daughter for a few weeks, one night she dreamt of 'Paradise'; her 'little cherub' was hiding her face in her mother's bosom: 'I heard her sweet cooing beat on my heart from the cliffs, and saw her tiny footsteps on the sands.'

In Shelley's mind the vision intermingled with words in Mary Wollstonecraft's last work, *Maria,* in which the grieving mother, her breasts overflowing with milk, imagines her lost baby: 'She heard her half speaking, half cooing, and felt the little twinkling fingers on her burning bosom.'[7] Baby and dead woman, mother and daughter, text and body, real and represented Fanny, merged as he wrote:

Thy little footsteps on the sands
   Of a remote and lonely shore −
The twinkling of thine infant hands
   Where now the worm will feed no more,
Thy look of mingled love and glee
When *one* returned to gaze on thee −

These footsteps on the sands are fled,
   Thine eyes are dark − thy hands are cold,
And she is dead − and thou art dead −

Evidently dissatisfied with this interplay of memories, Shelley folded the paper with the writings and drawing again and again.[8] Someone else smoothed it out, for Shelley's work, like Godwin's, was always significant.

AFTERWORD

IN HIS VENICE palazzo, surrounded by mistresses and a menagerie of monkeys, dogs and peacocks, Byron learnt of the birth of Claire's daughter Allegra. He was in no hurry to see either. Mary found there was to be no 'absentia Clariae' even with marriage: Claire and Allegra joined her and Shelley in Marlow, where several onlookers – including Godwin – assumed the child Shelley's. Indeed Godwin persisted in this way of thinking and rumours continued even when Byron had taken charge of Allegra.

Mandeville, in which Fanny had so passionately believed, was finished, just when Godwin also read his daughter's *Frankenstein*. Where her novel was an instant success, his was judged pedestrian, obsessive and tired. Gloomily he contemplated Shelley's new poem 'Laon and Cythna', with its tribute to himself as a 'mighty Spirit' before whom the 'tumultuous world' had stood mute. Given what was suspected of Byron with his sister and Shelley with Claire, he was unimpressed with the central theme of incest. The clarity of this was dropped when the poem became *The Revolt of Islam*; nonetheless the work thoroughly established Shelley's poetic notoriety with the public.

In September 1817 Mary bore a baby, Clara; the following March they were all en route for Italy, in part so that Byron would acknowledge Allegra, now duly dispatched to him. The departure angered Godwin and the old dramas were replayed. Before leaving, Shelley had obtained another expensive post-obit but the ever-needy Godwins received only a small fraction of it. Scolding and coldness followed; soon Godwin was openly reviling his son-in-law.

In Italy Claire faced patently absurd but troubling rumours that Byron was planning to raise Allegra only to debauch her. Desperate to see her daughter, she insisted on going with Shelley from Bagni di Lucca, their temporary home, to Venice. Shelley knew Byron would be furious if he arrived with Claire alone; so, needing to pretend that Mary and the children were there too, he demanded they follow at once. Clara, only a year old, was ailing and could not tolerate the long journey: she died of convulsions in her mother's arms in Venice. Intending consolation, Godwin told Mary that 'only persons of a very ordinary sort, & of a pusillanimous disposition ... sink long under a calamity of this nature ... We seldom indulge long in depression & mourning, except when we think secretly, that there is some-thing very refined in it, & that it does us honour.'[1]

Three months after the death of Clara, a child called Elena Shelley was born in Naples; she was registered as Shelley's and Mary's. The baby may have been Shelley's by an unknown woman or by Claire – perhaps it tells against the latter idea that Claire had been up Mount Vesuvius a few days before the birth and that later Mary swore by the life of her surviving child that the baby was not her stepsister's – though Claire may have been carried up the mountain and Mary may not have known the truth. Their dismissed servant declared to everyone she could reach that Shelley and Claire had certainly had a child and that it had been sent to the foundling hospital; Byron responded by forbidding any contact between Claire and Allegra, whom he soon placed in a convent. Elena Shelley died at seventeen months.

The Shelley ménage continued travelling. In Rome they stayed in the usual patrician lodgings, lingering to have their portraits painted. Little Will-mouse was high spirited but delicate, and sultry Rome did not agree with him. Mary was eager to go north to a cooler climate but, before they could do so, Willmouse caught malaria. On 7 June 1819 he died and was buried in the Protestant cemetery. His corpse was soon moved; so he too, like his Aunt Fanny who had so loved him, remained in an unmarked grave.

Childless, though again pregnant, Mary fell into a renewed and deeper depression. It alienated her from Shelley, who resented her sexual withdrawal and feared that she had left him 'in this dreary world alone'. He determined not to follow her to 'Sorrow's most obscure abode'. Cut off from those surrounding her – Claire was still an irritation – Mary thought much of suicide and perhaps now Fanny and Harriet came into her mind in a way they had not before. If so she was as discreet as ever. There is no mention of either in letters or journals.

Deep in his own troubles – he was threatened with eviction from Skinner Street for unpaid rent – Godwin could think of little but trying to get money from Shelley; again he deplored his daughter's excessive, selfish grief. Perhaps it suggested that she might imitate her mother and sister by attempting suicide; she was after all 'a Wollstonecraft'. With so little human sympathy Mary turned to writing about her misery, in a bleak novella called *Matilda* concerning an incestuous love of a father for a daughter who too much resembles her dead mother. The passion blights their lives and causes the suicide of the father; after she has rejected a Shelleyan poet who, she fears, will simply use her as grist to his poetry, the remorseful daughter wills herself to death. Mary sent her work to Godwin, who pronounced it 'disgusting & detestable'.[2]

In November Mary's and Shelley's fourth and last child, a son whom they named Percy Florence, was born. They moved to Pisa staying in a succession of fine lodgings near Lady Mount Cashell, who managed to persuade Claire to stay for a time in Florence and leave Mary in peace. Pining for Claire and distanced from Mary, Shelley grew infatuated with young Emilia Viviani, whom he planned to rescue from her expensive convent. After he had written an intensely sexual poem, *Epipsychidion*, in praise of free love, the impulse passed and Emilia made an arranged marriage. At much the same time he and Mary met Edward Williams and his common-law wife Jane; the latter, a striking, dark haired, man-directed woman, further aroused Shelley. Mary looked on wearily at the flirtations and tried to cope by nurturing her only child.

Having poured out his moody self-blame in *Manfred,* Byron now became Byronic and satiric by turns, finishing the first canto of his long, final poem, *Don Juan,* in 1819 and starting *Cain* in 1821. He had ceased his flamboyant promiscuity and settled into a curious relationship with a married Italian countess, the plump, amiable Teresa Guiccioli, whose family were political agitators against Austrian rule. Dissuading Teresa from fleeing to Geneva, Shelley urged them both to come to Pisa. Mary welcomed their arrival since it would keep her stepsister away. Travelling out of Pisa, Claire passed Byron in his Napoleonic coach, trailing his menagerie.

At the end of the month Claire, the Shelleys and the Williamses moved to a crowded house in the village of Lerici near La Spezia. Claire had had wild plans of kidnapping Allegra from the convent, but before she could act the child died of typhoid on 19 April. The news was kept from the mother until 2 May. 'In this life, one dies of anguish many times before one really dies,' Claire later wrote.[3] An unexpectedly grief-stricken Byron decreed that Allegra should be buried back in England, in Harrow churchyard with a plaque naming her in the nave. But he was thwarted by the churchwarden, who believed that commemorating a bastard would set a bad example to young Harrovians.

The following month Mary almost died of a miscarriage. She was still ill and depressed when, on 8 July, Shelley, Edward Williams and a young English boat attendant sailed out, met a storm and were drowned. Shelley was twenty-nine. As the *Courier* remarked, 'now he knows if there is a God or no'. His putrid, mutilated corpse was burnt on the seashore with Byron and other friends watching.

In the same year Shelley's and Harriet's friend Elizabeth Hitchener died. After her period of turmoil she had revived, travelled as governess to the Continent and married an Austrian army officer, from whom she swiftly separated. She returned to England and set up a school in Edmonton with her sisters.[4] Retaining her strong interest in Roman republican history, she used many of its examples in her *Enigmas* or riddles for children and family use. When she wrote number 28 describing a shipwreck, perhaps she remembered her time with the Shelleys:

> See, see the whirlpool yawn,
> Prepared t' engulf them all!
> Within its fatal influence drawn,
> In vain for help they call.

Yet in 'Apologetic Stanzas' preceding her last poem, after lamenting an intellectually deprived childhood, she declared she had been awakened by 'a vision' of someone 'wise, and great, and fair', who 'could loftiest, noblest strains inspire,/And to sweet cadence, tune thy wildest air'. It sounds as though she held a candle for Shelley to the end.[5]

Still only twenty-four when Shelley died, Mary responded with self-lacerating remorse, regretting her cold neglect, averted eyes and closed heart;

Shelley at once became a 'Celestial Spirit', a man unequalled by any human being that had ever existed. Nonetheless she spent the next months close to Byron, moved and excited by his presence, perhaps as much as Claire had once been, and like her stepsister copying out his poetry: there was some relief in being with a man who, unlike Shelley, delighted in the real rather than 'the abstract and the ideal'.[6] Then Byron moved away and the following year, bored with political wrangling and perhaps with Teresa, he offered to help Greek insurgents in their fight against their Turkish occupiers. Equipping himself with an antique helmet he sailed to Greece and prepared a fighting expedition. Before it was ready he fell ill, was purged and bled into dehydration. He died on 19 April 1824. He was thirty-six.

His body was returned to London, where Mary watched through a window as his cortège passed by – she had arrived back in August 1823. She was now determined to raise Percy Florence as an ordinary gentleman: without Shelley there was more chance that he would both reach adulthood and be commonplace. Jane Williams had also returned and was soon, like Harriet and Mary before her, courted by Shelley's friend Hogg, whose common-law wife she became.

Mary lodged near Godwin and Mary Jane. The pair had left Skinner Street and continued their trade in crowded rooms in the Strand. In Francis Place's phrase, Godwin 'shuffled on for some time' after Shelley's death; then in 1825 he became bankrupt and the Juvenile Library closed. It seemed no great matter and friends remarked that both events were long overdue. Despite *Mandeville*'s failure he wrote two more novels, both repeating the old themes and both disappointing. In 1832 his son William, a modest journalist who had, like Charles Clairmont, failed to live up to the high Godwinian standard, died in a cholera epidemic.

Two years later the dilapidated old radical obtained a government sinecure of Office Keeper Yeoman Usher of the Exchequer with an annual salary of £220. The Godwins were now more comfortable than they had been for years, but Mary Jane continued hostile to Mary, disliking her renewed intercourse with her husband, while Mary still thought of her stepmother as the 'grand annoyance'.[7] Yet, after Godwin's death in April 1836 at the age of eighty, the two women found themselves oddly friendly – perhaps Mary had already softened, since in the 1831 edition of *Frankenstein* she removed her swipe at stepmothers and, in 'The Mortal Immortal: A Tale' written about this time, although the ugly old mother tries to stop her adopted daughter Bertha running off with her lover by uttering the unpleasant words, 'Back to your cage – hawks are abroad!' in fact she is right, for the lover is a wizard's apprentice and immortal; as he remains young, Bertha grows old, peevish, rouged and jealous, in a way turning into her stepmother.[8]

Godwin was buried next to Mary Wollstonecraft in St Pancras' church-yard in the tomb where Mary and Shelley had reputedly first made scan-dalous love. Mary Jane Godwin, grown feeble-minded, died in 1841 and was buried alongside her husband and predecessor. Two years later Everina Wollstonecraft joined them in the churchyard. It is unlikely that she or Godwin had met Fanny's father again. Apparently a man called Gilbert Imlay died aged seventy-four in 1828 on the island of Jersey, a good spot for shady dealers between England and France. An epitaph on the tombstone makes no mention of any family but demands that the passerby tell the dead how society is advancing, for 'Transient hope gleams even in the grave.'[9]

When Sir Timothy lifted an earlier ban on the publication of Shelley's poetry Mary brought out a four-volume edition which established her husband as one of the great geniuses of the era; prudently his political and sexual ideas were submerged in his uplifting spiritual message. The notes omitted mention of Godwin, Fanny, Harriet and Claire (although after Peacock and Hogg protested at her deletion of the dedication of *Queen Mab* to Harriet Mary did restore the verses, exclaiming 'Poor Harriet to whose sad fate I attribute too many of my own heavy sorrows as the atone-ment claimed by fate for her death').[10] When introducing Godwin for a new edition of *Caleb Williams,* Mary wrote out Fanny from his story as well as the offending *Memoirs*: she implied that she was the only daughter of a conventional pair who had married before she was conceived. So too in an introduction to *Frankenstein* she effaced Harriet by suggesting that Shelley and she were man and wife before they left for Switzerland in 1816. The past had to conform to present needs.

To help support herself and Percy, Mary continued writing novels, none nearly as popular as *Frankenstein*. The heroes sounded remarkably like Lord Byron – as Claire contemptuously remarked: 'To think a person of your genius' should spend her powers embellishing 'what was the merest compound of vanity, folly, and every miserable weakness'. In *Lodore* (1835) for the first time she used the name of Fanny. The book drew on the years when she and Shelley were dodging creditors and bailiffs and perhaps the recollection recalled the willing go-between. In her novel plain Fanny is a foil to the pretty heroine; she is unappreciated by her vulgar mother, although she is talented, home-loving, kind-hearted and true. She waits tenderly on her eccentric father while he instructs her and later serves as comfort and helper to the central lovers; she fights for the oppressed whenever she can. Fanny ends the book unpartnered, heading for a varied fate of 'uncontaminating' sorrow. Mary gave her created Fanny one advantage over the real-life woman: a legacy that made her independent.

Perhaps this use of her own life and Fanny's name opened up a seam of memory, for in the following year Mary again used her sister's name in a short story 'The Parvenue'. In this 'Fanny' is like Mary in being fair and loved by an aristocrat who is constantly dunned for money by her imprudent family; finally they destroy her husband's love. There is, however, one touch of the real Fanny: since Mary's heroine lacks the profligate manners of aristocracy she is called 'sordid' by her lord, the word with which Mary had so upset her sister shortly before her death.

After Shelley drowned, Claire joined her brother Charles in Vienna, where the pair were watched by a jittery government as dangerous associates of the radical generation. Two years later she was in Russia as a governess to a Muscovite court minister, keeping her political views and radical past to herself. Refusing at least one offer of marriage she declared that her ten minutes of '*happy passion*' had inoculated her against further love.[11] She worked in Germany, France, Italy and England as governess or companion, sometimes in ill health, sometimes vibrantly happy, at others learning to be happy without happiness, often low spirited, understanding now Fanny's and Mary Wollstonecraft's horror of the dependent state – indeed she had a friend who killed herself rather than be a governess. She wrote often to Mary but quarrelled with her when they met. She never forgave the closeness to Byron after Allegra died: when with her stepsister she felt as if a 'Death Worm' were crawling along her veins.[12] In turn Claire made Mary 'more uncomfortable than any human being'; Claire, she wrote, 'poisoned my life when young … my idea of Heaven was a world without Claire'. In old age she dreaded being left alone with her.[13] Yet the sisters were bound together, mutually generous in time of need and anxious whenever they lost touch. Claire always accepted, with varying emotion, that Mary was the 'great authoress', the only one from Skinner Street to fulfil their father's hopes.

In 1844 Sir Timothy died at the age of ninety, leaving a much mortgaged and depleted estate. With Charles Bysshe, Shelley's neglected son by Harriet long dead, Percy Florence became Sir Percy, a proper, stolid and solid Englishman. In religious matters he may have had some unorthodox views, since he must have agreed to the publication of his father's subversive works on Christianity. But in the main he thought exactly as others thought; in this he was helped by a suitable wife, Jane, an older widow whom Mary much approved and who totally disapproved of Claire. They had no children and Jane devoted her energies to securing the respectability and fame of her husband's family, in part by destroying incriminating archives. The Regency period, which had been fascinated by wicked geniuses, was long past; now a writer's private life should conform to the highest domestic standards.

Mary died in London on 1 February 1851, aged fifty-three, having suffered for many years from a growing brain tumour. Sir Percy buried her in the seaside town of Bournemouth, near where he and his wife were living. He also arranged for Godwin and Mary Wollstonecraft, now made respectable, to be exhumed from St Pancras' and reburied next to her. They were accompanied by Shelley's heart, snatched from the flames on the Italian beach. To Claire's indignation Mary Jane Godwin was left behind in St Pancras' to be disturbed by the new railway being constructed round her.

Claire never achieved the limited respectability of her stepsister. With her own Allegra dead she had loved little Percy, calling him '*Percino,*' her 'darling boy', and fantasising that he would replicate his poet father. But the adult Sir Percy dismissed her as a 'stranger in the Shelley family'.[14] She moved to Paris, possibly involved with a lover. On Sir Timothy's death she received the huge bequest Shelley had meant for her and Allegra but lost most of it in mistaken property deals including a supposedly rentable opera box in the Haymarket; after Charles's death in 1850 she generously supported his widow and children – for her brother had turned out to be almost as improvident as his stepfather. In 1845 she came to England, continuing her wandering life there and in France. In 1859 she was back in Florence, where in 1870 she was joined by her unconventional Shelleyan niece Pauline with her illegitimate daughter. Two years later Edward Augustus Silsbee from Salem, Massachusetts, passionate devotee of Shelley's transforming poetry, arrived at their house eager to gain access to the papers of the great Romantic poets, which he presumed Claire held. Over many years, while aunt and niece vied for his attention, he recorded in his notebooks Claire's rambling, fitful memories of a Shelley who was always true to his principles, always justified in what he did, and who was remembered for his 'undying spirit, the contempt of pain and Death his carelessness of riches ... the calm majesty of a constant communion with high thoughts'.[15]

Silsbee's questions gave him glimpses of a demonic Byron as well as of Fanny, Mary and Harriet, Godwin and Mary Jane, all the actors of the crowded years. Henry James heard of the pursuit and turned it into literature in *The Aspern Papers* (1888), with Claire as Juliana Bordereau. The real Claire died on 19 March 1879 aged eighty. At her request she was buried with a shawl Shelley had given her more than half a century before.

NOTES

The following abbreviations have been used throughout the notes:

Abinger MSS: Abinger manuscripts held in the Bodleian Library, University of Oxford

BLJ: *Byron's Letters and Journals*, ed. Leslie A. Marchand, Vol. 5: *1816–1817, 'So late into the night'*; Vol. 6: *1818–1819, 'The flesh is frail'* (London: John Murray, 1976)

BWH: Berry, Wollstonecraft and Hay papers, State Library of New South Wales (ML MSS 315/90: CY Reel 3150)

CCC: *The Clairmont Correspondence: Letters of Claire Clairmont, Charles Clairmont, and Fanny Imlay Godwin*, ed. Marion Kingston Stocking, Vol. 1: *1808–1834*; Vol. 2: *1835–1879* (Baltimore, London: Johns Hopkins University Press, 1995)

CCJ: *The Journals of Claire Clairmont*, ed. Marion Kingston Stocking (Cambridge, Mass.: Harvard University Press, 1968)

CKG: Charles Kegan Paul, *William Godwin: His Friends and Contemporaries*, 2 vols. (London: H. S. King, 1876)

Crabb Robinson: *Henry Crabb Robinson on Books and Their Writers*, ed. Edith J. Morley, 3 vols. (London: Dent, 1938)

Hogg: Thomas Jefferson Hogg, *The Life of Percy Bysshe Shelley* (London: Routledge, 1906)

MSJ: *The Journals of Mary Shelley: 1814–1844*, ed. Paula R. Feldman and Diana Scott-Kilvert, 2 vols. (Oxford: Clarendon Press, 1987)

MWL: *The Collected Letters of Mary Wollstonecraft*, ed. Janet Todd (London: Allen Lane, 2003)

MWSL: *The Letters of Mary Wollstonecraft Shelley*, ed. Betty T. Bennett, Vol. 1: *'A part of the elect'* (Baltimore: Johns Hopkins University Press, 1980); Vol. 2: *'Treading in unknown paths'* (Baltimore: Johns Hopkins University Press, 1983), Vol. 3: *'What years I have spent!'* (Baltimore: Johns Hopkins University Press, 1988)

MWW: *The Works of Mary Wollstonecraft*, ed. Janet Todd and Marilyn Butler, 7 vols. (London: William Pickering, 1989)

N&M: *Collected Novels and Memoirs of William Godwin*, ed. Mark Philp, 8 vols. (London: Pickering & Chatto, 1992)

PBSL: *The Letters of Percy Bysshe Shelley*, ed. Frederick L. Jones, Vol. 1: *Shelley in England*; Vol. 2: *Shelley in Italy* (Oxford: Clarendon Press, 1964)

PBSP: *The Poems of Shelley*, ed. Geoffrey Matthews and Kelvin Everest, Vol. 1: *1804–1817* (London and New York: Longman, 1989); Vol. 2: *1817–1819* (London and New York: Longman, 2000)

Peacock: Thomas Love Peacock, 'Memoirs of Percy Bysshe Shelley', in *The Works of Thomas Love Peacock*, ed. H. F. B. Brett-Smith and C. V. E. Jones, Vol. 8 (London: Constable, 1934)

PPW: *Political and Philosophical Writings of William Godwin*, general ed. Mark Philp, (London: Pickering & Chatto, 1993), Vol. 2: *Political Writings II*; Vol. 3: *An Enquiry Concerning Political Justice*; Vol. 7: *Religious Writings*

SC: *Shelley and His Circle 1773–1822*, Vols. 3 and 4, ed. Kenneth Neill Cameron (Cambridge, Mass.: Harvard University Press, 1970); Vol. 5, ed. Donald H. Reiman (Cambridge, Mass.: Harvard University Press, 1973); Vol. 10, ed. Donald H. Reiman and Doucet Devin Fischer (Cambridge, Mass.: Harvard University Press, 2002)

SPP: *Shelley's Poetry and Prose*, ed. Donald H. Reiman and Neil Fraistat, 2nd edn (New York and London: W. W. Norton & Co., 2002)

Chapter 2

1. W. Clark Durant, *Memoirs of Mary Wollstonecraft, edited, with a preface, a supplement chronologically arranged and containing hitherto unpublished or uncollected material* (London: Constable, 1927), pp. 218–19; *Letters of Anna Seward written between the years 1784 and 1807*, ed. A. Constable (Edinburgh, 1811), Vol. 3, p. 117.

2. *The Spirit of the Age*, in *The Selected Writings of William Hazlitt*, ed. Duncan Wu (London: Pickering & Chatto, 1998), Vol. 7, p. 88.

3. *Morning Chronicle*, 10 January 1795.

4. PPW, Vol. 3, pp. 453–4.

5. 'Thoughts Occasioned by the Perusal of Dr Parr's Spital Sermon', PPW, Vol. 2, p. 165.

6. Harriet Boinville in SC, Vol. 3, p. 274.

Chapter 3

1. Percy Bysshe Shelley in MSJ, p. 6.

2. CCC, Vol. 2, p. 615; Edward Dowden, *The Life of Percy Bysshe Shelley* (London: Kegan Paul, 1886), Vol. 2, p. 547. Mrs Godwin's letters to Lady Mount Cashell were copied and edited several times by Claire Clairmont, so may be accurate only in parts. They were quoted and summarised in appendix B of Dowden's *Life of Shelley* and in appendix D of R. Glynn Grylls, *Claire Clairmont, Mother of Byron's Allegra* (London: John Murray, 1939).

3. Robert Gittings and Jo Manton, *Claire Clairmont and the Shelleys, 1798–1879* (Oxford: Oxford University Press, 1992), p. 15.

4. Percy Bysshe Shelley in MSJ, Vol. 1, p. 7.

5. Miranda Seymour, *Mary Shelley* (London: John Murray, 2000), p. 99.

6. CCJ, p. 31.

7. 'Journal of Cl. Clairmont written in the year 1814', SC, Vol. 3, pp. 350–51.

8. MSJ, Vol. 1, p. 20–1; *History of A Six Weeks' Tour* (London, T. Hookham, 1817), p. 69.

9. Grylls, *Claire Clairmont*, p. 274.

Chapter 4

1. *Letters from Sweden, Norway and Denmark*, MWW, Vol. 6; William Godwin, *Memoirs of the Author of a Vindication of the Rights of Woman*, ed. Richard Holmes (London: Penguin Books, 1987), p. 249.

2. MWL, pp. 239, 272, 279, 281.

3. *Letters from Sweden, Norway and Denmark*, MWW, Vol. 6, p. 269; *Letters to Imlay*, MWW, Vol. 6, p. 421.

4. MWL, pp. 326–7. Godwin replaced the names with dashes when he published the letter.
5. Ibid., p. 336.

Chapter 5

1. Henry W. Reveley, 'Notes and Observations to the "Shelley Memorials", after October 1859', SC, Vol. 10, p. 1136; Amelia Opie to Mary Wollstonecraft, 28 August [1796?], Abinger MSS, Dep. b. 210/6; Hannah Godwin to William Godwin, Abinger MSS, Dep. c. 811/1.
2. MWL, p. 359.
3. CKG, Vol. 1, pp. 237–8, 240.
4. MWL, pp. 416–20.
5. *The Wrongs of Woman; or, Maria*, MWW, Vol. 1, pp. 90, 95.
6. Gilbert Imlay to Joseph Johnson; Joseph Johnson to William Godwin, Abinger MSS, Dep. b. 229/1(b).
7. Everina Wollstonecraft to Elizabeth Berry, 30 September 1835, BWH.
8. Dowden, *Life of Shelley*, Vol. 2, pp. 50–52.
9. Everina Wollstonecraft to Elizabeth Berry, 30 September 1835, BWH.
10. *Political Justice*, PPW, Vol. 3, p. 92.
11. CKG, Vol. 1, p. 325.
12. William Godwin to an unnamed recipient, 2 January 179[8], Abinger MSS, Dep. b. 227/8.
13. Letter to the editor of the *Monthly Magazine*, 10 November 1801, PPW, Vol. 2, p. 212; William Austin, *Letters from London: Written During the Years 1802 & 1803* (Boston, Mass.: Printed for W. Pelham, 1804), p. 203.
14. Louisa Jones to William Godwin, Abinger MSS, Dep. c. 508.

Chapter 6

1. Godwin, *Memoirs*, pp. 242, 257.
2. 'A Lancashire Woman, R. W.' to William Godwin, 26 January 1799, Abinger MSS, Dep. b. 214/3.
3. Mary King's story is told in my *Rebel Daughters: Ireland in Conflict 1798* (London: Viking 2003); *Daughters of Ireland* (New York: Ballantine Books, 2004).
4. *St Leon*, ed. Pamela Clemit, N&M, Vol. 4, p. 48.

5. Ibid., pp. 36, 241.

6. *Mary Shelley's 'Literary Lives' and Other Writings*, Vol. 4: *Life of William Godwin*, ed. Pamela Clemit (London: Pickering & Chatto, 2002), p. 108.

7. MWL, p. 353.

8. Elizabeth Inchbald to William Godwin, [27?] December 1799, Abinger MSS, Dep. c. 509.

9. Mary Shelley, *Life of William Godwin*, p. 109.

10. CKG, Vol. 1, p. 294.

11. William Godwin to Maria Reveley, undated, Abinger MSS, Dep. c. 513.

Chapter 7

1. CKG, Vol. 1, pp. 325–6.

2. *Fleetwood*, ed. Pamela Clemit, N&M, Vol. 5 (London: Pickering & Chatto, 1992), p. 166.

3. *Collected Letters of Samuel Taylor Coleridge*, ed. Earl Leslie Griggs (Oxford: Clarendon Press, repr. 2000), Vol. 1: *1785–1800*, p. 553.

4. Harriet Shelley to Catherine Nugent, 4 August 1812, quoted in PBSL, Vol. 1, p. 320.

5. Postscript to Thomas Holcroft's letter, 20 June 1800, Abinger MSS, Dep. c. 511.

6. *Collected Letters of Samuel Taylor Coleridge*, Vol. 1, pp. 619, 588.

7. Abinger MSS, Dep. c. 606.

8. Everina Wollstonecraft to William Godwin, 24 February 1804, Abinger MSS, Dep. b. 214/3.

9. William Godwin to James Marshall, 11 July 1800, Abinger MSS, Dep. b. 214/5.

10. William Godwin to James Marshall, 2 and 3 August 1800, Abinger MSS, Dep. b. 214/5.

11. CKG, Vol. 1, p. 366.

12. William Godwin to James Marshall, 14 August 1800, Abinger MSS, Dep. b. 214/5.

13. Charlotte Howell to Everina Wollstonecraft, 2 January 1843, Abinger MSS, Dep. c. 767/1.

14. Archibald Hamilton Rowan to Everina Wollstonecraft, 8 March 1805, Abinger MSS, Dep. b. 214/3.
15. Elizabeth Berry to Everina Wollstonecraft, April 1835, Abinger MSS, Dep. c. 811/2.
16. MWL, p. 330. See Burtin R. Pollin, 'Fanny Godwin's Suicide Re-examined', *Etudes Anglaises*, 18:3 (1965), pp. 258–68.
17. *St Leon*, N&M, Vol. 4, pp. 47, 114.
18. William Godwin to W. T. Baxter, 8 June 1812, SC, Vol. 3, p. 101.

Chapter 8

1. CKG, Vol. 2, p. 58.
2. CKG, Vol. 1, p. 325.
3. See William St Clair, *The Godwins and the Shelleys: the Biography of a Family* (London: Faber, 1989), p. 253.
4. Crabb Robinson, Vol. 1, p. 105.
5. Mary Jane Godwin to William Godwin, 30 August 1811, Abinger MSS, Dep. c. 523.
6. William Godwin to Mary Jane Godwin, 28 October 1803; Mary Jane Godwin to William Godwin, September 1805, Abinger MSS, Dep. c. 523.
7. William Godwin to Mary Jane Godwin, 5 June 1806, Abinger MSS, Dep. c. 523.
8. *Fleetwood*, N&M, Vol. 5, p. 82.
9. Francis Place to Edward Wakefield, 23 January 1814, BL MSS, Add. 35,152. f. 30.
10. *The Fate of the Fenwicks: Letters to Mary Hays, 1789–1828*, ed. A. F. Wedd (London: Methuen, 1927), pp. 19–21, 215.
11. William Godwin to E. Fordham, 13 November 1811, Abinger MSS, Dep. b. 214/3.
12. CCC, Vol. 2, p. 627.
13. William Godwin to Mary Shelley, quoted in PPW, Vol. 7, p. 79.
14. CCC, Vol. 2, pp. 617–18.
15. Don Locke, *A Fantasy of Reason: the Life and Thought of William Godwin* (London: Routledge & Kegan Paul, 1980), p. 231.
16. Graham Wallas, *The Life of Francis Place: 1771–1854* (London: Longmans, 1898), quoted in *Lives of the Great Romantics III. Godwin,*

Wollstonecraft & Mary Shelley by Their Contemporaries, Vol. 1, ed. Pamela Clemit (London: Pickering & Chatto, 1999), p. 278.

17. Francis Place's sketch of characters he knew, written 27 November 1827, BL MSS, Add. 35,145, ff. 28–36.

Chapter 9

1. CKG, Vol. 2, p. 98.
2. *Conversations of James Northcote Esq. R. A. by William Hazlitt* (London: Frederick Muller Ltd., 1949), p. 2.
3. Charles Lamb to William Hazlitt, 10 November 1805, *Letters of Charles and Mary Anne Lamb,* ed. Edwin W. Marrs (Ithaca: Cornell University Press, 1976), Vol. 2: *1801–1809,* p. 188.
4. CCC, Vol. 1, p. 295.
5. Ibid., p. 2.
6. Seymour, *Mary Shelley*, p. 55.
7. William Godwin to Mary Jane Godwin, 24 May 1811, Abinger MSS, Dep. c. 523.
8. *The Private Journal of Aaron Burr* (Rochester, NY: printed for private distribution, 1903), Vol. 2, p. 341.
9. *Correspondence of Aaron Burr and His Daughter Theodosia,* ed. Mark Van Doren (New York: Covici-Friede Incorporated), p. 264.
10. *The Private Journal of Aaron Burr,* Vol. 2, p. 339.
11. Thomas Turner to William Godwin, 4 July 1803, Abinger MSS, Dep. c. 508; Maria Gisborne, diary entry for 22 August 1820, quoted in PBSL, Vol. 1, p. 456.
12. For Burr's observations in this section see *The Private Journal of Aaron Burr,* Vol. 2, pp. 286–7, 326, 351, 376, 398.
13. Ian Donnachie, *Robert Owen: Owen of New Lanark and New Harmony* (East Linton: Tuckwell, 2000), p. 116.
14. CKG, Vol. 2, p. 186.
15. Thomas Holcroft to William Godwin, 10 September 1797, Abinger MSS, Dep. c. 511.
16. William Godwin to Francis Place, 5 September 1813, BL MSS, Add 35,145. ff. 39–40.

Chapter 10

1. H. R. Woudhuysen, 'A Shelley Pamphlet Come to Light', *Times Literary Supplement*, 14 July 2006, p. 12.
2. PBSL, Vol. 1, p. 42.
3. See Richard Holmes, *Shelley. The Pursuit* (London: Flamingo, 1995), p. 26.
4. Louise Schutz Boas, *Harriet Shelley: Five Long Years* (London: Oxford University Press, 1962), p. 20.
5. Amelia Opie, *Adeline Mowbray*, ed. Shelley King and John B. Pierce (Oxford: Oxford University Press, 1999), p. 236.
6. Quotations in this and the previous two paragraphs are from PBSL, Vol. 1, pp. 80, 131, 140, 163.
7. Harriet Shelley to Elizabeth Hitchener, 14 March 1812, quoted ibid., p. 273.
8. On 'Memoirs of Prince Alexy Haimatoff', *The Prose Works of Percy Bysshe Shelley*, ed. E. B. Murray (Oxford: Clarendon Press, 1993), Vol. 1, p. 142.
9. *The Cenci; A Tragedy in Five Acts*, PBSP, Vol. 2, p. 858.
10. PBSL, Vol. 1, p. 231.
11. Dowden, *Life of Shelley*, Vol. 2, p. 542.
12. William Godwin to Percy Bysshe Shelley, 30 March 1812, quoted in PBSL, Vol. 1, pp. 278, 307.
13. Harriet Shelley to Elizabeth Hitchener, 27 February 1812, quoted ibid., p. 265.
14. Ibid., p. 196.
15. Ibid., p. 314.
16. Ibid., p. 336.
17. See Roger Ingpen, *Shelley in England: New Facts and Letters from the Shelley-Whitton Papers* (London: Kegan Paul, 1917), pp. 552–3 and Kenneth Neill Cameron, *The Young Shelley. Genesis of a Radical* (London: Victor Gollancz Ltd, 1951), p. 366 n.61.
18. Harriet Shelley to Mrs Nugent, 14 November 1812, quoted in PBSL, Vol. 1, p. 331.
19. Thomas Love Peacock, *Nightmare Abbey / Crotchet Castle*, ed. Raymond Wright (London: Penguin Classics, 1986), p. 83.

Chapter 11

1. William Godwin to Percy Bysshe Shelley, 7 July 1812, quoted in PBSL, Vol. 1, p. 313.
2. Ibid., p. 372.
3. Harriet Shelley to Mrs Nugent, 16 January 1813, quoted ibid., p. 350.
4. St. Clair, *The Godwins and the Shelleys*, p. 348.
5. Harriet Shelley to Mrs Nugent, October 1812, quoted in PBSL, Vol. 1, p. 327.
6. Ibid., p. 259.
7. Tatsuo Tokoo, *The Bodleian Shelley Manuscripts*, Vol. 23: *A Catalogue and Index of the Shelley Manuscripts*, p. 233.
8. CCC, Vol. 2, p. 657. See also Edward Augustus Silsbee's notes in the Silsbee Family Papers 1755–1907, Peabody Essex Museum, Salem, Mass., box 7, file 2.
9. Jane Austen to Cassandra Austen, 21–22 May 1801, in *Jane Austen's Letters*, ed. Deirdre Le Faye (Oxford: Oxford University Press, 1997), p. 89.
10. PBSL, Vol. 1, pp. 337, 291, 298, 136.
11. Ibid., p. 338.

Chapter 12

1. See Holmes, *Shelley*, pp. 187–198.
2. Harriet Shelley to Mrs Nugent, quoted in Boas, *Harriet Shelley*, p. 121.
3. *Queen Mab* and 'To Ianthe', PBSP, Vol. 1, pp. 270, 431.
4. *Maria*, MWW, Vol. 1, p. 85.
5. The story comes from Lady Shelley, Shelley's daughter-in-law, who heard it from Thomas Love Peacock.
6. Peacock, p. 69; Hogg, p. 526.
7. PBSL, Vol. 1, p. 384.
8. Hogg, p. 527.
9. Ibid., p. 491.
10. Harriet Boinville to Thomas Jefferson Hogg, 11 March 1814, SC, Vol. 3, pp. 274–5.
11. Shelley wrote in Latin and the sex of the speaker is not absolutely clear.
12. PBSL, Vol. 1, pp. 384, 402.

13. MSJ,Vol. 1, p. 34.
14. Grylls, *Claire Clairmont*, Appendix D, p. 279.
15. Peacock, p. 90; PBSL,Vol. 1, p. 402.
16. Reveley, 'Notes and Observations', SC,Vol. 10, pp. 1134–5.
17. 'Stanzas. – April, 1814', PBSP,Vol. 1, pp. 441–2.

Chapter 13

1. Dowden, *Life of Shelley*,Vol. 2, p. 542.
2. CKG,Vol. 1, pp. 289–90.
3. See his Essay XX, 'Of Phrenology', *Thoughts on Man, his Nature, Productions and Discoveries* (London, 1831).
4. CKG,Vol. 1, p. 294.
5. William Godwin to E. Fordham, 13 November 1811, Abinger MSS, Dep. b. 214/3.
6. 'Julian and Maddalo: A Conversation', PBSP,Vol. 2, p. 663.
7. Everina Wollstonecraft to Elizabeth Berry, 30 September 1835, BWH.
8. *A Defence of Poetry*, SPP, p. 535; Godwin, *Life of Geoffrey Chaucer, the Early English Poet* (London: Richard Phillips, 1803),Vol. 1, p. 370.
9. William Godwin to John Philpot Curran, 3 February 1801, Abinger MSS, Dep. b. 227/2.
10. *A Defence of Poetry*, SPP, p. 513.
11. Quoted in Susanne Zantop, 'The Beautiful Soul Writes Herself: Friederike Helene Unger and the "Grosse Goethe"', *In the Shadow of Olympus: German Women Writers Around 1800*, eds. Katherine R. Goodman and Edith J. Waldstein (Albany: State University of New York Press, 1992), p. 29.
12. Edith Waldstein, 'Goethe and Beyond: Bettine von Arnim's Correspondence with a Child and Günderode', ibid., pp. 95, 100.
13. *Correspondence of Fräulein Günderode and Bettina von Arnim* (Boston, Mass.: T. O. H. P. Burnham, 1861), pp. 194–7.
14. *Prometheus Unbound*, PBSP,Vol. 2, pp. 522–3.

Chapter 14

1. 'The Mourner', *Mary Shelley: Collected Tales and Stories*, ed. Charles Robinson (Baltimore and London: Johns Hopkins University Press, 1976), p. 92.

2. William Godwin to W.T. Baxter, 8 June 1812, SC,Vol. 3, p. 101.
3. *Conversations of James Northcote*, p. 2.
4. Edward J.Trelawny, *Records of Shelley, Byron, and the Author* (NewYork: The NewYork Review of Books, 2000), p. 155.
5. *Political Justice*, PPW,Vol. 3, p. 454.

Chapter 15
1. James Wollstonecraft to William Godwin, 25 March 1805, Abinger MSS, Dep. b. 215/1 and Lydia Wollstonecraft to William Godwin, 10 September 1805, Abinger MSS, Dep. b. 214/3.
2. Another possibility is Cresselly in Pembrokeshire since both Godwin and the Wollstonecrafts knew the gentlemanly family of the Allens who lived there.
3. MWSL,Vol. 2, p. 213; Everina Wollstonecraft to Elizabeth Berry, 30 September 1835, BWH.

Chapter 16
1. Hogg, p. 567; Peacock, p. 91.
2. Mary Shelley, ed., *The Poetical Works of Percy Bysshe Shelley* (London: E. Moxon, 1839),Vol. 3, p. 35.
3. PBSL,Vol. 1, pp. 402–3.
4. Harriet Shelley to Mrs Nugent, 20 November 1814, SC,Vol. 4, p. 773.
5. Holmes, *Shelley*, p. 233; PBSL,Vol. 1, pp. 388 n.2, 391 n.3.
6. Mark Twain, *In Defense of Harriet Shelley, and Other Essays* (NewYork & London: Harper & Brothers, 1918), p. 6.
7. MWSL,Vol. 1, p. 296.
8. Seymour, *Mary Shelley*, p. 96.
9. Dowden, *Life of Shelley*, Vol. 2, p. 544.
10. Charles Brockden Brown, *Ormond; or, The Secret Witness*, ed. Mary Chapman (Ontario: Broadview Press, 1999), pp. 133, 134, 165.
11. *Political Justice*, PPW,Vol. 3, p. 56.
12. MWL, p. 327.
13. St Clair, *The Godwins and the Shelleys*, pp. 361–2.
14. PBSL,Vol. 1, p. 403.
15. Peacock, pp. 91–2.

Chapter 17
1. CCC, Vol. 1, p. 103.
2. Thomas Constable, *Archibald Constable and His Literary Correspondents. A Memorial by His Son Thomas Constable* (Edinburgh: Edmonston & Douglas, 1873), Vol. 2, p. 67.
3. Dowden, *Life of Shelley*, Vol. 2, p. 546.
4. *Political Justice*, PPW, Vol. 4, p. 174.
5. Crabb Robinson, Vol. 1, p. 211.
6. CCC, Vol. 1, p. 63.
7. Everina Wollstonecraft to Elizabeth Berry, 30 September 1835, BWH.
8. CCC, Vol. 2, p. 628.
9. Dowden, *Life of Shelley*, Vol. 2, p. 549.

Chapter 18
1. PBSL, Vol. 1, pp. 394–5, 397–400.
2. Harriet Shelley to Mrs Nugent, 25 August, 20 November, 11 December 1814 and 24 January 1815, quoted in PBSL, Vol. 1, pp. 393, 421–2, 424.
3. MSJ, Vol. 1, p. 50.

Chapter 19
1. Crabb Robinson, Vol. 1, p. 56.
2. CCJ, p. 53.
3. Locke, *A Fantasy of Reason*, p. 209.
4. Ibid., p. 259; Gittings and Manton, *Claire Clairmont*, p. 23.
5. CCJ, p. 59.
6. MSJ, Vol. 1, p. 44.
7. Ibid., p. 53.

Chapter 20
1. MWSL, Vol. 1, p. 3.
2. *Mary Wollstonecraft, 'Mary' and 'Maria'; Mary Shelley, 'Matilda'*, ed. Janet Todd (London: Penguin Classics, 1992), p. 166.
3. PBSL, Vol. 1, p. 408.
4. Ibid., p. 412.
5. Peacock, p. 92.

6. CCJ, p. 58.
7. For Shelley's ailments see Nora Crook, *Shelley's Venomed Melody* (Cambridge: Cambridge University Press, 1986), pp. 102–3.
8. PBSL, Vol. 1, p. 54.
9. Percy Bysshe Shelley in MSJ, Vol. 1, pp. 32–3, 37; CCJ, p. 49.
10. Percy Bysshe Shelley in MSJ, Vol. 1, p. 35; CCJ, pp. 50–51.
11. CCJ, p. 58.
12. MSJ, Vol. 1, p. 44.
13. Ibid., pp. 45, 55, 56.
14. MWSL, Vol. 1, p. 9.
15. MSJ, Vol. 1, p. 72.
16. Ibid., pp. 68–72. Though it is possible that they – or Claire herself – did put an advertisement in *The Times* for a position for Claire; see Newman Ivey White, *Shelley* (New York, Alfred A. Knopf, 1940), Vol. 1, p. 694 n.116.
17. CCC, Vol. 1, p. 10.
18. Dowden, *Life of Shelley*, Vol. 2, p. 549.
19. St Clair, *The Godwins and the Shelleys*, pp. 497–503.

Chapter 21
1. Grylls, *Claire Clairmont*, p. 276.
2. Dowden, *Life of Shelley*, Vol. 2, p. 545.
3. PBSL, Vol. 1, p. 402.
4. *Epipsychidion*, SPP, p. 402; 'To Constantia', PBSP, Vol. 2, p. 338.
5. Dowden, *Life of Shelley*, Vol. 2, p. 549.
6. CCC, Vol. 1, pp. 9–10.
7. CCC, Vol. 2, p. 319.
8. CCC, Vol. 1, pp. 9–10; MSJ, Vol. 1, pp. 78–9.
9. MWSL, Vol. 1, pp. 15–16.
10. Ibid., p. 22.
11. *A Defence of Poetry*, SPP, p. 532.
12. PBSL, Vol. 2, p. 153.
13. Mary Shelley, *Poetical Works of Percy Bysshe Shelley*, Vol. 1, p. 139.
14. BLJ, Vol. 5, pp. 91, 228.
15. CCC, Vol. 1, pp. 24–5; BLJ, Vol. 5, p. 59.

16. William Graham, *Last Links with Byron, Shelley, and Keats* (London: L. Smithers & Co., 1898), p. 81.
17. 'Stanzas for Music', *Lord Byron, The Complete Poetical Works*, ed. Jerome J. McGann (Oxford: Clarendon Press, 1986), vol. 3, p. 379.
18. *Maria*, MWW, Vol. 1, p. 123.
19. CCC, Vol. 1, p. 241.
20. Ibid., p. 36.
21. Ibid., p. 38.

Chapter 22

1. MWSL, Vol. 1, p. 23.
2. CCC, Vol. 2, pp. 631–2.
3. Harriet Shelley to John Frank Newton, 5 June 1816, quoted in PBSL, Vol. 1, p. 477.
4. Boas argued the case in *Harriet Shelley*. The arguments against it are laid out in SC, Vol. 4, pp. 788–802.
5. SC, Vol. 4, p. 777; Crabb Robinson, Vol. 1, p. 211.

Chapter 23

1. 'Thoughts Occasioned by the Perusal of Dr Parr's Spital Sermon', PPW, Vol. 2, p. 170.
2. Mary Hays, *Memoirs of Emma Courtney* (London, 1796), Vol. 1, p. 71; Trelawny, *Records of Shelley*, p. 157.
3. Crabb Robinson, Vol. 1, pp. 14, 177.
4. *Collected Letters of Samuel Taylor Coleridge*, Vol. 2: *1801–1806*, p. 1072.
5. PBSL, Vol. 1, p. 450.
6. Ibid., p. 459; William Godwin's reply, 7 March 1816, quoted ibid., p. 461.
7. Locke, *A Fantasy of Reason*, p. 270.
8. Thomas Turner to William Godwin, 25 February 1816, SC, Vol. 4, p. 613.
9. PBSL, Vol. 1, pp. 454, 491, 509.
10. CCC, Vol. 1, p. 23.
11. Constable, *Archibald Constable and His Literary Correspondents*, Vol. 2, pp. 70, 72.
12. CKG, Vol. 2, pp. 235–6.

13. PBSL, Vol. 1, pp. 471–2.

14. Ibid., p. 477.

Chapter 24

1. CCC, Vol. 1, p. 59.
2. The *Cambrian*, 13 July 1816.
3. Henry Crabb Robinson to Mary Hays, 27 February 1815.
4. PBSL, Vol. 1, p. 223.
5. Donnachie, *Robert Owen*, p. 166.

Chapter 25

1. CCC, Vol. 1, p. 43.
2. PBSL, Vol. 1, p. 347.
3. *The Diary of Dr. John William Polidori: 1816, Relating to Byron, Shelley, etc.*, ed. William Michael Rossetti (London: Elkin Mathews, 1911), p. 101.
4. Ibid., p. 107.
5. Seymour, *Mary Shelley*, p. 153.
6. BLJ, Vol. 5, p. 92; Vol. 6, p. 127.
7. The famous night of ghost stories is now commemorated in a small nearby park called Byron's field, which instructs the reader not to disturb the tranquillity. But on the plaque fixed to the side of the Villa Diodati there is no mention of Shelley, Mary and Claire; only Byron as author of *The Prisoner of Chillon* and *Childe Harold's Pilgrimage*, Canto III is noted.
8. Mary Shelley's introduction to the 1831 edition of *Frankenstein*, quoted in *The Novels and Selected Works of Mary Shelley*, Vol. 1: *Frankenstein; or The Modern Prometheus*, ed. Nora Crook (London: William Pickering, 1996), p. 180.
9. Reveley, 'Notes and Observations', SC, Vol. 10, p. 1135.
10. BLJ, Vol. 6, p. 126.
11. PBSL, Vol. 1, p. 483; SC, Vol. 4, pp. 702–15.
12. BLJ, Vol. 5, pp. 71, 162.
13. CCJ, p. 184.
14. David Booth to Isabel Booth, 9 January 1818, SC, Vol. 5, p. 391.
15. BLJ, Vol. 5, pp. 86–7.

16. PBSL,Vol. 1, p. 497.
17. Ibid., pp. 479, 503 n.2; CCC,Vol. 1, p. 58.
18. PBSL,Vol. 1, p. 479.
19. BLJ,Vol. 5, p. 141.
20. PBSL,Vol. 1, p. 491.
21. PBSL,Vol. 2, p. 328.
22. BLJ,Vol. 5, pp. 92, 141.
23. CCC,Vol. 2, p. 341.

Chapter 26
1. CCC,Vol. 1, p. 49.
2. St Clair, *The Godwins and Shelleys*, pp. 407, 552 n.10.
3. CCC,Vol. 1, p. 49.
4. *Mandeville*, ed. Pamela Clemit, N&M,Vol. 6, p. 41.
5. PBSL,Vol. 1, p. 478.
6. MWSL,Vol. 1, p. 18.
7. CCC,Vol. 1, p. 48.
8. *Lord Byron. The Complete Poetical Works*,Vol. 4, p. 40.
9. CCC,Vol. 1, pp. 49, 54.
10. *A Defence of Poetry*, SPP, pp. 532–3.
11. CCC,Vol. 1, pp. 55–8.

Chapter 28
1. PBSL,Vol. 1, p. 505.
2. CCC,Vol. 1, p. 75.
3. BLJ,Vol. 5, p. 228.
4. William Godwin to Percy Bysshe Shelley, 28 June 1816, Bodleian MS Engl. Lett. c. 461 f. 144.
5. William Godwin to Fanny Godwin, 9 April 1816, Abinger MSS, Dep. c. 523.
6. Hogg, p. 314.
7. CCC,Vol. 1, p. 80.
8. MSJ,Vol. 1, p. 138.

Chapter 29

1. Lady Shelley to Alexander Berry, 11 March 1872, CCC, Vol. 1, p. 85 n.1.
2. Bodleian MS Shelley adds c. 4, Box 1, f. 68.
3. MWL, pp. 121–2.
4. Mrs Julian Marshall, *The Life & Letters of Mary Wollstonecraft Shelley* (London: Bentley & Son, 1889), Vol. 1, pp. 158–9.
5. *Prometheus Unbound* and 'Mont Blanc. Lines Written in the Vale of Chamouni', PBSP, Vol. 1, p. 545, Vol. 2, p. 592.
6. *The Diary of Dr. John William Polidori*, p. 121.
7. 'Julian and Maddalo: A Conversation', PBSP, Vol. 2, p. 672.
8. Silsbee Family Papers 1755–1907, box 8, file 4.
9. The *Cambrian*, May 1825.
10. 'Stanzas Written in Dejection – December 1818, near Naples', PBSP, Vol. 2, p. 450.
11. CKG, Vol. 2, p. 187; Reveley, 'Notes and Observations', SC, Vol. 10, p. 1139.
12. *Alastor; or, The Spirit of Solitude*, PBSP, Vol. 1, p. 486.
13. See the announcement in 6 September 1845 issue, printed below a column carrying the date of Friday Sept. 5: 'We should feel particularly obliged to Correspondents and Advertisers, if they would bear in mind, that the recent acceleration of the Mails, renders it imperative on us to proceed with our paper to press five or six hours earlier than previously, and therefore no communications, however brief, can be received later than seven o'clock on Thursday evening.' In other words they had been receiving new notices until at least midnight on Thursday.

Chapter 30

1. Silsbee Family Papers 1755–1907, box 7, file 2.
2. Reveley, 'Notes and Observations', SC, Vol. 10, p. 1139
3. *Proposals for an Association of Philanthropists, The Prose Works of Percy Bysshe Shelley*, Vol. 1, p. 47.
4. William Godwin to Percy Bysshe Shelley, 13 October 1816, Abinger MSS, Dep. c. 524.

5. See *The Cemetery: A Brief Appeal to the Feelings of Society in Behalf of Extra-Mural Burial* (London: William Pickering, 1848), p. 11; information kindly provided by Kim Collis.

6. 'On Burial Societies; and the Character of an Undertaker', the *Reflector*, No. 3, Article 11 (1811).

7. *Maria*, MWW, Vol. 1, p. 119.

Chapter 31

1. CCC, Vol. 2, p. 628.

2. CCC, Vol. 1, p. 108; Grylls, *Claire Clairmont*, p. 274; MWSL, Vol. 1, p. 54.

3. William Godwin to W. T. Baxter, 12 May 1817, quoted in White, *Shelley*, Vol. 1, p. 473.

4. Crabb Robinson, Vol. 1, pp. 203, 234, 235.

5. Maria Gisborne's journal entry for 9 July 1820, quoted in CCC, Vol. 1, p. 88 n. 5.

Chapter 32

1. The theory concerning Harriet's unborn child was first put forward by Boas in *Harriet Shelley*; see also Nicholas Roe in *Fiery Heart: the First Life of Leigh Hunt* (London: Pimlico, 2005), p. 281.

2. SC, Vol. 4, p. 778.

3. Henry Davis's *The Memorials of the Hamlet of Knightsbridge* was posthumously published by his brother, Charles; Davis identified Harriet's grave. For a full account of the death see 'The Last Days of Harriet Shelley', SC, Vol. 4, pp. 769–802.

4. PBSL, Vol. 1, pp. 520–21, 530.

5. Twain, *In Defense of Harriet Shelley*, pp. 4–5.

6. 'On Paradox and Common-Place', *Selected Writings of William Hazlitt*, Vol. 6, p. 130; MWSL, Vol. 3, p. 284.

7. SC, Vol. 4, pp. 805–6.

8. William Godwin to W. T. Baxter, 12 May 1817, quoted in White, *Shelley*, Vol. 1, p. 489; David Booth to Isabel Booth, 9 January 1818, SC, Vol. 5, p. 390.

9. William Godwin to Hull Godwin, 21 February 1817, Abinger MSS, Dep. c. 523.

10. Constable, *Archibald Constable and His Literary Correspondents*, Vol. 2, p. 84.

Chapter 33

1. MWSL, Vol. 3, p. 284.
2. MSJ, Vol. 1, p. 141.
3. MWSL, Vol. 1, pp. 24, 32.
4. Ibid., p. 52.
5. PBSL, Vol. 1, p. 526.
6. Silsbee Family Papers 1755–1907, box 7, file 2.
7. *Maria*, MWW, Vol. 1, p. 85.
8. 'Her voice did quiver as we parted', PBSP, Vol. 1, pp. 552–3. See G. M. Matthews, 'Whose Little Footsteps? Three Shelley Poems Re-addressed', in *The Evidence of the Imagination*, ed. Donald H. Reiman, M. C. Jaye and Betty T. Bennett (New York: New York University Press, 1978), pp. 254–60; B. C. Barker-Benfield, *Shelley's Guitar. An Exhibition Catalogue* (Oxford: Bodleian Library, 1992), no. 61.

Afterword

1. William Godwin to Mary Shelley, 27 October 1818, Abinger MSS, Dep. c. 524.
2. Seymour, *Mary Shelley*, p. 236.
3. Grylls, *Claire Clairmont*, p. 268.
4. See *The Complete Works of Percy Shelley*, ed. Roger Ingpen and Walter E. Peck, 10 vols. (London: Ernest Benn, 1926–1930), Vol. 8, pp. 28–9.
5. Elizabeth Hitchener, *The Weald of Sussex, a Poem* (London: Black & Co., 1822).
6. Mary Shelley, *Poetical Works of Percy Bysshe Shelley*, Vol. 1, p. xii.
7. MWSL, Vol. 1, p. 572.
8. 'The Mortal Immortal: A Tale', *Mary Shelley: Collected Tales and Stories*, p. 223.
9. Cited by Richard Garnett in 1903; Durant, *Memoirs*, pp. 245–6.
10. MSJ, Vol. 2, p. 560. In fact in 1821 Shelley himself had been pleased to find that some pirated copies of his poems had omitted what he had come to consider as 'a foolish dedication to my late wife, the publication of which would have annoyed me', PBSL, Vol. 2, p. 298.

11. CCC, Vol. 1, pp. 240–41.
12. CCJ, p. 432.
13. MWSL, Vol. 2, p. 271.
14. Gittings and Manton, *Claire Clairmont*, p. 238.
15. CCJ, p. 435.

SUGGESTED FURTHER READING

Prose and Poetry

Jane Austen, *Mansfield Park*, ed. John Wiltshire (Cambridge: Cambridge
   University Press, 2005)

George Gordon, Lord Byron, *The Prisoner of Chillon, Turkish Tales, Childe
   Harold*, in *Lord Byron. The Complete Poetical Works*, ed. Jerome J. McGann
   (Oxford: Clarendon Press, 1986)

Kubla Khan and *Christabel*, in *The Complete Poetical Works of Samuel Taylor
   Coleridge*, ed. Ernest Hartley Coleridge (Oxford: Clarendon Press, 1912),
   2 vols

William Godwin, *Caleb Williams, Fleetwood, St Leon* and *Mandeville*, in
   Collected Novels and Memoirs of William Godwin, general ed. Mark Philp
   (London: Pickering & Chatto, 1992)

William Godwin, *Political Justice*, in *Political and Philosophical Writings of
   William Godwin*, general ed. Mark Philp (London: Pickering & Chatto,
   1993)

William Hazlitt, *The Spirit of the Age*, preface by Michael Foot (Grasmere:
   The Wordsworth Trust, 2004)

Henry Mackenzie, *The Man of Feeling*, ed. Brian Vickers (Oxford: Oxford
   University Press, 2001)

Amelia Opie, *Adeline Mowbray; or, The Mother and Daughter: A Tale* ed.
   Shelley King and John Pierce (Oxford: Worlds Classics, 1999)

Thomas Love Peacock, *Nightmare Abbey* and *Crotchet Castle*, ed. Raymond
    Wright (London: Penguin Classics, 1986)
Jean-Jacques Rousseau, *Julie; ou La Nouvelle Héloïse* (Paris: Garnier Frères,
    1960)
Mary Shelley, *Frankenstein, Lodore* and *Matilda*, in *The Novels and Selected
    Works of Mary Shelley*, general ed. Nora Crook with Pamela Clemit
    (London: William Pickering, 1996)
Mary Shelley, *History of a Six Weeks' Tour* (Otley: Woodstock, 2002)
Mary Shelley: Collected Tales and Stories, ed. Charles Robinson (Baltimore
    and London: Johns Hopkins University Press, 1976)
Percy Bysshe Shelley, *Alastor; or, The Spirit of Solitude* and *Queen Mab*, in *The
    Poems of Shelley*, ed. Geoffrey Matthews and Kelvin Everest (London
    and New York: Longman, 1989)
Percy Bysshe Shelley, *A Defence of Poetry*, in *Shelley's Poetry and Prose*, ed.
    Donald H. Reiman and Neil Fraistat, 2nd edn (New York and London:
    W. W. Norton & Co., 2002)
Robert Southey, *Thalaba, The Curse of Kehama*, in *Poems of Robert Southey*,
    ed. Maurice H. Fitzgerald (Oxford: Oxford University Press, 1909)
Mary Wollstonecraft, *Lessons, Letters from Sweden, A Vindication of the Rights
    of Woman* and *The Wrongs of Woman; or, Maria*, in *The Works of Mary
    Wollstonecraft*, eds. Janet Todd and Marilyn Butler (London: William
    Pickering, 1989)

Memoirs, Letters and Diaries
The Private Journal of Aaron Burr (Rochester, NY: printed for private
    distribution, 1903)
Byron's Letters and Journals, ed. Leslie A. Marchand, 12 vols. (London:
    J. Murray, 1973–82)
*The Clairmont Correspondence: Letters of Claire Clairmont, Charles Clairmont,
    and Fanny Imlay Godwin*, ed. Marion Kingston Stocking, 2 vols.
    (Baltimore and London: Johns Hopkins University Press, 1995)
The Journals of Claire Clairmont, ed. Marion Kingston Stocking
    (Cambridge, Mass.: Harvard University Press, 1968)
Collected Letters of Samuel Taylor Coleridge, ed. Earl Leslie Griggs, 6 vols.
    (Oxford: Clarendon Press, repr. 2000)

Henry Crabb Robinson on Books and Their Writers, ed. Edith J. Morley, 3 vols.
    (London: Dent, 1938)
William Godwin, *Memoirs of the Author of a Vindication of the Rights of
    Woman*, ed. Richard Holmes (London: Penguin Books, 1987)
Thomas Love Peacock, 'Memoirs of Percy Bysshe Shelley', in *The Works of
    Thomas Love Peacock*, ed. H. F. B. Brett-Smith and C. V. E. Jones, Vol. 8
    (London: Constable, 1934)
The Journals of Mary Shelley: 1814–1844, eds. Paula R. Feldman and Diana
    Scott-Kilvert, 2 vols. (Oxford: Clarendon Press, 1987)
The Letters of Percy Bysshe Shelley, ed. Frederick L. Jones, 2 vols. (Oxford:
    Clarendon Press, 1964)
Shelley and his Circle, 1773–1822, eds. Kenneth Neill Cameron et al., 10 vols.
    (Cambridge, Mass.: Harvard University Press, 1961–2002)
Edward J. Trelawny, *Records of Shelley, Byron, and the Author* (New York: The
    New York Review of Books, 2000)
The Collected Letters of Mary Wollstonecraft, ed. Janet Todd (London: Allen
    Lane, 2003)

Biographies

Louise Schutz Boas, *Harriet Shelley: Five Long Years* (London: Oxford
    University Press, 1962)
Kenneth Neill Cameron, *The Young Shelley: Genesis of a Radical* (London:
    Victor Gollancz, 1951)
Edward Dowden, *The Life of Percy Bysshe Shelley*, 2 vols. (London: Kegan
    Paul, 1886)
Robert Gittings and Jo Manton, *Claire Clairmont and the Shelleys, 1798–1879*
    (Oxford: Oxford University Press, 1992)
Lyndall Gordon, *Mary Wollstonecraft: a New Genus* (London: Little, Brown,
    2005)
R. Glynn Grylls, *Claire Clairmont, Mother of Byron's Allegra* (London: John
    Murray, 1939)
Thomas Jefferson Hogg, *The Life of Percy Bysshe Shelley* (London:
    Routledge, 1906)
Richard Holmes, *Shelley: the Pursuit* (London: Flamingo, 1995)
Charles Kegan Paul, *William Godwin: His Friends and Contemporaries*, 2 vols.
    (London: H. S. King, 1876)

Don Locke, *A Fantasy of Reason: the Life and Thought of William Godwin* (London: Routledge & Kegan Paul, 1980)

Fiona MacCarthy, *Byron: Life and Legend* (London: John Murray, 2002)

Thomas Medwin, *The Life of Percy Bysshe Shelley*, 2 vols. (London, 1847)

Nicholas Roe, *Fiery Heart: the First Life of Leigh Hunt* (London: Pimlico, 2005)

William St Clair, *The Godwins and the Shelleys: the Biography of a Family* (London: Faber, 1989)

Miranda Seymour, *Mary Shelley* (London: John Murray, 2000)

Janet Todd, *Mary Wollstonecraft: a Revolutionary Life* (London: Weidenfeld & Nicolson, 2000)

Claire Tomalin, *The Life and Death of Mary Wollstonecraft* (London: Weidenfeld & Nicolson, 1974)

INDEX